Casing Interpersonal
COMMUNICATION

Case Studies in Personal and Social Relationships

Dawn O. Braithwaite ◆ Julia T. Wood

Kendall Hunt
publishing company

Book Team

Chairman and Chief Executive Officer   *Mark C. Falb*
President and Chief Operating Officer   *Chad M. Chandlee*
Vice President, Higher Education   *David L. Tart*
Director of Publishing Partnerships   *Paul B. Carty*
Editorial Manager   *Georgia Botsford*
Senior Editor   *Angela Willenbring*
Vice President, Operations   *Timothy J. Beitzel*
Assistant Vice President, Production Services   *Christine E. O'Brien*
Senior Production Editor   *Mary Melloy*
Permissions Editor   *Caroline Kieler*
Cover Designer   *Mallory Fondell*

Cover image © Jacob Lawrence

Kendall Hunt
publishing company

www.kendallhunt.com
Send all inquiries to:
4050 Westmark Drive
Dubuque, IA 52004-1840

Contents

Acknowledgments

Although our names appear as the Editors of this book, we could not have completed this project without the help of many people. Our greatest debt is to the scholars who made time to write the cases included in this book. The research they have conducted and the insights they bring to interpersonal communication make their cases as rich and vital as human relationships themselves.

We also wish to thank Paul Carty and Angela Willenbring at Kendall/Hunt, whose enthusiasm and support made it a pleasure to work on this book. Throughout the development and production processes they embodied the key principles of effective interpersonal communication.

We also want to express appreciation to our students. They are unfailing sources of ideas for cases. In our classes, they tell us what issues they are facing in their relationships. In addition, they let us know which concepts and theories they find particularly difficult to understand without concrete illustrations.

Finally, we thank our families. For both of us, our families include two-footed and four-footed members with whom we have blood or legal ties as well those who are family for other reasons. Dawn thanks Chuck Braithwaite for his unfailing support, his incredible meals, and the fun in their lives. She appreciates her stepfamily and those voluntary family members who make life worth living (and communication even more worth studying). Julia thanks her sweetheart, Robbie Cox, her puppy Cassidy, and her other family members Linda Becker, Carolyn, and Todd. Our family members are the ongoing case studies in our lives!

About the Contributors

Brenda J. Allen (Ph.D., Howard University) is an Associate Dean in the College of Liberal Arts and Sciences, and a Professor in the Department of Communication at the University of Colorado Denver. She studies and teaches organizational communication, diversity, and critical communication pedagogy. Among her numerous publications is a groundbreaking book entitled *Difference Matters: Communicating Social Identity* (2004, Waveland Press). In 2008, she was named a Master Teacher by the Western States Communication Association.

Betsy Wackernagel Bach (Ph.D. University of Washington) is Professor and Chair of the Department of Communication Studies at the University of Montana, after spending eight years in administration. Although trained in organizational communication, she has turned to studying communication in voluntary kin relationships. She is the author of 30 articles and one book. She served as President of the National Communication Association in 2009 and is a Past President of the Western States Communication Association.

Leslie A. Baxter (Ph.D., University of Oregon) is F. Wendell Miller Distinguished Professor of Communication Studies at the University of Iowa. Her research interests are centered in communication and relating in personal and familial relationships. She has over 120 publications and seven books. She is a Distinguished Scholar of the National Communication Association, recipient of NCA's Brommel Award in Family Communication, and Woolbert Award. She is a Past President of the Western States Communication Association.

Dawn O. Braithwaite (Ph.D., University of Minnesota) is Willa Cather Professor of Communication at the University of Nebraska–Lincoln. She examines how those in personal and family relationships communicate during transitions and challenge, studying rituals, relational dialectics, and supportive communication. She has published 80 articles and five books. She received the National Communication Association's Brommel Award in Family Communication, is Past President of Western States Communication Association, and President of the National Communication Association in 2010.

Carol J. Bruess (Ph.D., Ohio University) is an Associate Professor in the Department of Communication and Journalism, and Director of Family Studies, at the University of St. Thomas, St. Paul, Minnesota. Her research and teaching interests are in family and interpersonal communication with a focus on ritual. She is the author of many articles and book chapters, and co-author of the books *What Happy Couples Do* and *What Happy Parents Do* (Fairview Press, Minneapolis).

Patrice M. Buzzanell (Ph.D., Purdue University) is Professor and W. Charles and Ann Redding Faculty Fellow in Purdue's Department of Communication where she specializes in gendered career, work-life, and leadership issues. Author of approximately 100 books, articles, and chapters, Buzzanell has edited *Rethinking Organizational and Managerial Communication From Feminist Perspectives* (2000), *Gender in Applied Communication Contexts* (2004, with H. Sterk and L. Turner), and *Distinctive Qualities in Communication Research* (2010, with D. Carbaugh).

William R. Cupach (Ph.D., University of Southern California) is Professor of Communication at Illinois State University. His research pertains to problematic interactions in interpersonal relationships, including such contexts as embarrassing predicaments, relational transgressions, interpersonal conflict and criticism, social aggression, and obsessive relational pursuit. He previously served as Associate Editor for the *Journal of Social and Personal Relationships* and is a past President of the International Association for Relationship Research.

Wendy S. Davies-Popelka (M.A., University of North Carolina–Chapel Hill) is the employee communications manager for John Deere's Worldwide Construction & Forestry Division in Moline, Illinois. She is also an adjunct instructor at St. Ambrose University in Davenport, Iowa. She first examined women's intrapersonal communication about their weight while writing her master's thesis.

Suzy D'Enbeau (Ph.D., Purdue University) is an Assistant Professor in the Department of Communication Studies at University of Kansas. Suzy specializes in feminist theorizing, work-life issues, and popular culture. She has authored and co-authored articles in *Feminist Media Studies* and *Qualitative Inquiry*.

Kathryn Dindia (Ph.D., University of Washington) is Professor and Undergraduate Director in the Department of Communication at the University of Wisconsin in Milwaukee. Her research interests are self-disclosure, communication and relationship maintenance, and sex differences in communication. She teaches graduate and undergraduate courses on interpersonal communication and gender and communication and quantitative research methods. She received the UWM Distinguished Undergraduate Teaching Award in 1996.

Sarah E. Dirks (M.S., Illinois State University) is a doctoral candidate in Communication Studies at the University of Nebraska–Lincoln. She studies communication surrounding stressful life events within interpersonal contexts.

Marcia D. Dixson, (Ph.D., University of Iowa, 1993) is an Associate Professor and Chair of Communication at Indiana-Purdue University of Fort Wayne, teaches graduate and under-graduate communication courses in family, personal relationships, gender, research methods and nonverbal communication. Her research explores parent-child communication, relational communication, and communication pedagogy. She is also the mother of two young adults, Lance and Lindsay.

Steve Duck is Daniel and Amy Starch Distinguished Research Chair, Departments of Communication Studies and Psychology, University of Iowa. He has written/edited about 50 books, was founding Editor of the *Journal of Social and Personal Relationships,* edited two editions of the *Handbook of Personal Relationships,* and was first President of *the International Network on Personal Relationships.* He won the National Communication Association's G.R. Miller Book Award for his *Meaningful Relationships: Talking, Sense, and Relating* (SAGE, 1994), and, in answer to a reviewer of the first version of this case, he is not 17 years old: he can just adapt his writing style to fit the case. ROTFL.

Belle A. Edson (Ph.D., University of Denver) is Director of Undergraduate Studies and teaches at the Hugh Downs School of Human Communication at Arizona State University. Her research and teaching interests include feminism and communication, rhetorical theory and criticism, and social-movement theory. She was awarded the College of Liberal Arts and Sciences Distinguished Teaching Award in 2006.

Karen A. Foss (Ph.D., University of Iowa) is Regents Professor and Professor of Communication & Journalism at the University of New Mexico. The focus of her scholarship is feminist perspectives on communication, the discourse of marginalized groups, and social change. Her awards include Gender Scholar of the Year, Presidential Teaching Fellow, Francine Merritt Award, and Scholar of the Year. In 2006, she served as Fulbright Senior Specialist to the University of Southern Denmark.

Paige Garber (M.A., Northern Illinois University) has taken positions as Development Director for a non-profit organization in Minneapolis and another position as Director of Marketing for a company in the audio visual industry since completing her M.A. Currently Paige is a small business owner, assists her husband with his sales and marketing company and telepresence/video-conferencing center, and is a mother of two young boys.

Kate Lockwood Harris (M.A., University of North Carolina at Chapel Hill) is a Ph.D. student and Graduate Instructor at the University of Colorado–Boulder. She studies the communicative aspects of gender, violence, sexuality, and subjectivity.

Stephanie Hsu (M.A., University of Wisconsin-Milwaukee) is a first generation Chinese-American. Stephanie keeps her intercultural ties with her relatives and other native Chinese through speaking the language. In addition to the Chinese language, Stephanie is fluent in French. Her goals include working with U.S. businessmen and women on cultural adjustment and cross-cultural conflict prior to overseas assignments in French- and Chinese-speaking countries. Stephanie hopes to further her education with a Ph.D. in Intercultural Communication.

Naomi Johnson (Ph.D., University of North Carolina–Chapel Hill) is an assistant professor of Communication Studies at Longwood University, Farmville, VA. Her teaching and research interests include gendered communication, mass media, and marketing. Her research on several popular teen romance series was discussed in *The New York Times, Newsweek, NPR,* and a number of other news sources.

Douglas L. Kelley (Ph.D., University of Arizona) is Associate Professor of Communication Studies at Arizona State University. His research and teaching focus on interpersonal communication and forgiveness as represented by two recent books, *Communicating Forgiveness* and *Marriage at Midlife: Counseling Strategies and Analytical Tools.* He has also published in such journals as *The Journal of Social and Personal Relationships* and *Human Communication Research* and is coordinator of educational initiatives for the *Family Communication Consortium.*

Kendra Knight (M.A. Arizona State University) is a Doctoral student in the Hugh Downs School of Human Communication at Arizona State University in Tempe. Her research explores interpersonal and family communication across the lifespan. A major focus of her work is the experience of "casual" sexual interaction (e.g., hookups, friends with benefits relationships) among emerging adults. She has published a journal article and an encyclopedia entry, and has authored and coauthored seven conference papers.

Haley Kranstuber (M.A., Miami University) is a doctoral candidate in Communication Studies at the University of Nebraska–Lincoln. Her research focuses on the way family practices influence the psychological and physical well-being, identity, and worldview of family members. Specifically, her areas of research include narratives, boundaries and messages within adoptive families, family messages as they relate to childhood obesity, and the intergenerational transmission of family stories.

Aimee Lau (M.A., University of Wisconsin–Milwaukee) taught at Wisconsin Lutheran College for two years before deciding to pursue a Ph.D. in Communication. She is currently a Ph.D. student in the Department of Communication at the University of Wisconsin–Milwaukee. Aimee plans to focus her dissertation research on uses of social networking technologies to develop interpersonal relationships in educational settings.

Andrew M. Ledbetter (Ph.D., University of Kansas) is an Assistant Professor in the Department of Communication Studies at Texas Christian University. He examines how friends, family, and romantic partners use mediated communication to maintain their relationships. He has published over 15 articles in peer-reviewed journals on these topics. Ledbetter has also been recognized for outstanding teaching and service to students.

Jennifer A. Linde (M.A., Arizona State University) is a lecturer in the Hugh Downs School of Human Communication at Arizona State University. Her scholarly and teaching interests include performance studies, adaptation of traditional scholarship to the stage, education through performance, civil dialogue as public communication practice, and feminist criticism.

Kristen Lucas (Ph.D., Purdue University) is an assistant professor at University of Nebraska–Lincoln, where she specializes in organizational communication with an emphasis on blue-collar workers and organizations. She has conducted research on how family communication influences ongoing socialization experiences of people from blue-collar families as they pursue white-collar careers. She has published in *Journal of Applied Communication Research, Women's Studies in Communication, Western Journal of Communication,* and *Who Says? Working-Class Rhetoric, Class Consciousness, and Community.*

Joseph P. Mazer (Ph.D., Ohio University) is an Assistant Professor in the Department of Communication Studies at Clemson University. He examines the role of emotion in teaching and learning and how communication technologies function in interpersonal, familial, and organizational contexts. He has published articles and book chapters on virtual social networking, social and academic support, and measurement issues and trends in communication research. Mazer has also been recognized for outstanding teaching, research, and service.

Sandra Metts (Ph. D., University of Iowa) is a Professor in the School of Communication at Illinois State University. She teaches courses in interpersonal communication, communication and aging, and emotion theory. Her research interests focus on emotion experience and expression in relationships and the communicative management of problematic relational episodes including relationship disengagement, deception, sexual communication, and conflict. She is an Associate Editor for *Journal of Social and Personal Relationships* and past president of the Central States Communication Association.

Paul A. Mongeau (Ph.D. Michigan State University) is a Professor at the Hugh Downs School of Human Communication at Arizona State University in Tempe. His research focuses on modern sexual and relational norms on college campuses, communicative conundrums, and social influence processes in these contexts. He has served as editor of *Communication Studies* and *Journal of Social and Personal Relationships*. He has published over 35 journal articles and book chapters and coauthored a book on persuasive communication.

Tim Muehlhoff is an Associate Professor of Communication at Biola University. He received his Ph.D. in interpersonal communication from the University of North Carolina at Chapel Hill. He is the co-author of, *Authentic Communication: Christian Speech Engaging Culture* and his research interests include marital communication, social justice, and gender. He is currently involved in a project focusing on the often devalued and silenced narratives of rural Indian women in New Delhi, India.

Sayaka (Sai) Sato Mumm (M.A., Illinois State University), is a doctoral candidate in Communication Studies at the University of Nebraska–Lincoln. She studies communicative and redemptive aspects of close relationships, such as relational transgressions, hurtful events, forgiveness, and reconciliation.

Clark D. Olson (Ph.D. University of Minnesota) is a professor in the Hugh Downs School of Human Communication at Arizona State University where he has taught for twenty-six years. He regularly teaches interpersonal theory and research and has published over 30 articles and book chapters, winning the National Communication Association's *Golden Monograph* award for his research in 2005. He is interested in how environments impact social relationships. He volunteers as a docent at the Phoenix Art Museum.

Loreen N. Olson (Ph.D., University of Nebraska–Lincoln) is an Associate Professor of Communication at the University of Missouri–Columbia. Her primary research emphasis concerns the communicative elements of intimate and familial violence as well as a new area of scholarship called "communication of deviance." Other topics she has examined include luring communication of child sexual predators, emotion regulation within families, and the discursive construction of identity.

Sandra Petronio (Ph.D., University of Michigan). Professor in the Department of Communication Studies and School of Medicine, IUPUI and Senior Affiliate Faculty Member in the Charles Warren Fairbanks Center for Medical Ethics. She has expertise in privacy, disclosure, and confidentiality and has developed the evidenced-based theory of Communication Privacy Management. She has numerous publications, authored five books, and received national and international recognition for her scholarship.

Emily A. Rauscher (M.A., Western Kentucky University) is a doctoral candidate in the Department of Communication at the University of Missouri–Columbia. Her primary research interests include communication about family planning and communication in and about families constructed through adoption and in vitro fertilization. Other areas of interest include issues of communicating private information about egg/sperm donation and how egg/sperm donation is framed in the media.

Mary E. Rohlfing is a farmer. She received her Ph.D. from The University of Iowa in Communication Research in 1993, taught for 12 years, and chucked it all to become an organic farmer.

Paul Schrodt (Ph.D., University of Nebraska–Lincoln) is the Philip J. & Cheryl C. Burguières Distinguished Professor and Associate Professor of Communication Texas Christian University. His primary interests are in interpersonal and family communication, focusing on communicative cognitions and behaviors that facilitate stepfamily functioning and the stepparent-stepchild relationship. He has published more than 50 articles and book chapters, and is a Past Chair of the Family Communication Division of the National Communication Association.

Debra-L Sequeira (Ph.D., University of Washington) is Professor of Communication and Associate Dean of the College of Arts and Sciences at Seattle Pacific University. Her research focuses on culture and language studies, with articles published in *Text and Performance Quarterly* and *Research on Language and Social Interaction,* among other journals. She has also contributed book chapters in interpersonal communication/family communication, cultural communication, and spiritual/religious communication.

Christina Shaw (M.A. Northern Illinois University) is a Doctoral Student in the Hugh Downs School of Human Communication at Arizona State University in Tempe. Her research focuses on gender-based processes and consent in sexual interactions studied from a number of methodological perspectives. Her dissertation focuses on the pertinence of hookup culture to the lives of college women. She has published one journal article, encyclopedia entry, and been part of eight papers presented at professional conferences.

Brian H. Spitzberg (Ph.D., University of Southern California) is a Senate Distinguished Professor of Communication at San Diego State University. His areas of research include interpersonal communication skills, conflict, jealousy, infidelity, intimate violence, sexual coercion, and stalking. He serves as an active member of the San Diego District Attorney's Stalking Case Assessment Team, and is an active member of the Association of Threat Assessment Professionals. He received Western States Communication Association's Distinguished Scholar Award.

Paige W. Toller (Ph.D., University of Nebraska–Lincoln) is an Assistant Professor in the School of Communication at the University of Nebraska–Omaha. She has been studying communication and grief since writing her Masters' thesis in 2000. She teaches courses in interpersonal, family and small group communication as well as a graduate course in qualitative methods.

Erin K. Willer (Ph.D., University of Nebraska–Lincoln) is an Assistant Professor in the Department of Communication Studies at the University of Denver. Her research focuses on the ways individuals manage relational difficulty, such as social aggression and inter/intragroup conflict, in contexts including girls' cliques and gangs. She has received Top Paper awards from the National Communication Association and the Western States Communication Association and was selected as an American Association of University Women Dissertation Fellow in 2009.

Julia T. Wood is the Caroline H. and Thomas S. Royster Distinguished Professor of Graduate Education and the Lineberger Professor of Humanities at the University of North Carolina at Chapel Hill. Since completing her Ph.D. (Pennsylvania State University) at age 24, she has conducted research and written extensively about communication in personal relationships and about gender, communication, and culture. In addition to publishing over 60 articles and chapters, she has authored or edited 25 books. The recipient of fourteen awards for distinguished scholarship and thirteen teaching awards, Professor Wood divides her professional energies between writing and teaching.

Professor Wood lives with her partner, Robbie Cox, who is also a professor of Communication Studies at the University of North Carolina and is actively involved with the national Sierra Club, and their dog, Cassidy. When not writing and teaching, Professor Wood enjoys traveling, legal consulting, and spending time talking with students, friends, and family.

Introduction: Teaching with Case Studies

Imagine two scenarios. First, imagine that you are in an interpersonal communication class and your teacher tells you this: "Romantic partners often experience tension between the desire to be independent and the desire to feel connected." Your teacher then illustrates by saying, "For example, you may really want to be with your girlfriend or boyfriend one day and prefer not to see her or him the next day because you want some time alone."

Now imagine a second scenario. In it, your teacher asks you to read this story: Cecile feels really confused about her relationship with Josh. They've been dating exclusively for six months and for most of that time, they couldn't get enough of each other. All they wanted to do was see each other, talk to each other, be together. But that's changed in the last two weeks. Lately Cecile has sometimes felt crowded by Josh, and she starting to resent the way that being with him keeps her from being with other friends. Josh seems to be pulling back, too. There are times when he doesn't seem really engaged with her when they're together and times he doesn't want to see her. She knows they love each other, but she's confused by wanting time apart. Cecile wonders if it's possible to love someone and not want to be with him all the time. Isn't it inconsistent to want to be with Josh sometimes and to want to be away from him at other times? Cecile wants to tell Josh what she's feeling, but she's not sure what it means or how to talk with him.

Which scenario was more effective in giving you insight into the tension between autonomy and connection that occurs in most interpersonal relationships? In the first scenario you were given a clear definition and an example of the tension between wanting independence and connection. You understood the idea and felt confident that you could recall the definition for a test.

In the second scenario, you read about Cecile's relationship with Josh. Perhaps you could identify with her confusion because you've had similar feelings at times in your own relationships. Perhaps you've wanted some private time or time with other friends while still knowing you love another person and want to sustain an intimate relationship with that person. Perhaps you empathized with Cecile's concern that she wanted to talk to Josh but didn't know how to do so without hurting him.

Did you understand the tension between desires for independence and connection better from the explanation in the first scenario or the story in the second one? If you're like most people, each approach offered you distinct insights. The first scenario presented you with conceptual information that is essential to analyzing dynamics of interaction. The second scenario provided you with a rich example of how this tension surfaces in a concrete relationship. It allowed you to see how the abstract idea of tension between desires for connection and autonomy plays out in a real relationship with real people. The story provides a context for understanding conceptual information about tensions between desires for autonomy and connection. It also invites you to participate actively in learning by identifying with Cecile's situation and thinking about what she might do to communicate effectively with Josh.

This book is designed for people who want to learn by exploring conceptual information in real-life situations. The cases in this book invite you to use abstract and conceptual knowledge that is drawn from theory and research to analyze and address concrete circumstances. This is active learning because it requires you to understand how concepts, theories, and principles apply in actual situations. Studying interpersonal dynamics in practical situations develops your skill in applying what you learn to your own relationships. It also helps you expand your personal repertoire of communication choices so that you can adapt effectively to diverse contexts, individuals, and relationships.

This book provides you with case studies that are based on research and theories in the field of communication. Each case was written by individuals who have extensively studied the particular issues covered in the case. Analyzing the cases allows you to apply concepts, theories, and principles you've read about to concrete, real-life issues, problems, and processes in human relationships. Because the cases are written from the perspectives of different people, you'll learn to appreciate multiple perspectives on communication and the situations in which it occurs.

In this opening chapter, our goal is to explain the role of case studies in learning about interpersonal communication. We first describe the tradition of case study as a method of teaching, and we identify distinct values of case studies as a method of learning. In the second section of this chapter we link the case method of teaching and learning to narrative theory. Our discussion highlights the richness of a narrative approach to knowledge. The third section of this chapter describes ways you can approach the case studies in this book to enhance your knowledge of interpersonal communication. Finally, we preview the organization of this book, so that you understand why we've arranged cases in a particular sequence, and so that you can decide how you can most effectively learn from case studies in this book.

Case Studies As A Means to Learning

There are many ways to teach and to learn. The most conventional methods are lecture and discussion. These methods are effective in presenting concepts, principles, theories, and research. Yet, lecture and discussion are not especially effective in helping us learn how to *apply* concepts, principles, theories, and research to real-life communication situations. Presentational methods can be effectively supplemented by case studies, which foster rich understandings and practical skills how to use knowledge.

In 1997 Robert Diamond, Assistant Vice Chancellor of Syracuse University, asserted that conventional methods of education do not prepare students to function in the real world after they leave college. According to Diamond, students must not only learn information; they must also learn how to apply it effectively. In other words, education should help students develop skill in applying knowledge in pragmatic ways. When we really know something, we know how to use it to improve our effectiveness in personal, social, and professional interactions.

Agreeing with Diamond is management professor Larry Hartman who advocates teaching methods that "enable students to learn by doing" so that students leave college with experience in applying "individual communication skills, intellectual skills, and interpersonal skills" (p. 41). Knowledge consists not just of information, but also of insight into how to use it effectively.

Case studies are one means to foster skills in using knowledge effectively. Case studies are extended descriptions of particular events, situations, and people. A case tells a story, complete with the kinds of details and intricacies that characterize real life. Because cases are narratively rich, they allow us to see the complexities that mark human behavior and to appreciate the different ways that given behaviors might be interpreted. William Naumes, a management professor the University of New Hampshire who teaches about case writing, tells us that a case presents a good story, with a theme that we can think about when we have finished reading it. A good case will help us apply concepts or theories to our everyday lives and teach us about ourselves. Cases also encourage us to identify options for interpretation and behavior and to generate understanding and effective action.

The Case Study Tradition

The case study method of education enjoys a long and distinguished history in many fields. Perhaps the most familiar use of case studies is in religious and moral education. For centuries religious instructors of Ancient Chinese, Hebrew, and Greek teachers used parables to teach moral principles. This tradition persists in contemporary religious teaching—parables figure prominently in Christian, Jewish, Islamic, and Buddhist religious education.

Case studies also have an established place in secular education. Larry Hartman notes that since 1908, law schools have featured case studies prominently in teaching. Cases allow law students to discover how legal theory applies to the intricacies of particular situations. The same is true of business schools, which rely on case studies to teach students how to assess organizations and develop plans for improving efficiency, employee morale, and so forth. Intercultural workshops and training programs also rely heavily on case studies to teach people about diverse customs, assumptions, and expectations in different cultures. Public Administration Programs, such as those at Harvard and the Kennedy School of Government, feature case studies prominently.

The principles that make cases appropriate for training in law, business, and intercultural relations also render cases ideal for learning about communication. In 1990 Professor Beverly Sypher published *Case Studies in Organizational Communication,* which featured realistic cases that allowed students to apply communication concepts to organizational processes. Eileen Berlin Ray, a professor of communication at Cleveland State University, has led the way in introducing case studies in teaching about health communication. In 1993 she edited a book of case studies in health communication. Three years later she edited a book of case studies in communication and disenfranchisement within the health-care system. The cases in Ray's books give readers complex and useful understandings of multiple and interacting issues in health contexts. More recently, Erika Kirby and Chad McBride (2009) edited *Gender Actualized,* a book of case studies on gendered dynamics in human interaction.

This book extends the case study method to the study of interpersonal communication. In it, our goal is to show how theories, concepts, and principles of interpersonal communication operate in realistic situations and relationships.

Values of the Case Study Method

Case studies are widely used educational tools because they have distinct values—ones that are less prominent in conventional methods of education. Three primary values of the case study method are a focus on application, ability to represent real-world complexity, and practice in problem solving and management of tensions in human communication.

Application to Specific Situations. A key value of case studies is that they allow students to apply concepts. Doing so allows students to learn how to adapt general principles to specific circumstances in their own and others' lives. For example, contract courses in law school teach students that a contract is "a meeting of minds." That abstract definition, however, cannot teach students what contracts mean—or even when they exist—in particular cases. Is there "a meeting of minds" if one person is intoxicated when a contract is signed? What if a person who signs a contract feels coerced by others? What if a person doesn't understand the binding nature of a contract? Is "a meeting of minds" possible when one person doesn't understand the obligations inherent in a contract? Working with the particularities of specific cases allows law students to appreciate the nuances and complexity of the abstract definition, "a meeting of minds." Working with cases helps law students realize that any abstract definition must be translated to fit multiple details of a concrete situation.

Let's consider an example of how case studies can help us learn about communication in interpersonal relationships. Interpersonal communication scholars define self-disclosure as revealing information about oneself that others are unlikely to discover on their own. Yet, knowing this abstract definition doesn't show us what self-disclosure means, or how it takes place, in specific contexts.

Going beyond abstract concepts, a case study helps us analyze self-disclosure within particular settings and under specific conditions. Is it self-disclosure if a woman unintentionally reveals something about herself? Is it self-disclosure if a man who is told something personal by a friend doesn't realize the information is private and not shared with anyone else? Is it self-disclosure if a person routinely reveals private information to others? Is self-disclosure equally common and does it mean the same thing in cultures that emphasize privacy and in those that emphasize revealing oneself to others?

A case study allows us to look at self-disclosure in particular circumstances. This encourages us to recognize that what self-disclosure means and how it affects relationships vary across time and contexts. We learn not only what self-disclosure is in an abstract sense, but also how it operates and what it means in specific settings. As a result, we gain a more sophisticated appreciation of self-disclosing communication.

Real-Life Complexity. Another virtue of working with case studies is that they can highlight interaction among aspects of communication. Traditional methods of education introduce students to concepts individually—one concept at a time. This makes it difficult to appreciate how multiple concepts interact, and how they work together to shape what happens in human interaction. Realistic case studies can give us insight into multiple processes and issues that are simultaneously present and interacting in interpersonal communication.

A good case study of self-disclosure provides insight into how self-disclosing and the meaning of doing so are shaped by issues such as trust, relationship history, and self-concepts of communicators. We gain concrete understanding of how people decide when and to whom to reveal private information. We might also learn how self-disclosing affects those who disclose and those who are recipients of disclosure. Does learning another person's secrets increase feelings of closeness? Does disclosure by one person encourage reciprocal disclosure by another person? We might also discover how different responses to self-disclosures—acceptance, disapproval, betraying confidence, reciprocating—affect trust, self-esteem, and willingness to invest more in the relationship.

Because case studies provide layered narratives, they invite us to recognize the complexity of interpersonal communication. They help us realize there are links between self-disclosure and previous interactions in a relationship, as well as what is likely to follow. Case studies can illuminate other issues such as timing, context, and style of communication, and trace how these issues affect self-disclosure and responses to it.

Practice in Diagnosing and Managing Problems. A third value of studying cases is that it encourages thinking about how communication can help us deal with interpersonal problems and improve our relationships. When you examine a case thoughtfully, you can identify patterns of communication that lead to conflict, misunderstanding, or other problems. For example, you might ask whether Cecile and Josh should bring up their feelings with each other instead of trying to understand individually. Are they being dishonest not to share their feelings of wanting time apart? Is the lack of communication about feelings fueling resentment toward each other? Once you recognize patterns and their likely consequences, you are able to make more informed choices about which patterns to foster and avoid in your own relationships.

Cases invite you to figure out a way or ways to address problems and deal with the conflicts and tensions that are inevitable in human relationships. You might ask how Cecile and Josh could meet her needs for independent time without jeopardizing their relationship. What could she say to Josh to assure him that her desire for time apart doesn't mean she doesn't love him? Thinking about how Cecile and Josh might work out their problem helps you generate practical strategies and skills for analyzing and improving communication in your own interpersonal interactions.

Narrative Theory as a Foundation for Cases

The case method of education is built on the assumption that knowledge can be gained from detailed accounts of people, situations, and events. This assumption is shared by narrative theory, which is well established in the communication discipline. One of the scholars who developed this theory is Walter Fisher, a professor at the University of Southern California. Fisher believes that humans are naturally storytelling beings. We tell stories to make sense of our experiences and to share them with others. We listen to others to understand who they are and what their lives are about. According to Fisher, we continuously learn about ourselves, others, and the world through the process of telling and hearing narratives. Interpersonal communication scholar Jody Koenig Kellas (2008) of the University of Nebraska–Lincoln explains that narratives helps us understand the ways human build and make sense of their identities (who we are), our relationships, and our lives.

What is a narrative? Most simply defined, it is a good story. A good story involves believable characters who experience events that are organized in a deliberate way to give them coherence and meaning. In addition to providing an ordered presentation of events, stories also involve characters and plots. We encounter people and learn about their motives—why they do what they do. We learn about their backgrounds, goals, fears, and dreams, and all of this information helps us understand their actions. We also see plot lines develop as particular events and interactions make certain lines of future action likely and foreclose others. We see where a character's choice at one point in a story sets the stage for what can and cannot happen later.

Narratives are not just interesting stories. They are carefully constructed accounts, or explanations of human action. They give us insight into why certain things and not others happen and why characters do some things and not others. Narratives are not objective or true in an absolute sense. Rather they make sense from—and only from—particular perspectives. Many narratives are told from one person's point of view, so our insight into the account is shaped by that subjective point of view. Sometimes narratives switch between more than one character's point of view so that we gain insight into different, sometimes conflicting outlooks on what is happening and what it means. Because narratives reflect particular points of view, they teach us about individuals' perspectives on life and interaction. When we really enter into a narrative on its own terms, we gain understanding of how the narrator or character(s) sees the world.

Because narratives reflect specific points of view they have the power to increase our understanding of multiple perspectives and some of the reasons for them. For example, suppose you read a story about a woman who avoids conflict in her relationships. Told from her husband's point of view, the narrative portrays her as closed and unwilling to work through tough issues. His story highlights his frustration when his wife refuses to deal with conflict. The husband's point of view reveals that he has had conflicts in his friendships and in past romantic relationships and he is comfortable confronting them in dialogue.

Told from the wife's point of view, however, the story tells us that she feels paralyzed and profoundly scared when conflict threatens to arise in her marriage. Her story enlightens us about the abuse and violence that regularly erupted in her parents' marriage. We learn how helpless and scared she felt as a child watching vicious episodes between her mother and father. This insight, in turn, might make us more sympathetic to the woman and her reasons for avoiding conflict at all costs.

Which narrative is more accurate—the one reflecting the husband's or wife's point of view? It's not useful to ask whether one story is more accurate in some objective sense. What we need to appreciate is that each narrative gives us insight into how one person feels feel and why that person acts as she or he does. If we can discover the reasons for each person's feelings, actions, and desires, then we can better understand unsatisfying patterns of communication and how they might be changed.

Case studies allow us to examine how events unfold and how relationships are affected by the choices that people make. What we learn enlarges our understanding of a range of people and the ways they communicate. In addition, what we learn develops our abilities to analyze communication patterns and processes in our own interactions, so that we can create relationships that are healthy and productive.

Learning from Case Studies

If you have not had classes that feature cases, you may wonder how you should approach this book. Human Resource Management professor George Stevens suggests a three-stage process. First, he advises you to read a case in its entirety to gain an overall understanding of the characters, issues, and context. Set the case aside for a while, then reread it, this time making notes to yourself—perhaps in the margins of the pages. You might use notes to identify communication concepts, principles, and issues, as well as ways of approaching the case. Then put the case aside again so that it's on the back burner of your mind. Finally, read the case a third time and refine the notes that you made on the second reading. Now is the time to elaborate conceptual issues and applications.

After you have thought about a case and made notes on your own, it's a good idea to discuss a case with others. You will discover that you can learn a great deal by exploring others' views of a case—how are their perspectives similar to and different from your own? What do their experiences allow them to see that you didn't see on your own? Differences in how people perceive cases remind us that interpretations of communication are personal and subjective. Discussion of a case also allows you to refine your skills in presenting your ideas and responding to those of others. Finally, discussing a case provides an opportunity to broaden your own perspective and your repertoire of communication choices by learning from the unique experiences, insights, and approaches of others.

You may find it useful to let three questions guide your individual analysis of cases and your discussion with others. These questions direct your efforts to apply theories, principles, and concepts. First, ask what each case teaches you about interpersonal communication. Second, ask how and why various people in the case might interpret the situation differently and how each point of view makes sense from a specific individual's perspective. Finally, ask how you might respond to each case if you were in that situation. We'll elaborate how to use each of these questions when reading the cases in this book.

What Does This Case Teach about Interpersonal Communication?

The initial question to ask as you read a case is what it teaches you about interpersonal communication. George Stevens, who is in the field of Human Resource Management, asserts that case studies are extremely effective in providing opportunities to learn how theories and research findings apply to actual situations. As you read each case, ask whether it emphasizes a particular theory, concept, or set of concepts, communication principle, or relational process? When you can identify the conceptual focus of the case, ask what you learn. Do you gain a better understanding of a concept such as self-disclosure? How is your understanding enlarged? What do you now know that you didn't before reading the case? What questions remain unanswered?

When thinking about what you learn from a particular case, also ask yourself how issues in this case relate to ones presented in other cases and to other topics you've discussed in your class. As we noted earlier in this chapter, in interpersonal communication multiple issues are simultaneously present and interacting. Looking for connections among issues and concepts will lead you to recognize the complexities of interpersonal relating. For example, Case 1 focuses on decisions about keeping or changing names upon marrying. How might this topic be linked to issues of autonomy and connection that are covered in Case 6? Can you identify connections *between* patterns of development in blended families, covered in Case 10, and efforts to balance needs for couple time with needs for family time that are discussed in Case 14?

Can I Understand Alternative Perspectives on Interpersonal Communication in This Case?

The second question that should guide your reading of cases is whether you can understand alternative perspectives presented in the case. This is critical because understanding different, sometimes conflicting perspectives is one of the main skills of effective interpersonal communicators. You may not *agree* with all perspectives, and that's okay. The point is for you to understand different points of view and the reasons behind them. This gives you insight into people who think, act, and feel differently than you do. Thus, it enlarges your understanding of human communication.

Understanding alternative perspectives on situations also helps you communicate more effectively, especially with people who differ from you. In our earlier example, did you identify more with the husband who was frustrated by his wife's avoidance of conflict or the wife who perceived conflict as frightening and dangerous? Can you stretch to understand the perspective with which you didn't originally identify? If so, then you increase your ability to recognize, respect, and deal constructively with orientations to conflict that are unlike your own. In turn, this makes it more likely that you can communicate effectively with people who do not share your views of what conflict means and how to deal with it.

How Might I Address the Problem in This Case?

The case studies in this book offer you opportunities to generate concrete ways to address common problems in interpersonal relationships. As you read the cases, ask how you might deal with the tensions or problems presented. What would you tell Cecile she should do about her feelings of claustrophobia in the relationship with Josh?

What would you advise the husband and wife about how to manage their conflicts constructively?

Your ideas for approaching interpersonal communication problems should reflect what you've learned in the course this book accompanies. Thinking about how to address the issues in cases is an opportunity for you to apply the concepts you've learned and to see how they can be used to improve interpersonal communication.

Your ideas for resolving problems should also respect the perspective of each person in the case. Interpersonal literally means *between* people. Thus, interpersonal communication problems occur between people. They involve more than one person. By extension, effective resolutions of problems must also involve more than one person. We would be unwise to suggest the wife should simply recognize that couples need to deal with their conflicts. This advice ignores her deep-seated fear of conflict, so it's likely to be ineffective in changing conflict patterns. That advice might even make her feel guilty, which could create further problems in the marriage.

For the same reason, it's not helpful to suggest the husband should simply accept his wife's inability to confront conflict, since that neglects his need to talk about problems in the marriage. This would do nothing to relieve his frustration and would not help the couple learn to deal with their conflicts constructively. A good approach to the situation would begin with respect for both the husband's and wife's feelings and perspectives. Following that, it would be effective to make communication choices that reflect respect for both perspectives.

It's important to realize that there is seldom only one good way to address problems in interpersonal communication. Usually there are multiple, potentially constructive approaches to addressing problems in human relationships. An important value of discussing cases with others is that you increase your awareness of alternative ways of resolving tensions and keeping relationships healthy and enjoyable.

Extending Cases in the Classroom

There are additional ways you can work with the cases in this book to sharpen your skills in applying your conceptual knowledge to real-life situations. One option is to rewrite a case so that choices made early in it are revised to lead to different outcomes later in the case. How might a different response to anger or disclosure affect what happens between people in a case? A variation on this is to enact a case and to stop it at key points, so that you can create alternative trajectories for the story. You might stop a case at a key juncture and have one or more characters make different choices about how to communicate. Then you can follow through by enacting what might happen given the different choices. A third option is to write a continuation of a case. Working individually or with others in your class, you might compose the next chapter in a case to explore what is likely to happen, given what you know about the characters, situation, context, and choices made so far in the case.

The Organization of This Book

The cases in this book reflect current theories and research about human communication processes. The cases are organized into five topical areas that represent major foci of research and theory in the communication field. Within each area, the cases follow a standard format that is designed to facilitate your analysis.

Grouping of Case Studies

The cases in this book are organized into five major sections. The first set of case studies focuses on how we use communication to announce, negotiate, and alter personal identity. Each case in this section of the book presents you with a specific situation in which identity is at stake. One chapter, for example, explores the issue of whether to change one's name upon marrying. Another case concerns how some women talk themselves into unhealthy diets. These two cases, as well as others in Section I, ask you to think seriously about how communication shapes and reflects personal identity, and to consider how communication changes in response to changes in our identities over our lifetimes.

The second section of the book presents cases involving communication during the process of developing closeness. How does communication help us define our relationships, negotiate needs for autonomy and connection, and deal with gender-related differences in interaction style? These are among the issues that we examine in the section focused on the evolution of friendships and romantic intimacy.

In the third section of the book we consider common communication processes in established and ongoing relationships. One case highlights some of the issues involved in balancing career and family commitments. Another case illuminates the ways in which intimates use rituals to sustain intimacy in long-term relationships.

The fourth section of the book focuses on the dark side of interpersonal relationships. The cases in this section deal with betrayals of trust, date rape, stalking, alcoholism, and racial-ethnic biases. Each case allows you to appreciate complex communication processes that operate when relationships are troubled by major crises. These cases also invite you to think about ways to avoid serious problems in relationships you are building and how you might deal with problems and their aftermath in other relationships in your life.

In the final section of the book we provide cases that show how communication changes over time in long-term relationships. The case of caring for a parent reveals how parent-child communication patterns alter when a child assumes the role of caregiver for a parent. Another case in this section illustrates some of the communication patterns that are typical in long lasting friendships. These cases provide insight into the dynamics of enduring bonds.

The five sections in this book provide you with in-depth narratives of communication processes and problems that are common in the various relationships in our lives.

Studying them will help you make sense of your own past and present interactions, and to anticipate ones that may be part of your future. In addition, studying these cases should enhance your understanding of others' perspectives so that you gain an appreciation of the multiple ways people communicate and interpret what happens between them.

Format of Individual Case Studies

Each case is written by one or more scholars who have expertise in the particular topic of the case. This means that although the cases are presented as stories, they reflect theory and data from research. Thus, in reading the cases you will learn what has been discovered by scholars who investigate human communication.

To facilitate your study, all of the cases in this book follow a standard format. The authors open the cases with a list of key words to alert you to communication concepts, theories, and principles that are embedded in the case. Then authors present a focused narrative that sheds light on a particular topic in interpersonal communication. Typically, the authors create a story that allows you to understand what different people in the story feel and think and how they perceive what is happening.

Following the case, the authors pose a few questions to guide your analysis and discussion of the case. The questions that follow each case need not limit your reflection and discussion. In other words, the questions at the end of each chapter should stimulate your thinking, but not restrict it. Feel free to explore issues beyond those raised in the questions we pose.

Each case concludes with a short list of references. These references are not comprehensive bibliographies of research in an area. Instead, they highlight primary research that is reflected in the case they accompany. These references will lead you to further information about particular topics that interest you.

We hope that studying the cases in this book will prove valuable to you as you seek to learn more about human communication in your life and the lives of others.

Julia T. Wood
The University of North Carolina at Chapel Hill

Dawn O. Braithwaite
The University of Nebraska–Lincoln

References

Diamond, R. (1997, 1 August). Broad curriculum reform is needed if students are to master core skills. *Chronicle of Higher Education*, p. B7.

Eisenhardt, K.M. (1989). Building theories from case study research. *Academy of Management Review, 5,* 501–508.

Fisher, W. (1984). Narration as a human communication paradigm: The case of public moral argument. *Communication Monographs, 51,* 1–22.

Fisher, W. (1987). *Human communication as narration: Toward a philosophy of reason, value, and action.* Columbia, SC: University of South Carolina Press.

Hartman, L.D. (1992). Business communication and the case method: Toward integration in accounting and MBA graduate programs. *The Bulletin, 55,* 41–45.

Kellas, J.K. (2008). Narrative theories; Making sense of interpersonal communication. In D.O. Braithwaite & L.A. Baxter (Eds.), *Engaging theories in interpersonal communication: Multiple perspectives* (pp. 241–254.). Thousand Oaks, CA: Sage.

Kirby, E., & McBride, C. (Eds.). (2009), *Gender actualized: Cases in communicatively constructing realities.* Dubuque, IA: Kendall Hunt.

Naumes, W. (2006). *Art and craft of case writing.* Armonk, NY: Sharpe Reference.

Ray, E.B. (1993). (Ed.). *Case studies in health communication.* Mahwah, NJ: Lawrence Erlbaum.

Ray, E.B. (1996). (Ed.). *Case studies in communication and disenfranchisement: Applications to social health issues.* Mahwah, NJ: Lawrence Erlbaum.

Stevens, C.F. (1996). *Cases and exercises in human resource management.* Chicago: Richard D. Irwin.

Sypher, B.D. (Ed.). (1990). *Case studies in organizational communication.* New York: Guilford.

Part I

Negotiating Personal Identity in Relationships

1

What's in a Name? Negotiating Marital Name Changes

Karen A. Foss, Belle A. Edson, and Jennifer A. Linde

Key Terms

commitment, decision making, marriage, names, relational perceptions, self-disclosure, self-identity

---

Madeline Anderson took a sip of her iced tea and sighed. It still amazed her that this man who sat across the table smiling and speaking casually in Spanish to the server was going to be her husband in less than six months. She gazed absentmindedly at the closed menu in front of her, certain that she could order the Frontier Special in Spanish if she really wanted to try. Perhaps it was easier to let Martín do the ordering and save herself the embarrassment of sounding too much like a Minnesota girl trying to roll her "r's" She missed the time that she and Martín had when they first started dating: time for impromptu Spanish lessons, time for easy conversation, and time for lots of flirting. But Madeline also cherished the changes in their relationship over the last two years. Martín Romero had become many things to Madeline—classmate, friend, Spanish teacher, confidant, lover, and partner—and soon he would be her husband.

Another sigh escaped her lips, and this time, Martín caught her eye and winked. Madeline wondered how he could read her mind so easily. She wondered how he knew her as well as he did. It seemed to her that her parents were such strangers to one another, even after 26 years of marriage, even after living in the same house together for all that time. She marveled that she and Martín already had a way of relating that seemed absent from her parents' marriage. Madeline knew that her ability to share her feelings with Martín and to listen and argue and work at communicating had not come from her upbringing; she wondered where she had learned it. She certainly had discovered herself in these four years of college, and she felt a twinge of sadness that graduation was just a month away. Soon she'd be saying good-bye to the routine of the University of New Mexico and the beautiful Albuquerque sunsets.

MARTÍN: Is it that serious? (*Madeline was startled out of her thoughts.*)
MADELINE: What?

MARTÍN:	You stopped smiling a few minutes ago, and now you look far too pre-occupied for a Friday night. Is everything OK?
MADELINE:	Yup. What am I eating tonight?
MARTÍN:	Cartón y plátanos. [Cardboard and bananas].
MADELINE:	That sounds delicious. Does it come with jalapeños?
MARTÍN:	(*laughing*) Your Spanish is awful—remind me again why I'm marrying you.
MADELINE:	I'm going to make a lot of money.
MARTÍN:	That's right! Within a year, you'll be the head of engineering for some big company, and I'll get a job in a nearby school district. Then we'll have four babies, and my mother will come to visit frequently.
MADELINE:	Do you expect me to make a mother-in-law joke now? I'm sorry, sweetie, but I like your mother. She can come visit us anytime she wants.
MARTÍN:	That's good—because she and Dad are coming up from Socorro next weekend.
MADELINE:	Cool. Are they staying at your apartment?
MARTÍN:	No, they'll stay at Aunt Yolanda's. Mom doesn't want to know that you and I are living together, and this is her way of ignoring it.
MADELINE:	I don't have to stay there if it bothers them.
MARTÍN:	I've told you I'm not going to lie to them. Besides, I don't think it really offends them; it's just all that Catholic guilt.
MADELINE:	How come *you* don't have it?
MARTÍN:	I'm just a weekend Catholic.
MADELINE:	I still don't understand what you mean by that.
MARTÍN:	Do Lutherans go to mass on Wednesdays and Saturdays?
MADELINE:	We don't have mass.
MARTÍN:	(*laughing*) You engineers are so literal. My point is that if I were a full-fledged Catholic, I'd be in church a lot more during the week. (*After a short pause*) Sometimes I actually miss it.
MADELINE:	Martín, are you really okay about getting married in my church?
MARTÍN:	I'm okay with everything, mi amor: a chilly fall wedding in St. Paul, hoards of passionate Romeros doing the wedding dance to the rhythm of a polka band, mi abuelo bonding with your grandfather and inviting him to come spend winters in Española, and a quaint Norwegian wedding cake made by your cousins Uffda and Lefse.

Madeline found herself laughing loudly at Martín's descriptions. She knew that it was his way of letting her know that he intended to make the best of this Midwest-meets-Southwest wedding. They had been planning the wedding since January, and both were tired of the stress. At times it seemed like more hassle than it needed to be, and she and Martín had certainly had a few arguments because of it.

Madeline hated conflict. She remembered their first huge fight and how sick to her stomach she had felt. Martín seemed so comfortable with expressing emotion, probably a result of being raised by parents who encouraged their children to talk and work through problems. Martín still called his sister every weekend in San Francisco and often drove to Socorro during the week to go to his little brother's baseball games. In both relationships, she had noticed open displays of affection and displeasure. Madeline wondered if it bothered Martín that she often side-stepped disagreements. He was pretty good at drawing her out, and she was working on being more direct about expressing herself—but she hated to make him responsible for guessing her feelings.

And that made her remember something she had been avoiding. For several weeks, she had been wondering how to talk to him about her decision to keep her family name, Anderson, *when they married. She worried that Martín wouldn't understand and worse—that he would be hurt or angry. Madeline grinned at Martín as he finished his entertaining description of their wedding and decided that now was as good a time as any to bring up the name issue.*

MADELINE: Martín, since we're on the subject of the wedding, there's something I want to talk to you about, something that's been on my mind.

MARTÍN: Okay.

MADELINE: I've decided to keep my name when we get married.

MARTÍN: (*pausing*) Okay . . .

MADELINE: It's not that I don't like your name—you *know* that I really love the name Romero. It's just that it's not *my* name.

MARTÍN: All right.

MADELINE: (*pausing*) Is that all you're going to say?

MARTÍN: I'm thinking. Don't rush me. I'm just a little surprised. Do you mean you want to keep your name for professional situations?

MADELINE: Well, that, too. I don't want to change my name at all. I hope you're not hurt by this.

MARTÍN: Yeah, it hurts a little but that's not really the point, Maddy. I'm just trying to figure out why. Why don't you want to have my name?

MADELINE: Because I don't want to give up *mine*.

MARTÍN: Why? Because it's a hassle to change your driver's license, credit cards, and passport? Sorry if taking my name is such a hassle.

MADELINE: God, Martín, I'm not *that* shallow! This has nothing to do with convenience. I don't want to change my name because I don't know who I would be if I wasn't Madeline Anderson.

MARTÍN: You'd be Madeline Romero.

MADELINE: Exactly. I don't know who that is.

Martín took a deep breath and tried to control the fear that was creeping into him. The idea of Madeline not changing her name bothered him more than he wanted to admit. If she didn't want his name, what else didn't she want? His mind was racing with a thousand questions and a thousand reasons not to ask them. Maybe Madeline wasn't ready for this commitment, maybe he had rushed her into getting married too soon, maybe they didn't know each other as well as he thought.

Martín's love for Madeline was very much a part of his wanting to marry and raise a family with her. He felt lucky to have grown up with parents who still laughed together and played and held hands in public. He liked the idea of marriage and the goal of building a life together. He had met Madeline in a rock climbing class at UNM during their sophomore year, and he could still recall how funny and smart and beautiful she was to him that semester. There was no doubt in his mind that she was the one he wanted to be with for life. His family had been very support- ive, and even his abuela had gotten past the idea that he was going to marry an Anglo. Martín's stomach dropped at the thought of having to explain this to his mother and grandmother. He didn't want them to think that Madeline did not love him or that she did not fully embrace his family. He knew that he needed to ask Madeline a very difficult question.

MARTÍN:	Madeline, do you really want to spend your life married to me?
MADELINE:	Of course I do! Martín, this isn't about *us* and our future together. I simply want to keep my name because it represents who *I am,* just as your name represents who you are.
MARTÍN:	So you think being an individual is more important than being in a relationship?
MADELINE:	I didn't say that! I want our marriage to be a partnership of two indi- viduals; our relationship adds to who we are without taking anything away. I'm just trying to tell you that I've worked hard to create Made- line Anderson, and I don't want to throw all that away.
MARTÍN:	By marrying me?
MADELINE:	(*loudly*) That is ridiculous! I'm having a hard enough time talking about this without your questioning my commitment to you. My name is simply important to who I am—that's all. You don't even have to think about your name—you know you'll keep it. Why should it be any different for me?
MARTÍN:	Don't get so angry!
MADELINE:	Well, I think you're being pretty selfish.
MARTÍN:	Ditto.
MADELINE:	(*after a pause*) Let's just talk about this, okay?
MARTÍN:	Maddy, I'm trying very hard not to let this bother me, and I'm not re- ally sure why I feel so upset—but I do. I guess there are a few issues around this that we need to talk about.
MADELINE:	(*taking his hand across the table*) I'm ready to listen.
MARTÍN:	I'm worried that my family will see this as your not accepting our cul- ture. My grandmother thinks women should use the traditional Span- ish "de" when they get married.
MADELINE:	Madeline de Romero?

MARTÍN:	(*laughing*) No, you would be called Madeline Elaine Anderson de Romero. And don't forget to roll your r's!
MADELINE:	It would take me forever to sign checks!
MARTÍN:	I love my abuelita, and I want her to accept you.
MADELINE:	(*speaking softly*) Just like I love my grandparents. Do you see how keeping *Anderson* is one way I can honor them? What else are you concerned about?
MARTÍN:	I'm wondering what our friends will think. Won't they think it's pretty weird?
MADELINE:	I'd be surprised if they do. Most of the women I know plan to keep their family names when they marry.
MARTÍN:	You're kidding! What is this, some kind of female conspiracy? How come guys aren't in on the conversation?
MADELINE:	(*with a smile*) It's just our way of taking over the world. Keeping our names is simply the beginning. Our next move will be to stop wearing make-up and tight shoes . . . maybe we'll even stop shaving our legs!
MARTÍN:	Hmmm . . .
MADELINE:	Seriously, though. Women think about it because they have to make a decision about it—and men don't. Although that raises an interesting point—you could become Martín Anderson.
MARTÍN:	Radical thoughts, amor mío!
MADELINE:	Actually, I'm serious. It is an option, just as both of us taking a completely new name is, or both of us hyphenating our names. But I like my name and my identity, so I've never thought seriously about doing any of those other things with my name. But what else are you thinking about besides female conspiracies?
MARTÍN:	What about children? Whose name will they have?
MADELINE:	Yours, or maybe both of ours. Or we can give the girls my name and the boys yours. Can't we figure that out when we have them? Or maybe they could choose when they got older? What do you think?
MARTÍN:	Madeline, as much as I want to swallow all this and tell you I understand, I just can't. I don't think this is just your decision to make, and I don't think you've considered all the angles. I'm sorry.

Martín wondered if Madeline truly wanted to know what he was thinking. He took pride in the fact that he was open and honest with her most of the time, but on this occasion he was beginning to feel that raw honesty was just going to get him into trouble. He wanted Madeline to have his name; it was that simple. Yet, he also understood her desire to stick with Anderson. He had taken a gender and communication class last semester where this very topic had come up. He remembered feeling absolutely confused by the reasons women in the class had given for wanting to keep their names. He also recalled thinking that they were pretty radical thinkers and that their experience would never be his own. Funny how life comes back to bite you sometimes!

Martín was having a hard time sorting out his feelings. He certainly didn't want Madeline or anyone else to think that he associated marriage with ownership, or that she was not important as an individual, but he also saw this move as one that would destroy yet another tradition that men and women were used to sharing. Martín hated that. He thought that the loss of rituals was a danger to modern cultures, and he didn't want to participate in such a loss.

Madeline and Martín sat silently eating their meal. Each felt hurt and confused, and neither felt closer to a solution.

For Further Thought and Reflection

1. In what ways do Martin and Madeline use language to persuade or influence one another?
2. What are the reasons Madeline and Martín give for their married-name preferences?
3. Considering both Madeline's and Martín's perspectives, what are the possible decisions this couple might make?
4. In what ways do married-name choices suggest different styles of marriage relationships? Identify the characteristics of marriage for Martín and for Madeline.
5. To what degree do cultural issues affect married-name choices?
6. What issues of power and control are playing out between the couple in their relational decision-making process?

References

Clarke, V., Burns, M., & Burgoyne, C. (2008). Who would take whose name? Accounts of naming practices in same-sex relationships. *Journal of Community & Applied Social Psychology 18*, 420–439.

Duggan, D.A., Cota, A.A., & Dion, K.L. (1993). Taking the husband's name: What might it mean? *Names 41*, 87–102.

Foss, K.A., & Edson, B.A. (1989). What's in a name? Accounts of married women's name choices. *Western Journal of Speech Communication 53*, 356–373.

Goldin, C., & Shim, M. (2004). Making a name: Women's surnames at marriage and beyond. *Journal of Economic Perspectives 18*, 143–160.

Kline, S.L., Stafford, L., & Miklosovic, J.C. (1996). Women's surnames: Decisions, interpretations and associations with relational qualities. *Journal of Social and Personal Relationships 13*, 593–617.

Scheuble, L.K., & Johnson, D.R. (2005). Married women's situational use of last names: An empirical study. *Sex Roles 53*, 143–153.

Suter, E. A. (2004). Tradition never goes out of style: The role of tradition in women's naming practices. *Communication Review 7*, 57–87.

2

The Whole Package: Commodifying the Self

NAOMI JOHNSON

Key Terms

self-concept, consumption, marketing, mass media, celebrity culture

---

Ashley swept through her bedroom door, saucily placed her hand on her outthrust hip, and turned sideways for her best "red carpet" pose. She had learned the pose from her older sister Rachel's group sorority pictures posted on Facebook. Rachel told Ashley the "tea cup" pose helped create a "skinny arm" and made you look thinner in pictures.

"What do you think, girls?"

Ashley's best friends Suzie, Brittney, and Heather gazed at her and considered her question.

Brittney nodded in affirmation and sounded her approval. "Hot. Definitely a 10. That'll get Jake's attention!"

Suzie bit her lip. "I'm not so sure. Don't you think the skirt is a little . . . short? And maybe the stockings are a bit . . . over the line."

Ashley stomped her foot and sighed. "But, I'm not wearing them with heels, so it's not skanky. Look, it's Homecoming, so you're allowed to be a bit 'over the line,' Suzie! How else will I get Jake's attention?"

Ashley personally thought Suzie's Japanese parents made her a bit too conservative when it came to dressing.

"Yeah, it's just like in Cinderella—a little wave of the wand and *booyah*—a sparkly dress, new shoes, and, then *bam*—the love of a prince!" proclaimed Brittany.

Suzie rolled her eyes. "That's a movie. This is real life in Columbus, Ohio. Not exactly Disney. Besides, don't you remember that stupid Taylor Swift 'You Belong to Me' video that played over and over while we were in middle school? You get more attention for being an everyday girl in jeans than by trying to look like all sexy."

Heather finally piped up. "Is that your new Abercrombie skirt? That is fetch."

Ashley felt a small surge of pleasure from Heather's approval. She had just found the skirt with *the tags still on* at the Goodwill, but felt no need to let her friends know that it wasn't brand new from the store. Ashley didn't like for her friends to know that she couldn't keep up with their spending. Ever since her parents had gotten divorced, Ashley's mom had cut back on how much Ashley could spend on clothes. Her mom was always lecturing her about how it was all marketing anyhow, that Walmart's clothes were the same as anyone else's. Ashley didn't care how many lines of jeans Miley Cyrus sold at Walmart. It still didn't make it *cool* to shop there.

Ashley's family's newly reduced financial status was why she had suggested this sleepover with her friends to celebrate her 14th birthday. Before the divorce, one of their favorite activities had been shopping and a movie. But now it was watching DVDs and listening to the iPod at home. Ashley mentally shrugged. She didn't mind it much really. The girls had spent the evening watching MTV and chatting about high school life and the boys they liked, which had led to discussions about what to wear to Homecoming. This was the girls' first year of high school and they were looking forward to their first *real* dance with teenage boys instead of a bunch of middle-school nerds.

Heather, suddenly distracted from the discussion, turned up the volume on the first *Twilight* movie DVD that was playing on Ashley's bedroom television in the background. "Shhhh . . . this is my favorite part, where Edward carries her up the tree and they almost kiss!"

Ashley suffered a small pain of envy as Heather's attention moved away from her to the boy on the screen.

 "See, Bella is a simple jeans kind of girl, and both Jacob *and* Edward want her." Suzie interjected, unwilling to relinquish the point.

Brittany jumped in, "Oh my God! Aren't you *sick* of the whole *Twilight* thing by now? I mean, Bella has no personality. She just walks around getting rescued by Edward all the time when he's not threatening to hurt her until she gives up her life to become a vampire. Doesn't sound like a good relationship to me."

Heather laughed and pointed to her Hot Topic hoodie emblazoned in glitter with the words "Stupid Lamb," referencing Bella's characterization of herself from the first novel.

"Put me firmly in the Team Edward camp," Heather said with a grin, alluding to the popular "Team Edward" or "Team Jacob" Burger King advertising campaign that had sparked hot debates at their school about whether Bella should date Edward or Jacob. "Give me a boy that sparkles. I'd wear jeans and become a vampire anytime to be with him."

Brittany snickered and threw a pillow at Heather. "You *would* say that!"

Ashley smiled and looked over her friends. They were all different, but she loved how their differences didn't pull them apart. They had been best friends since the sixth grade. They all teased each other over these differences at times, but they also shared their deepest secrets, laughed together, and supported each other when times were rough.

Suzie, whose real name was Setsuko, had been Columbus Middle School's top sprinter. She and her mother currently were training to run in a half-marathon later in the fall, and Suzie was hoping to make the high school track team. A sporty girl, Suzie favored Nike tennis shoes and Under Armor workout gear over the type of sparkly shirt that Heather preferred these days. However, underneath all that, Suzie liked to be a little bit girly, too. Ashley knew for a fact from their shopping expeditions that Suzie favored Victoria Secret's Pink line of bras and underwear. "After all," Suzie had once reasoned to the group during a shopping expedition, "even though nobody sees them, I still like to feel pretty." She merely ignored it when Heather had wisecracked back in a sing-songy voice, "Sure it's not so you can look sexy for Kelvin?"

Thinking back on it, Ashley realized that this was a perfect example of how much Heather had changed over the last year. Among themselves, she, Suzie, and Brittany had voiced some worries about this change in their friend. Heather didn't know this, but some of the other girls at school had started calling her "Heather the Hussy" behind her back.

Ashley had admired Heather's beautiful figure ever since they were 12 and Heather's curves started filling out. To the envy of her friends and the often not-so-subtle admiration of some of their male classmates, Heather had the largest breasts of the four girls—34C's, in fact. (Ashley knew this from that Victoria Secret shopping trip and late night girlfriend chats). Lately, Heather had taken to showing her breasts off in form fitting t-shirts as she had gone quite "boy crazy" (as she herself termed it). At the moment, Heather was especially fond of her latest t-shirt acquisition from Aeropostale that proclaimed, "Hello, My Name is Hottie." Actually, the Hot Topic hoodie Heather currently was wearing was somewhat of a departure for her. Heather typically preferred the "preppy," yet "sexy" looks of Aeropostale or Abercrombie. "If I mix a little naughty with nice, it shows that I'm unpredictable!" she had once confided to Ashley.

Heather's reputation at school was starting to precede her. Even the teachers were noticing. Just last week, Heather had been sent home to change because she was in violation of the school dress code with her lacy black shirt over a red cami. Ashley had been nervous because she just so happened to have worn a similar lace shirt that day, but hers was white over a more modest blue cami. No one had made a remark about Ashley's choice of an outfit, but maybe that was because she didn't have half the bod that Heather had to fill it out. Really, it didn't seem fair at all, Ashley thought. No one cared about how much flesh the boys could show, but the girls had to wear shorts or skirts that were longer than their fingertips, and couldn't wear "revealing" tops.

Brittany took a bite of the Atkins diet bar that appeared to be her dinner for the evening. "Hey, don't you have some *Seventeens* or *Cosmos* or something? They might have some ideas for how to do our hair," Brittany suggested, interrupting Ashley's reverie.

Brittany, the fashionista of the group, could always be counted on to be "on trend." Brittany was going places. She was writing for the school paper's Style section regularly, even though she was only a first year student. An aspiring fashion designer, Brittany read fashion magazines and followed websites like gURL.com and cosmogirl.com religiously for the latest celebrity looks (and gaffes!). Brittany's work had paid off in a big way. Recently, a local marketing company called Ally had started asking for *her* opinion on their latest teen tastes. Once a month, Brittany met with other "cool hunters" (as Ally termed them), talked about the latest teen trends, and gave opinions on new lines of clothing and electronics. Ally even let her keep some of the products as a thank-you for her expertise! Then she would post her inside knowledge on her blog, "All Girl." Brittany wasn't just about fashion, though. Ashley could always depend on her for good advice on everything from parents to school to relationships.

"Suzie, since Heather is *obviously* busy, why don't you see what you can pull up on the laptop? Try gURL.com—they've got some good quizzes that'll be just what we need."

While Suzie started searching on her laptop, Ashley pulled out her magazines. Kristen Stewart, Selena Gomez, Dakota Fanning, Taylor Swift, and other stars gazed back at her with perfect hair, make-up, and features. The covers promised some answers to match these looks: "Diet Makeover: 10 Ways to a Healthier *Hotter* Body!" "5 Secret Celebrity Beauty Tips!" "Kissing 101—Get smoochable lips!"

"Which boob is bigger?" Suzie seriously intoned, staring at the laptop screen.

"What!" shrieked Ashley.

"Oh, my God. What is up with you?" giggled Heather.

"Hey, Brittany said she wanted to take a quiz. That's what gURL.com wants to know. Is it right, left, or I don't know?"

Brittany grabbed the laptop. "Stay focused here, girls. We've got a mission to make Ashley Jake-presentable."

Brittany ignored the ads for Spanx body shapers, Playtex Sport tampons, and a *Seventeen* magazine contest entry for a shopping spree that appeared on the webpage. She paused to check out the newest Miley Cyrus video that began playing in the corner of the screen with information about the latest song downloads. Brittany liked the fringed Ugg boots that Miley was sporting. She made a mental note to look them up on celebritystyle.com and post the link to the store that sold them on her next blog.

"Oh, eeeew. I can't stand Miley!" protested Suzie when the laptop began playing the song.

"I like her!" countered Ashley. "You're just mad because that Facebook app I sent you last week said that the Disney star that you're most like is Hannah Montana, and now that she's Miley Cyrus, she's not the same. She can't be Disney forever you know."

"Yeah, well, she was only 16 when she was dancing on a pole at the Teen Choice Awards. That's nasty," Suzie retorted.

"You know, my Mom's gym gives pole-dancing classes. It's not like it's just for strippers or something. It can be for exercise too," Heather chimed in. Just for effect, she jumped up, straddled a nearby floor lamp, and thrust her hips a few times. "There, my workout is done!"

Suzie looked uncomfortable. Ashley's pulse jumped a beat, and she quickly looked away.

"Okay, this will work," Brittany declared with satisfaction and entered the "gURL games" section that asked "Which celebrity hairstyle best fits your personality?" She logged into her gURL account so that the site would automatically send her the results with links to e-coupons on the various companies' websites for the products necessary to create the ideal look.

Meanwhile, Suzie contemplated the latest *CosmoGirl!* As usual, most of the models were white and didn't look anything like her.

"Hey, Ashley, what do you think of this? It says here that they recommend L'Oreal Perfect Curves cream to make smooth waves. You can use it to do this 'party ponytail.' That would look cute, but not like you're trying too hard." Suzie pointed to the product reviews and styling tips in the "Celebrate your Inner Diva" article while Ashley glanced at the Pantene ad on the adjoining page.

Ashley frowned and contemplated the choices her friends were laying out.

Getting Ready for the Dance

Ashley stared into her closet, but nothing seemed quite right. Her mom always talked about how good girls didn't need to look trashy to get a date. But, on the other hand, her mom was kind of old-fashioned. Did she really want to get fashion advice from her *mom*, of all people? Ashley thought about the products that Brittney had recommended for a sleek, smooth ponytail and pulled out the Spanx slimmer that Brittney had lent so that she could avoid "unsightly bulges" or the dreaded VPI (visible panty line). Of course, Ashley hadn't told her friend that she couldn't afford to buy the more expensive Bumble and Bumble hair glaze that Brittney swore by and recommended.

As she stared into her closet, Ashley contemplated the outfits and hairstyles the girls had worked out during the slumber party. Now that she actually was getting ready, Ashley felt less confident that she would stand out from the other girls. Not that she wanted to stand out *too* much, she quickly thought. Ashley wondered if Heather would listen to the girls' urging to wear a shrug over the low-cut, strappy red dress Heather had chosen. Heather had worn the dress once before when she and Ashley attended a wedding with Ashley's mom. Ashley remembered her mom's quickly hidden look of surprise when Heather entered the car. Privately, Ashley had thought Heather looked pretty sexy—not that Ashley would ever *say* that to anyone!

She quickly turned her thoughts away from Heather and toward her other friend's choices. Working from an inspiration garnered from an old *Cosmogirl Prom!*, Brittney had found the ideal dress for Suzie online. After a bit of begging, Suzie's parents had agreed to buy the sleeveless, high-necked dress that perfectly showcased her toned arms and slender athletic build.

As for Brittney, Ashley admired her friend's creative flair and knew that she would look amazing, as always. Brittany planned to combine a simple, vintage Audrey-Hepburn-style dress, spiced up with a chunky rhinestone necklace and two secretly purchased items: Victoria's Secret stockings with a seam running up the back and tall silver heels! Brittney confided to Ashley on the phone that she would don the last two items only *after* she left home and her mother could no longer stop her.

Now Ashley's Abercrombie skirt ensemble that the girls had collaborated on no longer seemed right. It's just not *me*, Ashley thought to herself. All the other girls had found outfits that expressed their identities.

Of course, maybe the real problem was that Ashley just wasn't sure who she was anyhow! When it came down to it, Ashley admitted to herself, she didn't really care about Jake or what he thought of her outfit at all. She even didn't care about clothes all that much. But, she wasn't a sporty girl like Suzie, or a fashionista like Brittany, or certainly not a boy-crazy girl like Heather.

So, who was she? A loyal friend to her girlfriends? A good girl, like her mother always said, who studied hard so she could go to college one day? Would she someday be Jake's girlfriend? Or was she someone else entirely? Perhaps . . . dare she dream . . . could she join the drama club and someday star in a reality TV show like her favorite, *Keeping up with the Kardashians?* Even now, Ashley still loved the show because of many good memories of sneaking in episodes with her friends when their parents weren't around. They had many whispered conversations about Kourtney, Kim, and Khloé's scandalous and glamorous lives and loves!

Quit dreaming, Ashley thought to herself dejectedly. You just don't have style, money, or a bod like any of the Kardashian sisters.

She pushed her clothes hangers aside in frustration. Whoever she was . . . whoever she was becoming . . ., Ashley doubted any of those answers were in her closet. She turned away in confusion.

For Further Thought and Reflection

1. In this story, how does marketing move beyond simple print or television ads? Do the girls themselves promote consumption through the interactions and activities that they do for fun?
2. List the products like beauty brands, music, and movies that are referenced from print, broadcast, or online media through this case. How do entertainment mass media *content* and celebrity worship complement and enhance marketing messages?
3. Looking at your product list from the second question, what do marketing messages about these products directly state or imply about socio-economic class, sexuality, and femininity? How does this influence each girl's self-concept, feelings of self-worth, and decision-making? How do the girls in this story both resist and embrace these messages?

4. What messages about idealized body types and sexual appearance are present in the marketing messages you identified in the first question? Identify two instances where one of the girls accepts the message. Identify two instances where one of the girls rejects or challenges the message. What interactions have led to this rejection or challenge? How do mass media messages and messages from other sources about sexuality and attractiveness contradict one another in this story?

5. Keep a log of marketing messages you encounter in one day of your everyday life including traditional ads, peer-to-peer marketing, product placement, "advertorials" (brand names included as creative content in magazines or programs), viral marketing (e.g., funny video on youTube), and other forms of online and digital (e.g., video games) marketing. Then answer the following: What types of idealized femininities, masculinities, socio-economic classes, and sexualities are portrayed? How might these repeated messages influence identity?

References

Currie, D.H. (1999). *Girl talk: Adolescent magazines and their readers.* Toronto: University of Toronto Press.

Duits, L., & van Romondt Vis, P. (2007). *Girls make sense: Girls, celebrities, and identities.* Paper presented at the annual meeting of the International Communication Association, San Francisco, CA.

Fisherkeller, J. (2007). How do kids' self-identities relate to media experiences in everyday life? In S.R. Mazzarella (Ed.) *20 questions about youth and the media.* (pp. 225–237). New York: Peter Lang.

Johnson, N.R. (2010). Consuming desires: Consumption, romance, and sexuality in bestselling teen romance novels. *Women's Studies in Communication, 33,* 54–73.

Labre, M.P., & Walsh-Childers, K. (2003). Friendly advice? Beauty messages in Web sites of teen magazines. *Mass Communication & Society, 6,* 379–396.

Lamb, S., & Brown, L.M. (2006). *Packaging girlhood: Rescuing our daughters from marketers' schemes.* New York: St. Martin's Griffin.

Mazzarella, S.R., & Atkins, A. (forthcoming). "Community, content, and commerce": Alloy.com and the commodification of tween/teen girl communities. In S.R. Mazzarella (Ed.). *Girl wide web 2.0: Revisiting girls, the Internet, and the negotiation of identity.* New York: Peter Lang.

Quart, A. (2003). *Branded: The buying and selling of teenagers.* Cambridge Center, MA: Perseus Publishing.

The author wishes to thank her nieces, Alisha, Amanda, and Marissa, for their invaluable suggestions for the storyline in this case.

Moving Up: The Challenges of Communicating a New Social Class Identity

Kristen Lucas

Key Terms

social class mobility, identity work, organizational socialization

---

ESPN Sports Center was on, but Jim Andrews wasn't listening. Instead he was lying on his couch in an otherwise dark room, the light from his television screen flickering across his blank face. He had a rough week—a rough couple months, to be exact—and he needed some time alone to gather his thoughts.

Since being hired as an entry-level attorney at one of the most prestigious law firms in the city, Jim was nagged by a little voice inside his head saying he didn't quite belong: *Kids from his working-class neighborhood grew up to work on the auto assembly line or to manage grocery stores or to enlist in the Army. They didn't become attorneys at high-powered law firms.* Whenever that pesky voice chimed in, Jim would do his best to silence it. He was smart, he graduated in the top 10 percent of his law school class, and he had an indefatigable work ethic. His logic just about licked that little voice until Monday afternoon.

Monday: The Performance Review

As he commuted into the city on Monday morning, Jim contemplated his to-do list for the day: conference call with his major client, file a couple motions in the case, spend a few hours researching case law, and put the finishing touches on a brief one of the senior partners had requested. The life of a young attorney was not nearly as glamorous as all those John Grisham novels made it seem. But it was definitely a good career with a lot of potential.

Jim kept busy all day, crossing items off of his to-do list and racking up billable hours for the firm. As usual, he ate lunch at his desk. He figured he could eat leftovers *and* put in another hour of work while everyone else ate out at some overpriced downtown restaurant. Eventually, the alarm on his watch beeped: 2:55 P.M. In only five minutes he would have his 60-day performance review with his immediate supervisor. He took a deep breath and headed over to his boss's office. His secretary, Carolyn, was out front. "Hello, Mr. Andrews. I'll let Mr. Hughes know you are here."

The hierarchical culture of the firm made Jim uneasy. The secretaries, paralegals, and other clerical workers were required to address attorneys by title, but attorneys addressed everyone in the firm by their first names. That rule didn't sit well with Jim. In the case of Carolyn, it just didn't seem right that a woman nearly 20 years older than he had to address him formally. Yet after many failed attempts, he had given up asking Carolyn to call him by his first name. "Thank you, Ms. Jackson," he said with a mix of respect for Carolyn and a twinge of defiance to the organization's rule. Carolyn smiled warmly back at Jim.

Marc Hughes opened the door, "Come on in, James." They started their meeting by making some small talk about the previous night's game, and Jim updated Marc on his case load. Then they got down to the real reason for the meeting, the performance review.

Jim was relieved to hear Marc's initial feedback. "We are impressed by you, James. You are a hard worker. You're billing an impressive number of hours. Your research and writing skills are top notch. And you've got a good analytical mind." Jim breathed a sigh of relief. This review was going better than he had expected. Perhaps all the rumors that this firm chewed up and spit out new attorneys were just that, rumors. Marc continued, "In these respects, we could not ask for more." Jim took notice of his words—"in these respects"—and he could feel the proverbial tide turning.

"Listen," Marc said to him, "We've got to talk about a few things. We know that you're a bright guy and a hard worker, but your success at the firm relies on some of the intangible things as well."

"What do you mean?" asked Jim.

Marc took a deep breath and shifted uncomfortably in his chair. "I don't know how to say this gently, so I'm just going to come out and say it directly. You're not projecting the image we need our young attorneys to project." Hearing the words out loud startled Jim, but the little voice inside his head said, "I told you so." Although Jim was prepared for a critique of his writing or his productivity, he wasn't prepared for the litany of little things that came his way in that performance review.

According to Marc, the senior partners thought that Jim was too rough around the edges. For starters, his language was not polished enough. *What does that mean? They already said that he had excellent writing skills. So what if he occasionally slipped up said "good" instead of "well" in casual conversation? And maybe he cussed a little here and there. But he really watched it around clients.* He did not dress well enough. *But he wore a suit and tie to work every day. He was never disheveled or in violation of the dress code. It shouldn't matter that his suits were off the rack at JC Penney. He doesn't need a whole closet of fancy clothes to do this job, right?* His car was not sending the right message to clients. *Are they serious? His*

Chevy? That thing got him through undergrad and law school. Maybe it was showing signs of its age, but he worked in an office building—not his car, for crying out loud. He was too friendly with the wrong people and not close enough with the right people who could get him somewhere in the firm. *Wrong people? Like Carolyn? The partners should be glad to know that one of their attorneys has taken time to get to know everyone in the firm and establish good working relationships with people from the janitorial staff who clean the offices, right up through the senior partners.*

It was a lot to take in. Marc ended the meeting by asking Jim to make a more conscientious effort to "fit in" to the culture of the firm. Shell-shocked as he was, Jim agreed to try. After all, this was a good job. He would be hard pressed to find something comparable, especially having only a couple months of experience.

Tuesday: Dressing for Success

After his morning run, breakfast, and a shower, Jim got dressed. This was normally the easy part of the day. He owned two suits—a dark grey one and a blue one—that he alternated. He also owned 10 shirt-and-tie "sets," the kind that come matched in a box. He hung each set together on the same hangar so he wouldn't have to worry about coordinating his clothes each morning. All he had to do was blindly grab one of the hangars. But today was different. Marc Hughes's comments were booming in his head and Jim could not help but look at the contents of his closet with despair. There was not much he could do about his wardrobe this morning. So he made do the best he could by mixing up one of his shirt and tie combos.

Rather than his usual mental to-do list preparation, Jim thought about suits, shirts, and ties his entire commute. It may be superficial, he reasoned. But if that is what is needed to be successful, then maybe he could try dressing a little differently. He promised himself that he would go shopping soon. A couple new suits might actually be a good thing. Maybe he would even try coordinating shirts and ties on his own instead of buying another boxed set. The thought of replacing his favorite watch was not as easy to swallow, though. He could see Marc's point about an expensive metal watch—one like all the other attorneys wore—looking more professional. But his digital watch was so practical. It had a timer and an alarm and a light. Instead of getting upset about it, Jim reminded himself that with a new position come new expectations. He should appreciate his boss raising these issues with him early so that he can make the adjustments necessary. If a new watch was what is needed to be successful at the firm, then a new watch it would be.

At the office, Jim found it more difficult than usual to concentrate on his work. Typically, he jumped right into it. But on Tuesday he found himself surveying what other men in the office were wearing. Jim was hoping that he'd be able to pick up on a couple trends and go shopping with a specific checklist. But maybe this clothing thing was trickier than he originally anticipated. Their suits looked pretty standard: blue, grey, black, and brown. Their shirts and ties were a variety of colors. How exactly did these guys look any different from Jim? More importantly, how was he going to figure out how to look more like them if he couldn't see the difference?

Jim was in the break room pouring himself a fresh cup of coffee when he heard a familiar voice ring out. "What's on your mind, James? You look like you're a thousand miles away." It was Kendra, a woman from Jim's law school class and his only real friend at the firm. He wanted to confide in Kendra about his review and the long list of things that Marc wanted him to change. But he also didn't want to expose himself too much.

"Oh, I don't know. Just tired, I guess." Kendra commiserated with him. The long hours were taking their toll on all the new hires. "Well," James started, "There is one thing I could use your advice on."

"Sure thing," Kendra said.

"Now that' I've had a few paychecks roll in, I've been thinking about going shopping for some more clothes. But I'm at a loss for where to start. Any suggestions?"

"Finally!" The enthusiasm of Kendra's voice made Jim realize that maybe he stuck out more than he originally thought. "If I were you, I'd get. . . ." Jim found a pen and eagerly wrote down the list in as much detail as possible.

By 4 o'clock, Jim knew he was just spinning his wheels and not making any real progress. He logged off his computer, grabbed his shopping list, locked his office door, and headed out to tackle the wardrobe problem head on.

Wednesday: Networking with the "Right" People

Jim had gotten behind on his case load, especially because he had been so preoccupied the first couple days of the week. But bolstered by his recent purchases—which totaled more than what he paid for his beloved Chevy—he was able to concentrate again. He felt almost like his old self and began making up for lost time. In fact, things were going so smoothly that he completely lost track of the hour until Kendra came by his office at 8 P.M. "Hey, James, nice tie," she said as she leaned in his doorway.

"Wait until you see my new suits. It'll be a few more days yet until the alterations are complete. But they are going to look real sharp! At least that's what the salesperson told me. Thanks, Kendra. You're a lifesaver. I couldn't have done it without you."

"A bunch of us are heading out right now for drinks and a bite to eat. We were thinking of going to that new sushi bar a few blocks from here. I know it's not your style to hang out after work, but why don't you join us?"

Jim briefly pondered why they never went out for beer and wings. It's all about the company, he reminded himself. "Know what? I'd really like to go this time."

The gathering at the sushi bar was nice. The firm really did have some incredible people working there. Jim felt a certain privilege being out with this group. They were all young, intelligent, and driven. And they also were a lot of fun. He appreciated how the banter flowed between college rivalries, to political debate, to crazy law school stories, to talking about the firm. Marc was right. Hanging out with these people really could be an advantage. Maybe he could even learn from them how to project this so-called image. So he decided to take on more of an observer role and to really figure out how they presented themselves: how they told stories, what kinds of jokes were appropriate, what topics of conversation were taboo.

Thursday: In a Jam

By late Thursday afternoon, Jim had wrapped up most of his work for the week. When he walked past the copy room, he saw Carolyn struggling with the copier. "Hey, can I give you a hand with that?"

Carolyn waved off his offer to help, but Jim could tell that she was stressed out. She was flipping all the trap doors open and shut, twisting hidden knobs, and peering between gears. But the copier still was blinking "Error—Paper Jam." "Really, it's no problem at all," Jim said as he took off his suit jacket and rolled up his sleeves. "These copiers can really be a pain in the . . ." Jim paused momentarily to adjust his language, ". . . neck."

"You can say that again," Carolyn said. "I've been working on this paper jam for 40 minutes, and now I'm right up against the deadline for Mr. Hughes." Jim saw the panicked look on Carolyn's face and saw tears welling up in the corner of her eyes.

"I bet you didn't know I have a black belt in copy jam removal." Jim had a knack for finding humor in stressful situations. "Give me five minutes and I'll have this copier begging for mercy." He opened, closed, twisted, and pulled until found the offending piece of paper stuck in the rollers. "Ta da!" Jim waved the crumpled white sheet in front of Carolyn, then shot it basketball-style into the nearby recycling basket.

Just then, Marc Hughes walked by. "Excuse me, Carolyn, do you have those files ready?" he asked sternly.

"Yes, sir."

"Good. And James, may I see you in my office?" It was unusual for Marc to call spontaneous meetings. He looked serious. And he slapped the doorframe as though to indicate there was some urgency to his request. Jim's curiosity was piqued.

"Well, my work here is done," Jim said to Carolyn. "You can handle it from here, I assume."

"Absolutely. And . . ." She waited until Marc was out of eyeshot and earshot, then quietly mouthed, "Thank you, *James*." Jim smiled to himself as he walked towards Marc's office.

Marc quickly knocked Jim back to reality. "James, can you tell me what was going on back there?"

"Sure. I walked past the copy room and saw Carolyn wrestling with the copier. I figured because she looked so stressed out and I was winding down for the day, I'd give her a hand."

Marc was not impressed by Jim's team spirit. "When I see a problem, James, I feel the need to nip it in the bud. That way, the problem doesn't get out of control. Remember our talk on Monday?" How could Jim forget? It had consumed almost all of his energy the rest of the week. "Well, we need you to be focusing on being the best attorney you can be. And just now, it looked like you were working on being an *assistant* to a *secretary*. We didn't hire you to fix our copiers. We have people like Carolyn for that. You're too important to be stooping to that level."

Jim interjected, "But I wasn't stooping. I was helping. It was a job that needed to be done."

"Well, if you're looking for work, come talk to me and I can get you additional assignments. But from now on, leave the paper jams to the little people. Okay?"

Up until that point, Jim was handling Marc's critique quite well. He adjusted his wardrobe, watched his language a little more carefully, and even made a point to network with other associates at the law firm. But this was going too far. "Little people"? What did Marc mean by the comment? Jim thought of his own mother who worked as a secretary while he was growing up. He knew how hard she worked and was infuriated to think about anyone considering her a "little person."

Friday: Going Home

Jim parked on the street in front of his parent's house. The familiarity of the neighborhood environment was comforting and a welcome relief from his stressful week at the office. The front porch light was on, and he could hear laughter. He opened the door without knocking and joined the festivities. "Jimmy!" a chorus of voices rang out. His parents, brother, sister, Aunt Mary and Uncle Frank greeted him. The seven adults squeezed around the kitchen table.

"Can I get you a beer?" his Uncle Frank boomed.

"I'd love one," said Jim.

"So what took you so long?" Jim's dad asked.

"I stayed late at work tonight." Jim's mother warmed him a plate of leftovers in the microwave.

"They better be paying you overtime for that, Jimmy," his dad said.

"No, dad, I'm on salary. So I don't get any overtime." Jim wolfed down the pot roast and potatoes his mother served.

"I just don't get why you'd work for them for free," Jim's dad shook his head in dismay. He worked as a mechanic in a union shop his whole life, so he genuinely didn't understand working without overtime pay. "You know, if you worked down at the garage with me, at least we'd pay you overtime. And with these 70-hour work weeks you're putting in, I'd be surprised if ya weren't seeing bigger paychecks than you are now."

"So how's life as a big shot treating ya?" asked his Uncle Frank, diverting the conversation.

"Big shot? I'm no big shot."

"Yeah, right. You're the only big shot this family's got." Jim knew that his family was proud of him. His father had been calling him the "family lawyer" since his first semester of law school. His mother cried through his entire law school graduation. He couldn't let them down. He really needed to make the job at the law firm work out.

"Yeah, Jimmy, you were always the smart one in the family," said his Aunt Mary.

"The smart ass, anyway," his younger brother retorted, and the whole family erupted into laughter.

* * * * *

Jim arrived back at his condo by about midnight. He picked up his remote control and mindlessly turned on the television. His head was swimming. How could so much happen in only a week? He had barely begun implementing the changes Marc wanted to see. He still had friendships to establish, mentors to seek out, communication habits to break, and others to make. He had a long road ahead of him.

Even if Marc thought he still had a long way to go, Jim knew that he was far from the starting line, too. Looking back, his transformation began in college when he started getting exposed to new ideas and a new worldview. Law school prompted even more changes, as it prepared him for life as an unequivocally white-collar professional. No one understood these changes more intimately than his family. Yes, they were proud of him for all of his successes. But he knew that they also lamented the distance that was growing between them. It wasn't for a lack of love. It was the difference that sprung up between them the further he went along this road to being the ideal professional Marc and the senior partners were grooming him to become. He no longer fit in completely with his family. They didn't understand his new world. So should he work harder to fit in with his coworkers? Or should he back off and revert to some of his old ways? How can he possibly reconcile these feelings of limbo he was experiencing? How could he prove to his boss that he is cut out to be an attorney? And how could he reassure his parents that he is the same old Jimmy they raised?

For Further Thought and Reflection

1. Kaufmann (2003) explains that in order to earn reciprocal middle class membership, people from working class backgrounds must engage in conscientious identity work, involving changing how they speak, attending to the nonverbal messages they use to represent themselves to others, and adjusting their relationships (e.g., prioritizing friendships with other middle class people). What specific examples of identity work did Jim engage in?

2. What kind of identity work do you think might be required of you in your chosen career field? What identity work is acceptable to make for the sake of a career? How much is too much?

3. In what ways might Jim's working class background be a hindrance to his success? In what ways might it be an advantage?

4. Social class mobility is often marked by feelings of being in "limbo" (Lubrano, 2004), in which someone feels that he or she belongs a little to two social classes, but not fully to either. What evidence do you have that Jim is experiencing limbo? Do you think that limbo is a legitimate feeling to experience during social class mobility?

5. Miller and Jablin (1991) explain that organizational newcomers seek information in a variety of ways in order to "learn the ropes" and get a better understanding of what is expected from them. But when social costs are high, newcomers resort to less direct tactics, such as observation, surveillance, and disguising conversations. What tactics did Jim use to find out what was expected? Why might he think that his working class background raises the social costs involved in information seeking?

References

Alvesson, M., & Willmott, H. (2002). Identity regulation as organizational control: Producing the appropriate individual. *Journal of Management Studies, 39,* 619–644.

Engen, D. (2004). Invisible identities: Notes on class and race. In Gonzalez, A., Houston, M., & Chen, V. (Eds.) *Our voices: Essays in culture, ethnicity and communication* (4th ed., pp. 250–255). Los Angeles: Roxbury.

Kaufman, P. (2003). Learning to not labor: How working-class individuals construct middle-class identities. *The Sociological Quarterly, 44,* 481–504.

Lair, D. J., Sullivan, K., & Cheney, G. (2005). Marketization and the recasting of the professional self. *Management Communication Quarterly, 18,* 307–343.

Lubrano, A. (2004). *Limbo: Blue-collar roots, white-collar dreams.* Hoboken, NJ: John Wiley and Sons.

Lucas, K. (in press) Anticipatory socialization in blue-collar families: The negotiation of contradictory messages of social mobility and reproduction. *Western Journal of Communication.*

Miller, V. D., & Jablin, F. M. (1991). Information seeking during organizational entry: Influences, tactics, and a model of the process. *Academy of Management Review, 16,* 92–120.

4 Mirror, Mirror on the Wall: Weight, Identity, and Self-Talk in Women

Wendy S. Davies-Popelka

Key Terms

body image, identity, intrapersonal communication, race/ethnicity, self-esteem

---

"Hurry up, Reece, we're gonna be late for class if we don't go eat lunch now!" shouted Emma exasperatedly, as she watched her roommate check her hair and makeup in the mirror for what seemed like the hundredth time that day.

"Don't worry, Emma, we have plenty of time," said Charelle, coming down the hall and stopping in the door to Emma's and Reece's dorm room. "And Reece, honey, you know you look gorgeous, so stop fussing and let's go!"

"Oh, you two, give me a break. I have to make sure my hair looks good, 'cause nothing else does today," explained Reece. She caught a glimpse of herself in the mirror: *You're fat, fat, fat*, the mirror told her.

Charelle looked at Emma with a question in her eyes. Emma nodded and then said, "Yeah, today's one of Reece's 'fat days.' She told me that before she even got out of bed this morning."

"Girlfriend, what do you weigh? All of 120?" asked Charelle.

"Fine, make fun of me all you want. You don't understand. I ate a bowl of cereal, two pieces of bread, a piece of cheese, two slices of pizza, and a chocolate chip cookie yesterday. I must have gained five pounds just since yesterday." Reece turned and glanced into the mirror on the wall above her dresser one last time, running her fingers through her streaked, shoulder-length blond hair. *They don't understand what's it like to be fat*, she thought to herself. *If only I had Emma's figure. She's so thin, and she never has to watch what she eats. I'm so fat. Today I will only eat vegetables and drink only water. And I have to spend 30 extra minutes at the gym. That should make up for yesterday's calories.*

Turning toward her friends, Reece grabbed her backpack off the bed and slung it over her shoulder. "Let's go then if you two are in such a hurry to eat lunch before class."

In the cafeteria, Reece grabbed a tray from the bin, and placed silverware and a napkin on the tray as she moved to the first station, the salad bar. She lifted a plate from the stack next to the salad bar and carefully selected an assortment of raw vegetables—carrots, celery, broccoli, cucumbers—ignoring the cauliflower, which she disliked with a passion. *Some ranch dressing would be really good with these veggies,* she thought to herself. *But I can't have those calories after the horrible day I had yesterday. I have to make up for all that bad food I ate. I shouldn't have eaten that cookie last night before I went to bed. I can't believe I did that. How stupid can I be!?* Turning back to her friends, who were piling their plates with salad—complete with lots of dressing, she noticed—Reece said, "I'm done. I'll grab us a table."

Reece turned and walked toward the checkout line, leaving Charelle and Emma standing there looking at each other, their mouths wide open. Emma recovered first, answering with Charelle's questioning look with a nod, saying, "Yeah, she's been on this weird diet kick lately. If she has a 'bad' day, like she eats something she doesn't think she should have, she tries to make up for the next day, by just eating raw vegetables and drinking water."

"That sounds like punishment to me," replied Charelle, shuddering at the thought. "And what's up with her listing off every single thing she ate yesterday? I've never heard her do that before."

"Oh, she does that every night. She calls it her private time," explained Emma. "She told me she lies in bed at night and lists out everything she ate that day. Then she decides what she can eat the next day based on that."

"I don't understand her obsession with her weight," said Charelle. "I mean, she's not fat. She's what? A size six?"

"Yeah, but when she was really young, she had a problem with her weight. Then she lost a whole bunch of weight in high school, but when she came to college she gained some of it back. Now she's trying to get back to where she was in high school," Emma explained.

At the table

Reece leaned back in her chair and tried not to watch Emma eat the piece of carrot cake she had chosen for dessert. Even after eating most of the vegetables and drinking a glass of water, she still felt hungry. *Well, that's what you get,* she said to herself. *If you hadn't made such a pig out of yourself yesterday, you might be able to have a piece of cake. But no, you had to be a pig. That's all you are, you know. A fat pig. Ever since third grade, when those kids made fun of you. . . .* Reece's thoughts drifted back to Mrs. Wright's third-grade classroom:

Reece glanced down at her shoes as she walked to the front of the classroom. Painfully shy, she dreaded having to be in front of other children. And now

Mrs. Wright had called on her to solve a math problem on the chalkboard! As she walked past Mary's desk, Reece heard Mary and Mary's best friend Lisa whispering and giggling. Then she heard Mary say under her breath, "Nice pants. Where'd you get 'em? Tents 'R Us?" Reece turned bright red and her footsteps faltered as Mary's cruel comment sunk in. *I can't help it,* she thought, *that my mom makes my clothes for me. If only I weren't so fat,* she chastised herself, *I could find clothes to fit me like normal people.* Reece continued her progression toward the front of the room, inwardly shaking at the cruelty from the two girls she so desperately wanted to be her friends. Then she heard the unmistakable whisper of Jimmy St. John coming from her left. "Boom. Boom. Boom," he chanted, ridiculing her as she walked haltingly up the seemingly endless aisle. Children around him began laughing as they heard his taunts. Reece turned an even brighter shade of scarlet and wished desperately that she could sink into the floor and disappear forever. *If only I were skinny,* she thought, *then they would like me. Then I would be popular and everybody would want to be my friend.*

"Hey, girlfriend, what are you daydreaming about? Aren't you going to finish your rabbit-food lunch before it wilts?" Charelle's voice interrupted Reece's painful recollection and brought her back to the present with a start. She mentally shook herself. *Now there's no need to be thinking about that still. You know that you have been working hard to lose weight ever since that day in third grade. If you hadn't regained a bunch of weight when you came to college, you would still be as thin as you were in high school. No matter what it takes, you have to get back there.*

"Hey Reece, you wanna try a bite of this carrot cake? It's even better than the chocolate cake they were serving last week," offered Emma.

"No thanks, Em," Reece said. "I'll never lose the last 10 pounds if I eat cake."

"Ten pounds!" exclaimed Charelle. "Where in the world do you think you're going to lose 10 pounds?"

"I have to lose 10 pounds to get down to 110," explained Reece. "That's what I'm supposed to weigh."

"According to whom?" asked Charelle.

"I don't remember where I read it," said Reece. "One of the fashion magazines had an equation in it to figure your ideal weight. You should weigh 100 pounds if you're five feet tall and then add five pounds for every inch over five feet. Since I'm 5'2", I should weigh 110."

"What does your dad think of that equation?" Emma asked with a slight frown.

"Well, my dad says it's not right, and I shouldn't follow it," Reece said. "He has a chart from the American Medical Association that came in one of his medical journals that he gave me to look at, but it said I should weigh more than 120. But that can't be right, 'cause I'd look fat. So I'm using the equation that says 110."

"Your father the doctor said to ignore the equation you read in some fashion mag, but you think he's wrong?" Emma asked, giving Reece a skeptical look.

"Well, if I want to look the way I should," said Reece defensively, "I need to lose at least ten pounds." As she picked up a carrot stick off her plate, Reece eyed the thick slice of carrot cake on Emma's plate. *I would really like to try that carrot cake,* she thought, instantly reprimanding herself for even thinking that. *How do you ever think you're going to lose weight and be beautiful if you can't even stay away from junk food?* Even as she chastised herself, though, Reece was contemplating the carrot cake again. She reached over and pinched off a tiny piece of the cream cheese frosting, placing it on her tongue and relishing its sweetness as it dissolved in her mouth. *What an idiot!* she screamed at herself. *You are so weak. You'll never be thin. You can't resist temptation, so there's no way you're going to be able to diet. You just need to stop eating completely. Obviously you can't even come down to the cafeteria without cheating, so from now on, you'll stay in your room and drink water.* She pushed her plate away from her, cringing at the harsh things she was saying to herself but unable to stop.

"You can't be full already," said Charelle. "You haven't eaten anything."

"Leave me alone," cried Reece. "I'm not hungry." She shoved her chair back from the table and stood, gathering her tray and her backpack. "I'm going to class," she said. "I have a few questions to ask Professor Lane before class starts." She turned abruptly and walked away from the table, leaving her two friends staring open-mouthed at her back, confused by her sudden burst of temper.

"What's up with that?" said Charelle. "I don't think I've ever seen her that upset. What did I say?"

"Oh nothing," said Emma. "She's like this sometimes when she's upset about her weight. She gets really quiet and withdrawn and is overly sensitive if you criticize her in any way."

"I don't understand," said Charelle. "She's not fat. I think she's beautiful just as she is."

"I know, I know. But she thinks she's fat. And nothing anyone says will change her mind."

"I just don't get why she's so hard on herself."

"I know; I don't either."

In class

"Okay, class, quiet down. Today we're going to continue our discussion of body image by talking with Dr. Susan Holland, an expert in eating disorders." Professor Lane introduced the guest speaker to her Psychology 125 class and took a seat at the back of the room.

Dr. Holland thanked Professor Lane and the class for allowing her to visit them and share information on eating disorders.

"Did you know that dieting has reached almost epidemic proportions?" she asked the class. "Depending on what study you read, it has been estimated that as many as 60–80 percent of adolescent girls are dieting at any given time. And an obsession with being thin can lead to eating disorders."

"But doesn't that just apply to girls?" questioned one young man in the front row.

"Well, it does seem to apply especially to women, but more and more men, particularly gay men, are beginning to worry about their weight as well. Research studies have found that women are generally more concerned and less satisfied with their physical appearance than men. Women are also more likely to weigh themselves, to describe themselves as fat, to think that that their current figure is heavier than their ideal figure, and to not see themselves as underweight even when they are," Dr. Holland continued. "I have a question for you to think about. You don't have to answer this out loud, but just think . . . how many years of your life would you give up to be your ideal weight?"

A wave of laughter and a few gasps raced through the class as the students thought about Dr. Holland's question.

I would probably give up a few years to weigh 110, thought Reece.

Emma considered the same question herself. *How can anyone give up years of their life to change their weight? Don't they know that life is precious? I can't imagine being so upset over your weight that you would actually give up years of your life!*

As the students pondered her question, Dr. Holland shared more information with them. "In response to the question I just asked you," she said, "fifteen percent of women and 11 percent of men in a national survey said that they would sacrifice more than five years of their lives to be their ideal weight. Twenty-four percent of women and 17 percent of men said they would give up more than three years."

"I can't believe anyone would willingly give up years of their life to be a different weight," stated a young African American woman in the back of the room. "I mean, I could probably stand to lose 20 or 30 pounds if I had to, but I would never give up years of my life to do it. I mean, God gave me life, and He's the only one who can take it away. And He loves me the way I am."

"I don't know," replied a young European American woman. "I can see where people might be willing to do that. There's an awful lot of pressure put on women to be thin. I have a lot of friends who do some pretty extreme things to try to lose weight. In fact, two of my roommates are anorexic and one of them is an exercise freak. Being thin is like an obsession with them."

"Unfortunately many women are obsessed with losing weight," said Dr. Holland. "Some people would do anything to lose weight. And their desire to lose weight may not always be linked to an actual weight problem. Who can think of things that thinness in women symbolizes in American culture?"

As soon as she asked the question, answers came flying from around the room. "Beauty."

"If you're thin, you have a lot of friends and people like you."

"Thinness equals success."

"If you're thin, you have control over your life."

"All of those things are true," said Dr. Holland. "In our culture, thinness has come to mean many different things, and many women—especially white women—have internalized the standard of thinness and use it to judge their own attractiveness."

"I don't understand what the big deal is," said a young European American woman. "What's wrong with our wanting to be thin and attractive?"

"It *is* a big deal," replied Dr. Holland, "when the desire to be thin begins to affect your health. And there are many health risks associated with being too thin: eating disorders can cause women to stop menstruating, cause severe damage to kidneys and other internal organs, and even lead to death."

"When women have internalized the cultural standard of thinness and use that standard to judge themselves by, they often don't measure up. And if they don't measure up to that arbitrary standard, they may feel less worthy, like they are less of a person. And this feeling may begin to affect their self-esteem and their self-confidence."

"I don't really understand," said a young man in the middle of the room. "Where do women get this pressure? I mean I've never said anything to my girlfriend about her weight, but she's constantly talking about losing weight."

"It's everywhere," cried the woman sitting beside him. "You hear it from the media, from your parents, from your friends, from guys . . ."

"Yeah, sometimes guys are the worst," said another young woman. "They are constantly making comments about really thin women, like 'She's so hot,' or 'What a body.' What are we supposed to think?"

"That's not true of all guys," exclaimed another woman in the class. "My guy friends who are African American say that they like women with a few curves. They don't want women who look like one of the Olsen twins."

"That brings up an important issue," said Dr. Holland, raising her hand to quiet the building conversation the last few comments had inspired. "There is often a difference among various racial groups. African American culture, for example, seems to be more accepting of weight than European American culture. Although African American women are heavier overall as a group, twice as many African American women as European American women are satisfied with the shape of their body as it is." At the end of class, Dr. Holland fielded a few final questions and then thanked the students for their lively participation. As the students filed from the room, Emma caught up with Reece and tapped her on the shoulder.

"Hey, friend," she said. "Want to go watch the women's field hockey game with me?"

"Can't," replied Reece. "I'm going to the gym to work out."

"Can't you wait and go later?" asked Emma.

"No," Reece said. "I have to put in an extra half hour today and then I have to go to the Student Advisory Board meeting. Then I have gobs of homework to do."

"Want to meet for supper then?" Emma asked.

"No thanks, I'm going to be too busy to eat tonight, I think," said Reece.

"Reece, come on, you have to eat. "Didn't you listen to what Dr. Holland said? Don't let the thin ideal run—or ruin—your life."

"Got to go," said Reece, ignoring her friend's question. "See you later."

Emma shook her head sadly as she watched her best friend head toward the gym. *What can I do to help her get over this obsession with her weight?* she wondered. *I'm afraid she's going to hurt herself, but she just doesn't seem to see what she's doing.*

As Reece entered the door of the gym, she mentally ran through her exercise plan for the day. *I'll stretch out and then use the Stairmaster for 30 minutes. Then I'll run two miles on the track and do another 30 minutes on the exercise bike. Maybe that'll make up for all that junk I ate yesterday. If I do 45 minutes on the exercise bike, maybe I can eat supper tonight,* she thought. Instantly, she corrected herself. *No, I can't. Those ten pounds are going to be hard to lose, and I can't let myself cheat.* As she headed for the locker room, Reece glanced in the mirrored wall by the stairs. *You're fat,* the mirror told her, *but if you work hard enough maybe someday you'll be thin.* Reece struggled in vain to ignore the hunger pangs in her stomach, and tried to envision looking in the mirror and seeing her new, thin body. *Whatever it takes,* she told herself, *that's what I'll do. Whatever it takes to be thin.*

For Further Thought and Reflection

1. How does Reece's intrapersonal communication about her weight affect her self-esteem? What messages does she send herself repeatedly that affect her self-esteem? Where did these messages come from?

2. How does your communication with yourself and with others affect your body image? What messages do you send yourself and where do they come from?

3. Not all people feel the same pressure to be thin. How much pressure do you and your friends feel to be thin? Do you hear people talking about wanting to be thin and measuring themselves against impossible standards? What might account for some people feeling an intense amount of pressure and others not feeling any pressure?

4. In this case, Reece strongly wants to lose weight and expresses her willingness to "do whatever it takes" to be thin. Do you think her desire to lose weight and her behavior are unhealthy? Does her friend Emma have a responsibility to say something to Reece about her behavior? What do you think Emma should do as Reece's friend to keep Reece from hurting herself?

References

Cash, T.F., & Henry, P.E. (1995). Women's body images: The results of a national survey in the U.S.A. *Sex Roles, 33,* 19–28.

Davies-Popelka, W.S. (1998). Listening to their voices: An interpretive study of women's intrapersonal communication about weight. Unpublished master's thesis, University of North Carolina, Chapel Hill.

Hesse-Biber, S.N. & Levy, P. (2006). *The cult of thinness* (2nd ed.). New York: Oxford University Press.

National Institute on Media and the Family. Retrieved June 8, 2007, from http://www.mediafamily.org/facts/facts_mediaeffect.shtml.

Schooler, D., Ward, M., Merriwether, A., & Caruthers, A. (2004). Who's that girl: Television's role in the body image of young white and black women. *Psychology of Women Quarterly, 28,* 38–47.

The Born (Again) Identity: Managing Change Associated with Religious Conversion

Douglas L. Kelley, Debra-L Sequeira

Key Terms

conversion, forgiveness, identity, looking-glass self, peer relationships, turning points

John stood in front of the mirror. He turned his body to one side and then the other, trying to get the best view possible of his lats. This morning, like every morning since he had joined the Jefferson High football team, the mirror confirmed John's own thoughts—he was a stud. Of course he would never have said this out loud to anyone, but who would have thought sophomore year, that he would become the key component of the Titan defense and one of the most popular students on campus?

A year ago last fall, during the Homecoming game, John intercepted a pass during the final seconds and ran it back for the winning touchdown. The next day at school John found himself in the men's bathroom at lunch, looking in the mirror to make certain that he was the same guy who had come to school the day before. His friends seemed friendlier; seniors who had never so much as given him the time of day before gave him a look that said, "You're in." Girls he didn't even know were suddenly finding him soooo interesting!

John's senior year also brought some new experiences in the form of partying with the guys on the team. Here, as well as on the football field, John expanded his popularity by being known as a risk-taker. Football and drinking allowed John to live life on the edge. And it was this edge that provided John with the "rush" that he increasingly needed to feel good.

In the winter of his senior year, the rush John needed came in the form of driving 65 miles per hour on an icy mountain road near his home. Beer and tequila shots subtly blurred his vision and dulled his senses. Lulled into a false sense of control, John couldn't compensate quickly enough and rolled his parents' Highlander two and a half times over an embankment. A Douglas fir was the only thing that kept the car and its driver from cascading 210 feet to the bottom of the ravine. This silent sentinel was the difference between death and life.

Death was more what it felt like to John, however, when he awoke from a five-day coma to find himself in a hospital bed, his mother by his side. Her bright eyes were a comfort to him at first, but her troubled smile betrayed the truth. The doctors were sure he would once again walk normally and regain full mobility. However, the college football scholarships he had counted on were out of the question. Then slowly it came to him—his seventeen-year old sister, Katie, had been in the car. John paused, afraid to ask, "Is, is Katie okay?"

His mom paused, tears in her eyes. "Katie is fine. She was bruised up a bit, but she's going to be okay."

* * * * *

John's first conscious week in the hospital was brutal. His friends were encouraging and uplifting, but he could sense their uncertainty about how to treat him. They tried to joke as they had before, but somehow it seemed forced and unnatural. The look in their eyes, the distance they kept, and their short stays were like a mirror reflecting John's changed identity. Secretly, he felt like they blamed him for screwing up his own life and putting his sister in danger.

Following surgery on his neck and right leg, an intense physical therapy regimen brought the ex-Titan football star to the point where he could get out of bed. As he moved slowly around the room with a walker, he paused and stood silently before a full-length mirror, taking in what others' eyes had told him—his hopes dashed, his spirit crushed. "Why me?" he whispered. "Why me?" He heard no reply. John was still standing in front of the mirror when his physical therapist, Mark, knocked on the door, "Hey, lookin' good. You've come a long way."

Looking down at his legs, John didn't think so. "Yeah, a long way to nowhere," he snapped sarcastically. "I've lost everything."

"Listen, man, you can't afford a pity party now. You've still got a lot of work to do. The doctors and I can help you learn to regain use of your legs, but the real healing is up to you."

John looked quizzically at Mark. What did he mean, "the real healing is up to me?" Each and every day since regaining consciousness John had punished himself for ruining everything. Katie had come to visit him shortly after he had regained consciousness. She still had bruises and cuts on her face. It could have been so much worse. When he found out that her face would always be slightly scarred, he felt even more strongly that he had no right to be healed himself.

Mark could sense John's mental resistance to healing so, later, in the exercise room, he asked John to come to the center of the workout area. With the aid of his walker, John slowly worked his way out until he stood eye to eye with Mark. "Give me the walker."

John recoiled. "I can't! You know that."

"Give me the walker, John."

Mark slowly began to pull John's walker away from him. "John, you're trying to do this with only upper body strength." Mark put his hand firmly on John's shoulder, "John, you need to trust me." John paused, then slowly let go of the walker. He stood silently, staring in disbelief at his legs that somehow were now supporting his body. When he finally raised his head, Mark was looking straight at him. "A little faith goes a long way, John." John could see a mixture of strength and compassion in Mark. This man seemed so certain, so assured. John wanted that, but thought, "Surely Mark has never let people down like I have."

After the session, Mark took John back to his room. "Good workout. I'll leave you alone to think about what happened today—especially how faith and trust might be part of your recovery. Oh, and here's some reading material that might help." Mark dropped a small book on John's lap, entitled, "God's Forgiving Love."

Over the next few days John devoured the book. He had never heard that God could love someone, even if they had made some huge mistakes. One night after finishing the book and continued physical therapy with Mark, John prayed and told God that he accepted God's forgiveness. John had never been much for forgiveness, he believed that each person should earn their way and "pay the price" for the choices they make. Yet, after praying and, for the first time in his life, feeling truly forgiven, John felt like a physical weight had been taken off of him.

The next morning he was ready for Mark to walk through the door. "So, John, what's up with you today? That's the first real smile I've seen from you since we started your physical therapy."

"Is it?" John felt slightly embarrassed. "I've been reading that book you gave me. I, uhm, decided to forgive myself for what I've done. I mean, if God can forgive me, I guess I can, too."

"Great," said Mark enthusiastically. "Now that's progress. If you're up for it, I have some challenging exercises planned for today."

From that point on, John began to feel like it was okay for him finally to work full out on getting better. He began to look forward to his physical therapy and his talks with Mark. In fact, the change was so dramatic that his family and friends remarked on how quickly his recovery was going.

One day Katie unexpectedly showed up. She hadn't visited John very often since that first day because of her own injuries and needing to catch up on missed schoolwork. "Sorry I haven't been by."

"Well," John said sheepishly, "I wouldn't blame you if you never wanted to see me again."

"No way. You're still my brother. We all make mistakes. You know, you may find this hard to believe, but I was afraid I'd lost you."

"I guess you'll always have a reminder of me"—John pointed to Katie's face.

"John, the scar will improve over time. I just want you to know . . . I mean . . . I just want it to be like old times."

John exhaled with relief at Katie's apparent forgiveness. After a long time of talking and catching up on the latest news about friends and school, Katie ventured into new territory, "So, John, I see you have a Bible on your bedside. It's like you're preparing to have the priest read you your last rites." With this she gave a somewhat uncomfortable laugh, trying hard to sound natural.

"Yeah, I thought that I'd better be ready in case you all have been kidding me about my actual improvement."

Both laughed, yet Katie couldn't decide if John didn't pick up on her discomfort or if he simply decided not to acknowledge it. She pressed on.

"You know, Mom told me last night that you had mentioned God quite a bit yesterday when talking to her."

"Yeah! I pretty much decided to give my life to God. I mean think of it, if it wasn't for that one tree I would have been a goner. And my physical therapist, Mark is a Christian. We've had some really great talks."

"John, you know . . . um . . . Well, it's great if that's helping you now. You've been through a lot, but when you come home . . . I mean, well. . . ." Katie rose to go. "I guess what I'm trying to say is that . . . well . . . we all go through phases, and, well . . . well, when you get home, everything will be able to get back to normal." With this she tousled his hair and headed out the door.

* * * * *

After being released from the hospital, John started attending church with Mark. It was after church one Sunday when John burst with excitement into Katie's room, "Katie, you've just got to hear what we talked about today in church."

Plunking down on her bed next to her, John could feel the tension in Katie's body and see the stressed look on her face. "Are you all right?" he asked.

"John you know I think you're the best big goon of a brother anyone could ever have, and I know you have just gone through the most traumatic time of your life, but something has happened to you. You just don't seem like you anymore."

"Look, I'm still me. The only difference is that God is part of my life, now."

"It's just that we used to fight and argue all the time, but there was always this real connection between us. I felt like we were so similar, you know? I mean, we could talk about anything."

"That's exactly what I'm still doing," John replied. "I'm still sharing with you what's most important to me. It just happens that God is a big part of that."

"I know," said Katie reservedly, "I mean, I guess I'm glad for you and all, but somehow it's just different between you and me now."

"It doesn't have to be that way," John quickly retorted. "I'm still sharing with you. It seems to me that you're the one who's changed. You're the one who isn't sharing with me!"

"But . . . look, never mind."

"Never mind what?"

"It's just that I'm not so sure that you really approve of me and my friends anymore."

"What do you mean?" John asked in confusion.

"Well," Katie began hesitatingly, "I mean, you don't really think drinking is cool anymore and, well, I know what you think about Jennifer and Amy."

"Well, Jennifer and Amy aren't good influences on you. You wouldn't drink so much if it weren't for them. And, remember it was drinking that caused that scar on your face. Besides, I really do want you to experience God's grace like I have."

"See what I mean!" Katie suddenly exploded. "What is this 'God's grace' crap? It's like you're talking in secret code. And, regarding drinking, it was *your* drinking, not mine, that gave me this scar. Just because you're still feeling guilty doesn't mean I shouldn't drink. Look, I've gotta go. Oh, and by the way, Tyler called and wants you to call him back."

As the door shut behind her, John sat staring at the full-length mirror that hung on the back of his door. Had he really changed? He knew that his encounter with God was real and that he wasn't the same person spiritually that he had been before. But, wasn't he the same brother he had always been? And, why was Katie so resistant to hearing about how God had changed his life? As he stared in the mirror longer, he thought, "I'm still the same. I just have God now, that's all. Katie just needs some time to get used to it. I'll show her I'm not so different. I'll call Tyler and get together with the guys." The call to Tyler lifted his spirits. They laughed, and he found out some friends wanted to get together that very night and John was to be the guest of honor.

Later that night, John walked nervously up the steps of Tyler's apartment. He took a deep breath and opened the door. As John entered the room, eyes lit up and a barrage of voices said how great he looked and how they had meant to call. The warm air, moving bodies, slaps on the back, and blur of faces were almost numbing.

"What'll you have?" someone shouted.

"Huh?" John was looking to put a face with the voice.

"What'll you have?" It was Tyler standing at the bar. People began chanting "Chug King. Chug King. Chug King." How had he forgotten? John had been the beer-chugging champion at various parties, and was affectionately called "Chug King" by his adoring fans. He stared at the chanting, hopeful faces. "Uh, well . . . I uhm . . ." John wasn't sure what to think. He hadn't been a Christian very long and wasn't quite sure what he believed about drinking.

Suddenly an open can of beer came flying from behind the bar. John caught it mid-flight as Tyler proposed a toast in his honor. "Friends, we've gathered here tonight to bring one of our own home. John's life has taken a few unexpected turns lately, but he's finally back with us." Tyler hopped the bar, put his arm around John, and raised his beer high. "Here's to John!" With this, beer cans clanked all around the room and John took his first sip of beer in ten weeks.

The next two hours of conversation went as well as could be expected—mostly shallow and surface stuff, no risks. But finally, the moment he had been dreading came. "Hey everybody, it's chugging time! Clear a path to let the Chug King and any challengers come forward." A cheer from the crowd went up; John and two reluctant challengers were pushed forward.

"Hey, you know they don't let you chug much in the hospital, so I'm kind of out of practice," John said weakly. "Maybe these two. . . ."

"Not to worry," Tyler interrupted, "we know this is your first time out of the chute since the accident." With this Tyler tossed a can of beer to each of the three contestants. "Ready, steady, you're. . . ."

"Wait, wait, I, well, I. . . ." interrupted John.

"What is it ol' Chug King?" Tyler said with an air of mock subservience. "What is your bidding?"

Well, it's just that . . ." John began.

"Just that John has found religion, that's all," came a familiar voice from the crowd.

John wheeled around quickly, only to see Katie and her friend Amy. "Katie, what are you doing here?"

"Amy and I were just hitting a few parties, oh Chug King," Katie said mockingly.

John slowly became aware of Tyler's voice, "Is this true? Has the Chug Master found religion?"

John stared at Katie's face, and at the mark that would be there forever because of his choices. "No. I haven't exactly found religion. . . ." John started.

"Good!" Tyler interjected.

"It's more like God just grabbed hold of my life. I just don't need the whole Chug King thing anymore."

The resulting silence in the room was deafening. John could hear nothing but his own heart pounding wildly in his chest. Slowly people began to turn away into their own small conversations. Tyler walked over to other friends and they began laughing, a little too enthusiastically. Finally, when Katie and Amy seemed distracted by a couple of his old friends, John slipped quietly out the door.

The drive home was painful. Why was this so hard? Had he really changed? Why couldn't they accept him with this new part of his life? And, most importantly, how could Katie have humiliated him like that?

When Katie came home a little after midnight, the light was still on in John's room. She knocked lightly on the door. "I'm not here!" John called. Katie slowly opened the door. "I told you, I'm not here. Isn't that what you said to me earlier? If I'm not me anymore, then I'm really not here, am I?"

"John, I'm sorry."

"Sorry for what? That I'm not here anymore or that you humiliated me in front of all of my old friends?"

Katie shot back, "Look, you're not exactly innocent you know. You stood there and made all of us feel that you are better than we are because you don't need to drink anymore. I guess God's grace and forgiveness only works one way, huh?"

For Further Thought and Reflection

1. Write the end of this story. Is reconciliation possible between John and Katie? How can they more productively communicate to rebuild their relationship?
2. Early in the story John had to accept forgiveness from God for his choices. How does one try to gain self-forgiveness?
3. It appears that both John and Katie need to forgive one another. Describe key elements to the forgiveness process and apply them to John and Katie.
4. Several times in this story people mention "getting back to normal." Is this a realistic goal? What do people want in their relationship when they talk about this?
5. Have you ever taken a position or held a belief that put you at odds with the majority of your peers? If so, how did you handle it? Can discomfort ever be positive in a relationship?
6. What were the turning points in John's relationships with his family? His friends? What types of turning points could occur that would strengthen or weaken his current relationships?

References

Baxter, L.A., & Bullis, C. (1986). Turning points in developing romantic relationships. *Human Communication Research, 12, (4)*, 469–493.

Mead, G.H. (1934). *Mind, self, and society.* Chicago, IL: University of Chicago.

Sherif, M., & Hovland, C.I. (1961). *Social Judgment.* New Haven, CT: Yale University Press.

Waldron, V. & Kelley, D. (2008). *Communicating forgiveness.* Newbury Park, CA: Sage.

Part II

Coming Together: Developing Closeness with Others

6

I Need Some Space: Friends through Good Times and Bad Times

KATHRYN DINDIA, AIMEE LAU, STEPHANIE HSU & PAIGE GARBER

Key Terms

relational dialectics, openness/closedness, autonomy/connection, novelty/predictability

Turning left and driving down the street, Ashley saw for the first time the dorm she would be living in for the upcoming school year. Butterflies began to flutter in her stomach. As her father pulled the van into the lot, Ashley took a deep breath to prepare for what was to come. Ashley and her parents got out of the car and began unloading her belongings.

Walking down the hallway toward her room, Ashley spotted her roommate and best friend of four years, Jacinta. It was a relief to see a familiar face with so many strangers around. As best friends, Ashley and Jacinta were excited to be attending the same college and sharing a dorm room. They were looking forward to learning new things and growing closer.

When Ashley's family left, Jacinta came back into the room. "Are you all right, Ash?" she asked. Ashley replied, "I'm okay. I think it's just going to take some time to adjust to living away from home and my family."

"I know exactly what you mean. Giving up the comforts and security of home will be tough, but the excitement of being independent and exploring life on our own will be a great experience. If you ever want to talk about something, I am always here for you."

"I know," Ashley replied. "And you know that you can always come to me too, Jacy."

* * * * *

For four months, Ashley and Jacinta were inseparable. They made the same friends, joined the same clubs, ate dinner together almost every night, and went out to the same places. But by the fifth month, Ashley felt like she was suffocating in her friendship with Jacinta and needed some space. It was nice to start college with the security of a built-in friend, but now Ashley was ready to venture out on her own, and make some other friends. On the weekends, she began to associate more with new friends outside of the circle of friends she and Jacinta shared. However, every time Ashley was invited to go somewhere with her new friends, Jacinta would tag along without asking. The situation grew to be such a problem that Ashley started to sneak out of her dorm room to be alone with her new friends.

There were several times when Ashley planned to tell Jacinta what she was feeling. She thought: "I need time to myself and I want some time with my new friends without Jacy. But I'm afraid that saying something to Jacy would hurt her feelings and our friendship."

Over the weeks that followed, Jacinta noticed that Ashley was not in the room as often, and wondered if something was wrong. She thought, "I really need to find out what is going on with Ashley. We don't really do much together anymore, which is really weird."

One day, Ashley came back to the room from class in a bad mood. She noticed a large pile of Jacinta's laundry on the floor. Just as Ashley walked out of the room, Jacinta walked in. "Jacy, what's all your junk doing all over the floor? I can't even walk through the room without seeing all of your crap lying everywhere!"

Jacinta apologized. "Look, I am sorry that everything is everywhere. I was just trying to organize some of my stuff. Besides, I didn't think you would be back for another hour because I thought you were going to be in the chemistry lab."

"Whatever!" Ashley snapped.

Jacinta ignored Ashley's comment and looked directly at her. "Ashley, we really need to talk about some things."

"Like what?" Ashley said harshly.

"Like the fact that over the last month or so, you have been incredibly moody, we barely do anything together, and you're never in the room anymore! I feel like our friendship is going downhill and I want to know what is going on. Ash, we've been best friends for a long time! You know you can tell me what's on your mind."

Ashley moved toward the couch and sat down. "You're right, Jacy. There has been something that has been bothering me and I should have told you right away, but I was scared you'd be mad at me."

"Ashley, tell me what it is! I care about our friendship and want to work things out."

"Jacy, I really care about you too. But the big problem is that I don't feel like I have any freedom in our friendship. Every time I tell you I am going somewhere with my friends, you never ask if you can come along. You always invite yourself. Don't get me wrong. I really love spending time with you, but I also like hanging out with other friends."

Jacinta was surprised. "Wow! I thought it was a given that we always do things together. I'm sorry that I got on your nerves, but it's not fair that you are so angry with me, Ash. You could have at least talked to me instead of getting so defensive about the situation."

"Yeah, I guess you're right, but it wasn't that easy to talk to you about it."

"What do you mean?" asked Jacinta.

"Well, I didn't want to hurt your feelings, make you angry, and hurt our friendship."

"The fact that you have been avoiding me for the past several weeks hurts more than if you would have just told me." After a moment of silence, Jacinta said, "Ashley, let's promise that if we ever have a problem, no matter what it is, we will tell each other right away, okay?"

"Deal!" Ashley replied.

* * * * *

Before the start of their sophomore year, Ashley and Jacinta agreed that it would be best to room with other people. They felt that more time apart would ease some of the strain in their friendship. For one thing, Ashley had a new boyfriend, Steve, and Jacinta wasn't too fond of him. Jacinta thought Steve was trouble and had told Ashley so. Ashley moved to an apartment complex with two friends from her French class, while Jacinta moved into an apartment building two blocks away. Although Ashley and Jacinta didn't see each other as often, they made it a point to stay in touch by phone, chatting on Facebook, or getting together for coffee. As the new semester progressed, Jacinta and Ashley's friendship grew stronger and they enjoyed the time they spent together.

One night, as Jacinta was online checking out some new pictures posted by one of her Facebook friends, someone who was not friends with Ashley, and she found a picture of Ashley's boyfriend Steve, kissing another girl. She noted that the picture was dated just a couple of days ago. She was upset and angry and wanted to confront Steve. At the same time, she felt like she should tell Ashley first. Jacinta was torn. Should she tell Ashley about the picture or should she pretend that nothing had happened? She decided, as a best friend, she needed to tell Ashley.

Jacinta sent a text message to Ashley. "Need to talk."

Ashley replied back, texting "about what?"

Jacinta hesitated. "tell you f2f. be at your apt soon."

Ashley was waiting outside for Jacinta when she arrived at her apartment. Once inside, Jacinta said, "I've been agonizing over what I am about to tell you and it's very serious."

"You're really scaring me, Jacy!" Ashley nervously replied.

"I want you to know that as my best friend, Ash, I care about you and only want what is best for you. I think you better sit down."

"I don't want to sit down. Just tell me!" Ashley demanded.

Jacinta took a deep breath. "Okay, here it goes. . . . Last night, I was online checking out some pictures that one of my other friends posted on her Facebook page and I saw a picture of Steve. He was with another girl . . . and they were kissing."

Immediately denying the accusation, Ashley yelled, "How could you say that? There's no way he would ever do that to me." Ashley caught her breath and said more calmly, "You probably saw someone who looks like Steve."

"No! I know it was Steve with another girl. I can show you the picture on Facebook if you want. I'm so sorry, Ash. I don't mean to hurt you, but I wanted you to know before the relationship got serious and you ended up getting hurt even more."

Running to her room and slamming the door, Ashley began to cry uncontrollably.

Jacinta wanted to do something to help, anything that would make her feel better. She hated seeing Ashley like this. After waiting five minutes, Jacinta softly knocked on Ashley's door. "Ashley, I am going to leave you alone. I know you need some time alone to think about things. When you're ready to talk, call me! Don't forget that I am here for you."

"Thank you, Jacy." Ashley softly replied.

The next day, Jacinta received a call from Ashley. They decided to meet at a coffee shop, where Ashley told Jacinta what happened after she had left her apartment. "I called Steve and asked him to come over. I confronted him about that other girl. At first, he denied it, but then I told him you saw the picture on Facebook and he admitted it. I couldn't believe he lied to me! I broke up with him because I could never trust him again. I can't believe that I was in love with that jerk! Jacy, I should have taken your advice when you warned me he was trouble. I guess I wanted to believe that he was a good person."

Jacinta squeezed her hand. "I know you did. For a long time, I tried to accept the fact that you were in a relationship with Steve, even though I did not like him. As long as you were happy, I was happy."

"Jacinta, I want you to know how much our friendship means to me. You really saved me from making one of the biggest mistakes in my life. I don't know what I would do without you. Thank you."

Jacinta smiled. "I know I don't say this as often as I should, but you've always been a big part of my life too, Ashley. You've supported me through a lot of things and even put up with my annoying habits!" Ashley and Jacinta began to laugh. "I know I can always count on you if I need someone to talk to. I'm so thankful for the friendship we have had for the past six years."

* * * * *

The summer had ended and Ashley and Jacinta's third year of college had begun. Ashley had decided to study in France for the spring semester. Jacinta wanted to go along, but opted to stay in the States because she just couldn't afford the extra costs of studying abroad for a semester. During the fall semester, Jacinta and Ashley decided to try living together again, but this time in an apartment. Two months went by without problems. Ashley still spent time with other friends and Jacinta began dating a new man.

Ashley was always curious about the guy Jacinta was dating. She constantly asked who he was, but Jacinta would always reply, "Oh, just a guy."

Ashley found it very awkward that Jacinta never mentioned his name or brought him to the apartment to introduce her. After four weeks, Ashley decided to ask Jacinta again about the mystery man. "So, when am I ever going to meet this boyfriend of yours?"

"One day," Jacinta quickly answered.

Later that week, Ashley stopped by the grocery store after class to pick up some items needed to fix dinner. As she walked past a checkout counter, she saw Jacinta holding hands with her mystery guy. Ashley could not believe who she was looking at. It was Steve! Ashley immediately realized why Jacinta had been so secretive about her relationship. Ashley was so stunned that she dropped the glass bottle she was carrying. Several people, including Jacinta and Steve, turned around to see what happened. Jacinta watched Ashley run out of the store. She tried to run after Ashley, but she was too fast. She knew that Ashley had seen her with Steve. Jacinta had been nervous for so long to tell Ashley about dating Steve because she was not sure how Ashley would take the news. As Ashley ran back to the apartment, she thought to herself, "How could Jacy do this to me? I thought she was my best friend!" Ashley unlocked the front door, went to her room, and buried her head under her pillow, and cried.

Jacinta knew that she would have to tell Ashley sooner or later, but this was not how she anticipated doing it. Jacinta arrived at the apartment and knocked on Ashley's door. "Ash, open up. It's Jacy."

"Go away!" Ashley demanded.

"Please Ashley! I'm sorry!"

"Don't talk to me ever again!" Ashley screamed.

Jacinta backed away from the door. She thought to herself, "There goes the greatest friendship I ever had. There is no way Ashley is going to forgive me for this. I thought that maybe because we are friends and she cared about me that she would try to be happy for me!"

One week passed, and not one word, not even eye contact was exchanged between Ashley and Jacinta. Tension was high whenever they were in the apartment together. Another two weeks went by and nothing changed. Finally, one afternoon during lunch, Jacinta tried to open the line of communication. "Ashley, I know how upset you are with me about seeing Steve. And I know I am a hypocrite for saying how bad Steve was for you. I can't explain how we even got together! Steve has grown up a lot and is a completely different person than he was when you dated him last year. All I can do is hope that you can forgive me. We can't ignore each other for the rest of our lives. Ashley, I would do anything possible to try to salvage our relationship! It means more to me than staying in a relationship with a guy."

Ashley turned to Jacinta. "Jacy, you know you really hurt me. How could you ever go out with a guy I dated, especially one who you saw cheating on me?"

"I really am sorry for all the pain I caused you Ashley. I swear, I didn't get together with Steve to intentionally hurt you."

"You know, Jacy, it's going to take a long time for me to build up trust in you again."

"I know it will," Jacinta sadly said.

* * * * *

The first semester ended and winter break approached. Jacinta and Ashley spent a good deal of time talking about the situation with Steve and where their friendship stood. Even though they sorted some of their problems out, both knew their friendship would not be the same. Trust between Ashley and Jacinta was still fragile. Spring semester arrived and it was time for Ashley to leave for France. She and Jacinta decided that they would take this time apart to think about how they could turn their friendship around. Jacinta went to the airport with Ashley and her family to send Ashley off. Ashley hugged her parents, but only waved good-bye to Jacinta and told her to take care of herself.

When Ashley arrived in France, she felt a sense of relief, relief from the pressures of home and friends. So much had happened between her and Jacinta that it was a wonderful feeling to get away from it all. At the same time, she knew she would miss Jacy and her family.

Two months passed since Ashley had left, and Jacinta had not heard from her. She had no idea how Ashley was doing or what she was doing. Jacinta made the effort to keep in contact through emails and text messages. No responses from Ashley made Jacinta feel lonely. Jacinta felt there were very few people at school who she could really talk with. Jacinta thought that maybe Ashley was still angry with her and the relationship with Steve.

Three weeks later, Jacinta finally received an email from Ashley. In the email, Ashley apologized for not writing sooner. She had been so busy with schoolwork and exploring Europe. She also wrote that she missed Jacy a lot. For the remaining time of Ashley's trip, she and Jacinta emailed back and forth regularly.

The day finally came when Jacinta and Ashley's parents went to pick up Ashley and they invited Jacinta to come along. As Ashley walked out of the terminal, her family ran to her and they all embraced. Jacinta stood back and watched. Ashley then approached Jacinta. "Hi Jacy. It's good to see you again!"

"Hi Ash. How was your flight?" Both of them acted awkward; they were both unsure about the status of their friendship. Gradually, they began to talk about what had happened to them since they had last emailed each other.

Summer vacation began and Ashley and Jacinta saw each other from time to time. Ashley shared stories about her time abroad. Ashley also told her that she had met someone in her program. His name was Jerome and she was planning to go back to France to visit him. Jacinta was happy to hear about it. Jacinta told Ashley that she had begun to see someone new and that she wanted to introduce him to Ashley. "Ashley, I am sorry about the way things were before you left for France. I still feel terrible."

"Jacy, after thinking about things in France, I learned to forgive and forget. I learned not to take things, especially our close friendship, for granted. I want us to be best friends again."

Jacinta smiled, "I would really like that, too."

* * * * *

Ashley's and Jacinta's final year at college approached. They decided that they would live together again. They promised each other they would make their last year a memorable experience. Neither knew what was going to happen after graduation. They had some ideas about plans after college, but nothing definite.

The entire year went without any major problems and before they knew it, graduation day arrived. Jacinta and Ashley could not believe how fast their four years in college had come and gone. They were both excited to start their new lives but at the same time, they were sad about leaving each other. Jacinta took a teaching job in Arizona and Ashley was leaving for France at the end of the summer to live with her French boyfriend, Jerome.

After the graduation ceremony, Jacinta and Ashley congratulated one another and hugged. "Ashley, when are we going to see each other again?"

"I don't know, but it definitely is going to be strange without you." Both Ashley and Jacinta began to well up with tears.

"I promise to write and call often." Ashley remarked.

"Me too," Jacinta said. "Let's promise to always be friends no matter what, Ash!"

"Friends forever. Jacy, that is something I will treasure for the rest of my life!"

For Further Thought and Discussion

1. According to Baxter (1988) there are at least three dialectical tensions inherent in all relationships, opposite tensions that individuals struggle to balance within a relationship: autonomy/connection, novelty/predictability, and openness/closedness. What are specific examples of each of the dialectical tensions in the communication that takes place between Ashley and Jacinta? Which dialectical tension is most predominant?
2. Relationship partners, knowingly or unknowingly, use strategies to deal with the dialectical tensions in their relationship. There are several strategies that researchers have identified for managing dialectical tensions (Baxter, 1998; Montgomery & Baxter, 1998; Wood, 2004) including selecting one pole of the tension over the

other, cyclic alternation between the two poles of the tension, topical segmentation such that some topics/activities engage one pole of the tension while other topics/activities engage the other pole of the tension, moderation in which one takes a middle-of-the-road approach to managing the tension, disqualification in which one pretends the tension does not exist, and reframing such that the poles are no longer seen as in opposition to each other. Which of these strategies did Jacinta and Ashley use to manage the dialectical tensions in their relationship? What was the principle dialectical strategy used to manage the openness/closedness dialectic in their relationship?

3. Dialectical tensions are often experienced in varying degrees of intensity and at different times by each partner in a relationship. Can you find specific examples of Jacinta and Ashley experiencing tensions to different degrees or at different times in their relationship? How did their different experiences of the dialectical tensions lead to conflict?

4. Dialectical tensions, and how relationship partners respond to them, influence relationship development. How did Jacinta and Ashley's relationship change as a result of their communication about dialectical tensions? What dialectical tension did you feel was most important for Ashley and Jacinta to manage to maintain their relationship?

5. Dialectical tensions are interrelated in personal relationships. How does the autonomy/connection tension affect the openness/closedness tension, and vice versa, in Jacinta and Ashley's relationship? How does the novelty/predictability tension affect the openness/closedness tension, and vice versa, in Jacinta and Ashley's relationship?

References

Baxter, L.A. & Montgomery, B.M. (1998). Rethinking communication in personal relationships from a dialectical perspective. In S.W. Duck (Ed.), *Handbook of personal relationships second edition* (pp. 305–351). London: John Wiley & Sons.

Baxter, L.A. & Braithwaite, D.O. (2008). Relational dialectics theory: Crafting meaning from competing discourses. In L.A. Baxter & D.O. Braithwaite (Eds.), *Engaging theories in interpersonal communication: Multiple perspectives* (pp. 349–362). Thousand Oaks, CA: Sage.

Dindia, K. (2000). Self-disclosure, identity, and relationship development. In K. Dindia & S.W. Duck (Eds.), *Communication and personal relationships* (pp. 147–162). London: John Wiley & Sons.

Montgomery, B.M. & Baxter, L.A. (1998). *Dialectical approaches to studying relationships.* New Jersey: Lawrence Erlbaum Associates.

Rawlins, W. (1992). *Friendship matters: Communication, dialectics, and the life course.* New York: Aldine de Gruyter.

Wood, J.T. (2004). *Communication theories in action: An introduction.* Belmont, CA: Wadsworth.

Wood, J.T. (2010). *Interpersonal communication: Everyday encounters.* Belmont, CA: Wadsworth.

7

Talking Family: The Discourses of Voluntary Kin

Dawn O. Braithwaite, Betsy Wackernagel Bach, Sarah E. Dirks, Haley Kranstuber, Sayaka Sato Mumm

Key Terms

fictive kin, voluntary kin, discourse dependent families, turning points

Miriam scurried around the kitchen, working on Thanksgiving dinner. She checked the dining room table and decided it was lovely, with her grandmother's linens and china that she used only for special dinners. She straightened the tall candles and the little Thanksgiving Pilgrim couple, figurines that had always graced her mother's table when Miriam was growing up. Her mom, Esther, had given the Pilgrim couple to her when Miriam and Mike were married. Seeing them on her table brought back great childhood memories, in spite of the fact that Franco, the man she called "Little Bro," teased her every year, claiming that the man Pilgrim was gay. "I mean, come on, look at those pants, those boots with the big buckle, and that hat," he would tease her. Now her son Matt was joining Franco in teasing his mom. "Little does Matt realize he'll inherit them" she smiled to herself. Miriam loved Thanksgiving and all the traditions associated with it—the turkey roasting in the oven, the cranberry salad, the wild rice dressing, and even Franco's jokes about her little Pilgrim man. She looked forward to the following day, as their tradition was to gather at Franco's and Steve's to watch the final football game of the season against their arch-rival. Miriam always made a big pot of turkey soup from Thanksgiving leftovers.

Miriam counted the place settings around the dining room table one last time. There were places for herself, Esther, Yuki, Franco, and Steve, and places for Dejon, her new colleague at work, and his wife, Krista. Miriam had a lot of trouble deciding how to place everyone at the long table—Mike always sat on one end and she on the other. This was the first time she had hosted a formal dinner since he left. Their divorce was final just two weeks ago. "Stop it. Don't start thinking about it," she told herself. She switched the places around one last time. She had put her mother in "Mike's chair," but was afraid that Esther would not be able to hear well, so she switched her

51

work colleague Dejon to the end of the table. This way no one in the family would have to sit somewhere new this first Thanksgiving without Mike.

Miriam returned to the kitchen and checked the "kids' table" in the corner. The kids would enjoy eating in the kitchen, where they could cut up and have a good time. Miriam hoped that Mike would get their son back home on time. Matt had spent the night with his Dad and Mike promised to get him home well before dinner. "He had better not get him back late like he did on Matt's birthday," she said to herself.

Miriam forced her attention back to more positive thoughts. She basted the turkey and put a large pot of water on the stove to boil potatoes. The cranberry dish was done and she checked the clock, as everyone would be arriving soon. She decided to wash up some of the dishes before she changed into that beautiful new sweater Yuki had given her. As she worked her way through the pile of pots and pans, her mind wandered. How many holidays, birthdays, homecoming games, and other events they had all spent together—Miriam, Mike, and Matt, Yuki, Mom, Steve, Franco, and the boys. They were inseparable, or so she had thought, and had often referred to themselves as "the family" when they were talking with each other. Steve and Franco's boys called Esther "Grandma" and had always called her "Auntie Miriam." Esther referred to Steve and Franco as "my boys" and always gave their sons Christmas and birthday presents, like she did for all her grandkids.

"Thank goodness for Mom," Miriam said out loud as she washed the last of the dirty pans. Esther had been a rock since the day Mike announced that he was leaving, and her financial support had kept Miriam afloat until she could refinance the house to cover the payments on her own. Then of course, there was Yuki—what would she do without the woman who was like a sister to her? She and Yuki had survived the sorority together and, after college, they grew closer than best friends. Miriam was an only child, and she could not imagine any sister closer than Yuki.

Even though she lived just a couple of miles away, Yuki had spent the night at Miriam's and right now she was upstairs taking a shower before everyone else arrived. Yuki often spent the night before a holiday. In fact, Yuki, Miriam, and Mike had a long tradition of making blueberry pancakes for breakfast and reading the newspaper together. This year Miriam was especially glad to have Yuki stay over so she wouldn't wake up alone in a too-quiet house. They decided to skip the pancakes and start a new tradition of home-made yogurt and granola. She and Yuki had Skyped with Yuki's parents in Tokyo last night. Even though they do not celebrate Thanksgiving in Japan, Yuki liked to talk with her parents on her American holidays, and Miriam was glad to join in and say a quick hello too—very quick—as they do not speak English!

Franco and Steve would be arriving any moment, as Steve had promised to come and help with the mashed potatoes and the gravy. Mike had always made the mashed potatoes and gravy. "They'll probably be late," she laughed to herself. While Franco was always on time, or even early, Steve was perpetually late, trying to fit one more task in, editing one more manuscript, putting the final touches on a gourmet dish that he was making, or picking out the perfect bottle of wine to bring along. Miriam's thoughts turned to Steve and Franco's 20th anniversary celebration just this past Spring. Steve made his famous homemade lobster ravioli and set an elegant table for all of them. It was the last time that the whole family was together. Steve and Franco's two boys looked so handsome, and so uncomfortable in dress shirts and slacks. It was the first time Miriam had ever seen the boys out of jeans since they had moved down the street seven years ago when the boys were in preschool. Mike joined the celebration, arriving late and leaving early. She appreciated that he made the effort to be there, and recognized that it took some courage, as he knew that Esther, along with Steve and Franco, were furious with him for leaving Miriam. Everyone was on their best behavior for Steve and Franco's sakes, trying just a little too hard to make jokes and outdo each other with funny stories, like the family had always done.

* * * * *

As Yuki got dressed after her quick shower, she thought back to the Skype conversation she and Miriam had with her parents in Japan. Yuki could not believe how much time has passed since she had come to the U.S. for her college education. She still vividly remembered how helpless and lonely she was at first, surrounded by strangers, and struggling to get a good grip on English as her second language.

Once she became more comfortable speaking in English, Yuki joined a sorority in order to acculturate herself further and make friends. In the sorority, Yuki did make many friends, but more importantly, she found her "Big Sister," Miriam. Miriam and Yuki were assigned to be "Big Sister" and "Little Sister" during Yuki's first week in the sorority, and their sisterly bond grew from there. Miriam became Yuki's "sister in America," and Yuki's family in Japan had been more than grateful that Yuki developed such a solid and special bond in the United States. Since Yuki was very close to her family, despite living thousands of miles away from them, she was excited to have Miriam talk to her parents on Skype. This, in Yuki's mind, kept Yuki's parents happy and assured about how Yuki and her sister in America were doing.

Although Yuki felt happy and blessed overall, she was not entirely without worries. Last night was the first night Yuki stayed overnight at Miriam's place since Mike moved out. As Yuki developed a strong sisterhood with Miriam, Miriam's other close ties, like her friends Steve and Franco, naturally became a part of Yuki's American family as well. Mike was no different. Now that Mike was gone, Yuki honestly was unsure about how this first Thanksgiving without him would go. Several questions ran through her mind. "How will the conversations go if everyone talks about past holidays, trips, and other occasions, when Mike was still one of us? Where are we going to sit at a Thanksgiving table without Mike? Who will make Mike's famous pumpkin pie?" Yuki was concerned about Miriam's feelings, and was sure that Miriam would be nervous about how this Thanksgiving would play out. She couldn't help but imagine that the whole family would feel a void this Thanksgiving without Mike.

On Monday, Yuki had stopped over at Steve and Franco's on the way home from work to get their perspectives on Thanksgiving dinner. Yuki had met Steve and Franco through Miriam at one of Miriam's infamous Cinco de Mayo parties. She felt very close to Steve and Franco right away because of Miriam's strong bond with them, but soon developed a warm relationship with them on her own. Yuki considered Steve and Franco her "museum buddies," and they attended museum and gallery events in town frequently. The three of them had become closer in the last months since Miriam and Mike split up. They devised plans for getting Miriam out of the house and having fun, or called to consult each other on how Miriam was coping.

During their talk on the Monday before Thanksgiving, Steve and Yuki came up with ideas for keeping Miriam's mind off of Mike, while Franco chimed into the conversation from the kitchen as he was making dinner. They decided to suggest some new games to play after dinner to establish new traditions. Because of their close relationship with Miriam, the three of them felt a responsibility to support Miriam as she adjusted to the divorce. They knew Miriam would drop anything to help them in a time of need, and they were committed to doing the same for her. While taking care of one another was something they all did on a voluntary basis, during tough times like this they felt an especially strong sense of obligation to take care of her. Without Miriam knowing it, in fact, Yuki had turned down a trip to Chicago the day after Thanksgiving in order to stay with Miriam. Even though she regretted missing the new exhibit at the Art Institute, she knew that staying with Miriam was the right thing to do.

Still contemplating the upcoming day, Yuki headed downstairs to check in with Miriam. Miriam was still bustling around working on final details. Even though Yuki could see everything was ready to go, she easily fell into place next to Miriam in her efforts to straighten the candles and the table settings until all was perfect. Knowing Miriam had a lot on her mind, Yuki decided to just make a simple statement to her, "Miriam, you know I love you, I'm so grateful you are my family here and I'm happy we can spend this holiday together, no matter what." Miriam looked at Yuki with moist eyes and smiled, and they kept working in silence. Both women continued to tidy up the house as they waited for Steve and Franco.

* * * * *

Steve and Franco were indeed running late and arrived with their sons in tow. Even though they just lived down the street, they drove to Miriam's because they had decided to make extra dishes for the dinner in addition to helping with the potatoes. Sensing Miriam's plight at hosting her first Thanksgiving alone, Steve had been cooking up a storm since yesterday. All four of them barged into the house like they always did, without waiting for Miriam to come to the door, each carrying something to add to the meal. Miriam was delighted, as she had confessed to Steve that since Mike had always planned their holiday dinners, she was at a bit of a loss at how to proceed without him. As usual, Steve delivered. Since Mike's departure, Miriam had come to depend upon Steve for moral support. They got together weekly just to drink wine and talk, and Miriam was most grateful for his friendship. He was always there for her when she needed to vent.

Miriam had known Steve and Franco since they arrived in the neighborhood. They had moved in down the street and their two boys were close in age to Miriam's son, Matt. The boys had all gone to preschool together, and now were all attending the same elementary school. Miriam, Mike, Steve, and Franco spent many warm summer evenings together at the baseball field. They would often bring a picnic dinner and eat when the boys finished their game. Miriam smiled when she thought of these times, because watching Little League games was always much more palatable when accompanied by the bottle or two of wine that the four adults shared with appetizers. Often, the two families and sons would stay at the field talking and eating until long after the game was over. Franco knew the constellations, so they would often lie on their backs in the grass by the field and star gaze well into the night. They would always have a contest to see who could find Orion's Belt first. She was pleased that she, Franco, and Steve continued the picnic tradition this past summer despite Mike's departure, particularly for the sake of the boys, as all three had suffered in his own way when Mike moved out. The three boys were like brothers, and in fact often referred to each other as, "my fake-real brother" when talking with others.

As Steve, Franco and the boys entered Miriam's home, Steve looked at Miriam and whispered, "See if you can cheer Franco up. He's had a rough morning." Miriam threw Steve a quizzical look, and he responded, "Since it's Thanksgiving, Franco called his parents. I warned him—but he was too stubborn to listen to me."

Exasperated, Miriam replied, "Good grief! What happened *this* time?

Steve rolled his eyes and said, "The usual. He should stop being such a faithful son to those people. They treat him so badly. They just won't acknowledge the fact that he is in a healthy, good relationship and is a father. It drives me crazy as his sister has been married three times and had a string of failed relationships, but they treat her like royalty. Franco tries his damndest and always calls his parents to wish them a happy holiday and say that he misses them, but they just won't engage in any meaningful conversation. They are polite, but that's about it. They give a very cursory report about what they are doing, ask about the law practice, and hang up. As usual, they never ask about me or about the boys. It's as if we didn't exist."

Steve continued, "I don't know why he keeps doing this to himself; he's just so sad after he talks with them. He says he believes he must keep some contact with them. I understand that he loves his family, and I know he thinks if he keeps at it, someday they'll come around, but I doubt it, I really do. Every holiday it's the same thing, over and over. I keep telling him not to call, but he still does. I just hate to see Franco get so torn up. And, it always wrecks our holiday for an hour or two until he snaps out of it. Thank God for you, Miriam, Yuki, and your Mom."

Nodding in agreement, Miriam replied, "Yes, I feel bad for Franco. I can certainly understand why he would want to try to keep contact with his family, and I know that it's hurtful and frustrating—for all you. That being said, I am so glad that we're here for each other, particularly around the holidays." "That settles it," Miriam told herself, "I'll be sure to sit next to Franco at dinner, as I can make him laugh."

* * * * *

"Goodness, the house smells wonderful with this great meal spread out before us," Dejon exclaimed from the head of the table. "Miriam, it is so kind of you to invite Krista and me for Thanksgiving. We are so far away from our families and it would not feel like a holiday with just the two of us. You have all been so welcoming and we appreciate the cooks. You can count on us for dish duty afterward!"

"I am glad to abandon my post!" Esther added.

Dejon continued, grinning "You bet. And, hey, I didn't expect you to ask me to sit in the 'seat of honor' at the head of the table!"

Dejon's last statement was met with dead silence around the table. Everyone had noticed Dejon was seated in Mike's chair and no one quite knew what to say. Finally, Franco broke the tension, "OK, I'll say it, We all miss Mike. It's better to say it, rather than pretend nothing has changed. Dejon, you had no way of knowing that this is where Miriam's former husband Mike sat for our dinners. This is the first holiday he hasn't been here." Everyone sneaked a peek at Miriam who had tears sliding down her cheeks, as did Yuki. Dejon looked embarrassed, "Oh, I, I am so sorry, Miriam!"

"You didn't say anything wrong, Dejon," Yuki said. "It's just that we've had this little family going for a number of years, since college for many of us. This is our first holiday without Mike and it is tough." Yuki turned to Miriam. "We are so sorry. We wanted everything to be just like it was, and a good day for you above all."

Miriam paused. She had dreaded facing these feelings of missing Mike and she had vowed to herself she would not cry and ruin everyone's dinner. But actually, it seemed worse to have Mike gone and pretend everything was normal. Acknowledging their absence felt like the right thing to do. "Hey, guys, it's okay. I appreciate that you are all trying to make this a good day for me. And this first holiday without Mike is of course rough. But I am also aware that this is a loss for all of us. We have long called ourselves a family. So this is a loss for our little family. Things are not the same, but here we are. I love you guys. Matt and I are both so grateful for your place in our lives. You've made these last months much more bearable. And it is good to have Dejon and Krista here too." Miriam managed a smile and wiped her eyes.

Franco rose from his chair and held his wine glass high. He looked around the table at these people he loved. "What is it about holidays that bring out all these strong feelings? Well, all I know is that we *are* family. A changed one, but family nonetheless. So, I propose a toast to family and to new friends." With that everyone stood, raised their glasses and joined in the toast. Steve chimed in, "And to the turkey, oh, and that bird on the table too." Franco laughed and sat down, exclaiming, "Okay, people, let's dig in!"

Steve carved the turkey and Yuki poured the wine. The kids came in to the dining room, plates in hand, and the parents dished out their food and helped them carry their plates back to the kitchen and get settled in. They could hear giggles and silliness coming from the kitchen. "You kids be sure to eat some vegetables too" Esther called after them. "Last year I think all Matt ate was pie."

Miriam looked around the table and was thankful for all the people here with her today. She took Franco's hand and squeezed it. "Thanks Little Bro. Today's not easy, and, of course, Christmas is right around the corner. Mike is talking about wanting to take Matt to visit his girlfriend's family in Los Angeles." Franco looked her in the eye, "One day at a time, Miriam, one day at a time." He turned to Esther to his right "Hey, Esther baby, pass the potatoes and prepare for a major defeat in our Scrabble tournament after dinner!"

For Further Thought and Reflection

1. How has communication changed among the different members of this voluntary family since Mike moved out?
2. Braithwaite and colleagues (2010) identified several types of voluntary families: (a) substitute (replacing family), (b) supplemental (long-term relationships that form due to lack of emotional closeness or geographical distance, or in addition to blood and legal family), (c) extended (two families become one), and (d) convenience (family-like relationships in a particular time or place in life, that may not continue beyond that time). How would you categorize relationships of the voluntary family in this case study?
3. What are major turning points (important points of positive or negative change) in the experiences of this voluntary family?
4. Galvin (2006) talks about non-traditional families as "discourse dependent," in that without cultural models and set roles, they have to interact and figure out how to be a family. How did these people come to regard themselves as family? How do they know what is expected of them?
5. Do you regard Miriam, Esther, Yuki, Steve and Franco and their children a *real* family? Explain.

References

Baxter L.A., Braithwaite, D.O. & Nicholson, J. (1999). Turning points in the development of blended family relationships. *Journal of Social and Personal Relationships, 16,* 291–313.

Braithwaite, D.O., Bach B.W., Baxter, L.A., Hammonds, J., Hosek, A.M., Willer, E., Wolf, B. (2010). Constructing family: A typology of voluntary kin. *Journal of Social and Personal Relationships, 27,* 388–407.

Gallagher, S.K. & Gerstel, N. (1993). Kinkeeping and friend keeping among older women: The effect of marriage. *The Gerontologist, 33,* 675–681.

Galvin, K. (2006). Diversity's impact on defining the family: Discourse-dependence and identity. In L.H. Turner & R. West (Eds.), *The family communication sourcebook* (pp. 3–19). Thousand Oaks, CA: Sage.

Muraco, A. (2006). Intentional families: Fictive kin ties between cross-gender, different sexual orientation friends. *Journal of Marriage & Family, 68,* 1313–1325.

Weston, K. (1991). *Families we choose.* New York: Columbia University Press.

8

He Says/She Says: Misunderstandings between Men and Women

Julia T. Wood

Key Terms

gendered communication patterns, speech communities, instrumental communication

---

Ginger walks out of her last class of the day to find Luke waiting for her, as he usually does on Tuesdays and Thursdays. She greets him with a hug and they fall into a matched pace that soon will lead them to the library.

"Becky got an offer from BellTech—her first choice," Ginger says, knowing Luke will be interested because Becky is a mutual friend of theirs.

"Yeah? That's great." Luke says, raising his voice to compensate for a nearby student who is talking on his BlackBerry at high volume. "We'll have to take her out to celebrate."

"Well, she hasn't accepted yet."

"What's she waiting for? A red carpet?"

"Chicago is pretty far away, you know, so it's a big decision," Ginger explains. She thinks how hard it would be for her to move away from Luke and all her friends and family. She adds, "And Ben doesn't want her to leave. He's not comfortable with a long-distance relationship. He's encouraging her to turn down the offer."

"That's selfish. They can visit and call. Lots of people have long-distance relationships."

"Maybe, but it's not the same as being together. Besides, I think she's worried that taking the job might end the relationship with Ben."

"Let's focus on the job offer, not the relationship," Luke suggests. "That's the issue for her right now."

"But the two are connected. How can Becky decide about the job without making a decision about Ben?" Ginger thinks about all short-term relationships Becky has had. "In the three years we've known Becky, she's never stayed with anyone for long. Whenever a relationship starts to get serious, she bolts. The question is whether she's going to do that again with Ben."

"So you think she won't take the job?" he asks, glancing at construction where a campus building is being renovated.

"What I really think is that this offer may be an easy way to end the relationship." Ginger tries to make eye contact with Luke, but his eyes remain focused on the construction. "I think her pattern of bailing out of relationships is because her parents divorced when she was 12. Maybe she doesn't trust a relationship to last."

"Maybe a job is more trustworthy," Luke says. "Besides, this is the time for her to launch her career. She can settle down later if she wants, but opportunities like Bell-Tech don't come along every day."

"Neither do relationships," Ginger says sharply.

"Well, I think she should take the job."

Ginger is irritated by Luke's assumption that his answer is the right answer. It's not his business to say what Becky should do. Ginger wonders how she would feel if her parents had divorced. Would she be wary of committing to a relationship? Wanting to share her thoughts with Luke, Ginger asks, "Do you think people whose parents divorced are less able to form commitments?"

"Beats me," Luke replies, only half listening to Ginger. He gets frustrated when she starts a conversation on one topic and then wanders onto another and another. He finds it hard to follow her thinking and there's never any closure on a topic.

Ginger looks at Luke and asks, "If your parents had divorced, do you think you would shy away from relationships? Do you think we wouldn't be together?"

"I don't know," he replies. How is he supposed to answer a hypothetical question? His parents didn't divorce, so he has no idea how he'd feel if they had. And what does any of this have to do with Becky and her job offer? Why can't Ginger ever stick with just one topic? "I don't have any idea. They didn't split up, so how can I tell you how I would have felt if they had? Can you get back to the point?"

"This *is* the point. The point is about Becky's feelings about relationships," Ginger snaps.

"You started it by telling me Becky had an offer from BellTech, and now we're talking about hypothetical family dynamics. Can we focus on whether she should take the job?"

"It's not my place to say what she should or shouldn't do, and it's not your place either. I'm trying to consider all of the issues that are connected to deciding about the job offer," Ginger says crossly. "Why can't you ever let a conversation evolve naturally?"

"There's a difference between a conversation that evolves and one that rambles all over," he growls. "I'd just like for you, for once, to stay on topic."

"I am on topic! Lots of things are linked together. Do you think what Becky does about BellTech's offer is irrelevant to Ben or her parents' divorce?"

"It's a job offer. She takes it or she doesn't," Luke replies. "Whether or not her parents divorced and whether or not she is serious about Ben, she has to decide about the offer. She's 21 years old. She should get on with her life."

Ginger lets out an exasperated sigh. She is so tired of trying to have a real talk with Luke and having him try to force the conversation into some narrow cubby hole or flood her with advice she hasn't asked for and doesn't want.

"Let's just drop it," she says.

"Fine with me," Luke replies. He is happy to drop this conversation—one more in a long line of ones where he and Ginger wind up irritated with each other. He loves her but feels frustrated when she wanders all over in their conversations. If she would just stick to the point . . .

* * * * *

Michelle drops by Luke's room that afternoon and says, "Hey, guy, what's happening?"

He smiles, glad to see Michelle. They first met during freshman orientation and become fast friends. In the four years since, Michelle and he have seen each other through academic anxieties, minor medical problems, and many, many relationships. He finds it so easy to talk with her about whatever is on his mind. He doesn't have to put up a false front and not show he is upset or feels vulnerable, like he does with his guy friends. Michelle always takes him as he is and empathizes with his feelings.

"Nothing much, really. I'm just kind of aggravated with Ginger," he replies, clearing his clothes off a chair so Michelle can sit.

"Trouble in paradise?" she teases. When Luke doesn't smile, Michelle asks, "So, is there a problem between you two?"

"No, not really—just a problem that keeps coming up when we talk. She starts a conversation about one thing and the next thing I know we're all over the map. She's unable to stick to a topic. The minute I try to respond to one thing she's said, she's bouncing off somewhere else." Luke describes what happened today to Michelle and then says, "I mean why bring up the job offer if she wants to talk about how divorce affects children?"

Michelle laughs, "Oh, that's easy. She wasn't just trying to talk with you about the job offer or divorce."

Luke's face reflects his perplexity. "Huh? She brought up those topics. What do you mean she didn't want to talk about them."

"Well, she did and she didn't," Michelle explains. "She was talking about them because they were on her mind, but mainly she just wanted to be in touch with you and share herself with you. It could have been other topics. It could have been plans for graduation day or anything."

"That's crazy."

"No, it's just not how you think and talk."

"But it's incoherent," Luke insists. "You can't have a conversation about one thing, like a job offer, if you're jumping to relationships and divorce and everything else."

"But, Luke, in Ginger's mind what Becky decides to do about the offer is related to her relationship with Ben and Becky's parents' divorce. She probably feels that Becky would be less likely to take the job in order to stay near Ben if her folks hadn't divorced. If you understand that, then you understand why Ginger would bring up those other things."

"Is that why she got angry when I offered advice?"

"She probably was more interested in having you tune into what she was thinking and feeling than in any advice. You don't always have to fix things, you know."

"But the only reason I give her advice is because I care about her," he protests.

"Maybe you two should talk about what you want in conversations," Michelle suggests. "It sounds to me as if you are really talking past each other."

* * * * *

That evening Ginger is hanging out with her roommate, Cassandra. She describes the earlier conversation with Luke and expresses her frustration that he never seems willing to talk in a free-flowing kind of way.

"I know what you mean," Cassandra says, nodding vigorously as their eyes connect. "The same thing happens with me and Aaron. I'll start talking about something and that will lead naturally to something else, and then he's all over my case for rambling. But it's not rambling to deal with a lot of issues that are all so related."

"Exactly," Ginger says. "And no matter what I bring up, Luke's first response is to give advice. That drives me crazy—like I need his advice or something. Mr. Answer Man."

"It used to drive me crazy, too," Cassandra agrees. "But in my Gender and Communication course I learned why this happens. It's not just you and Luke and me and Aaron. It's a problem a lot of women and men have when they talk."

"Really?"

"Yeah, really—we're not alone," Cassandra says. "When we were kids and learning how to interact with others, we played with other girls and Aaron and Luke played with other boys. Boys and girls play differently and communicate differently, so we learned different ways to interact."

"Such as?" Ginger prompts.

"According to an article I read for one of my classes, most girls learn to weave issues and people together in conversations, but guys generally learn to compartmentalize topics and people. So to them it feels logical to deal with one topic at a time, but to us it feels logical to mix everything together."

"So it's a basic gender difference?"

"Well, not entirely. Gender isn't the only thing that affects how we communicate," Cassandra qualifies. "We've read some research that shows there are differences between how, say, Black and White and Asian people communicate, so ethnic communities also affect how we interact. You can't say 'all women do this, and all men do that,' but you can say there are some general patterns."

Cassandra thinks back to her class. The teacher used the term "speech communities" to describe the different ways women and men generally communicate. Her teacher explained that researchers had observed young boys and girls playing, and had discovered that the boys and girls played in different ways. The boys tended to play games like football and war that were structured by rules (what counts as a touchdown; what counts as victory in battle), whereas girls tended to play games like house and school in which there were no clear-cut rules. The girls had to talk with each other to connect their worlds and work out how to play their games. As a result, girls were more likely to learn that talk builds relationships and is a way to link people together. In their games, the boys used communication mainly to define events (calling out a foul) and to plan strategy (the huddle). The researchers concluded that men learn to use communication to achieve specific things whereas women learn to use communication to create relationships. Thinking back over what she has learned in her class, Cassandra tries to translate it for Ginger.

"I think it's like this: You were talking to Luke about Becky's job offer more to connect to him than to report on the job offer, right?"

Ginger shrugs. "Sure, why else would we talk?"

"Exactly," Cassandra says. "But Luke probably saw the conversation as about the job offer, so he addressed that. He didn't understand the topic was mainly a way for you and him to relate."

"Weird." Ginger shakes her head. "Why would you talk to someone if you weren't trying to relate to them?"

"If you were a guy, you might talk to resolve an issue or accomplish something like telling news or solving a problem or giving directions or offering advice."

"But I didn't ask him for advice. I was just trying to talk with him about Becky and the connections between the job offer and her relationship with Ben and her parents' divorce. Why does he feel compelled to give advice instead of just listening or talking with me?"

"He was trying to help, trying to support you and Becky by figuring out what she should do."

"But why won't he connect with me first and then offer advice, if he feels he has to do that?" Ginger asks. "I mean, isn't that the point of talking, anyway?"

"To you, it is, but it may not be to Luke, because he may not perceive the point of conversation the same way that you do," Cassandra reiterates. "And he may find your way of talking just as confusing as you find his. He probably thinks it's really weird that you don't stick to just one topic. And he probably thinks it's really strange that you didn't want his advice. He was trying to help, after all."

Ginger laughs, "Boyfriends!"

"Amen to that," Cassandra agrees.

* * * * *

After class the next Thursday, Ginger finds Luke waiting in the usual spot. She walks over to him and hugs him hello. "Becky turned BellTech down," Ginger announces.

"Wow, that's news," he replies as they start walking.

"She decided to stay because of the relationship with Ben. We had a long talk about how she always ends relationships, and she said she didn't want to continue that pattern."

"So does she think it's because her parents divorced?"

Ginger stops and looks at him. "What's going on? You don't sound like yourself."

"Well, I'm beginning to understand a bit better why you put all these things together in a conversation, and I'm trying to follow the connections you make instead of always telling you what ought to happen or to stay on topic."

"That's so strange, because I talked with Cassandra the other night and she helped me understand why you like to tackle one topic at a time and that when you give me advice you are trying to help, not saying you think you have all the answers or that I can't solve my own problems."

"So Becky really turned BellTech down, did she?" he says to resume the conversation. Ginger nods. "Is she interviewing with other companies now?"

"Right now she wants to focus on the relationship with Ben and see where it might go," Ginger replies.

"But this is prime time for interviewing. She shouldn't delay that or she might not get a job at all."

"So your advice is that she should be interviewing?" Ginger asks with a mischievous smile.

He grins and says, "Even when you start to understand gendered patterns of communication, it's hard to break out of them, isn't it?"

Discussion Questions

1. Reread the conversations between Ginger and Luke, Ginger and Cassandra, and Luke and Michelle. What gendered patterns of communication can you identify in the three conversations? How similar are the conversations in these cases to your own experiences communicating with women and men?

2. Why do you think Luke talked with a woman friend instead of a man friend? Whom do you talk with when you are upset or frustrated?

3. How much does understanding the sources of gendered conversational patterns help men and women to avoid misunderstandings and frustrations in their interactions?

4. In this case Cassandra noted that gender is not the only aspect of identity that affects communication. Drawing on your experience and observation, can you point out ways in which communication is influenced by race, economic class, and other aspects of social identity?

Selected References

Maltz, D., & Borker, R. (1982). A cultural approach to male-female miscommunication. In J.J. Gumperz (Ed.), *Language and social identity* (pp. 196–216). Cambridge, UK: Cambridge University Press.

Metts, S. (2006).Hanging out and doing lunch: Enacting friendship closeness. In J.T. Wood & S.W. Duck (Eds.), *Composing relationships: Communication in everyday life* (pp. 76–85). Belmont, CA: Wadsworth-Cengage.

Wood, J.T., & Inman, C.C. (1992). In a different mode: Masculine styles of communicating closeness. *Journal of Applied Communication Research, 21,* 279–295.

Wood, J.T. (2008). Critical, feminist theories of interpersonal communication. In L. Baxter & D. Braithwaite (Eds.). E*ngaging theories in interpersonal communication* (pp. 323–334). Thousand Oaks, CA: Sage.

Wood, J.T. (2010). *Gendered lives: Communication, gender, & culture,* 9th ed. Belmont, CA: Wadsworth-Cengage.

Let Her Eat Cake: Recognizing and Coordinating Rules for Communicating

Betsy Wackernagel Bach

Key Terms

communication rules, implicit rules, explicit rules, rule-following, rule-breaking, organizational socialization

---

Ashley was excited. She could hardly contain herself. She had just waved goodbye to her father and was running up the stairs of her dormitory without waiting to watch him turn the corner so that she could wave one last time. It's not that Ashley didn't love her father. She did. And she knew that she would miss her father and her mom and two sisters—eventually. But not now. There was too much to do. She had the campus to explore, roommates to meet, and sorority rush to attend. Decisions had to be made about how to arrange the furniture and which posters to put up on the bare walls of her dorm room. She savored the moment of being on her own for the very first time, and breathed a sigh of relief. "I can finally have a life!"

Background

Ashley had grown up in Plains, a small agricultural community of 6,000, about 400 miles from Northern Rockies University, the place she was now glad to call home. She knew almost everyone in Plains, as the community was close-knit. All 40 people in her high school graduating class had been born and raised in Plains. She knew a great deal about all of her classmates, their families, and even their extended families. Although Ashley had been popular and well-liked in high school, she was thrilled at Northern, as the campus had more than 15,000 students. She was anxious to have some anonymity, as well as the opportunity to make new friends.

Ashley meets Melissa

Ashley arrived on campus early as she had signed up for sorority rush, a two-week event at which women wishing to join sororities could learn more about sorority life. During rush, women visited sorority houses, talked with sorority members and (if they seem compatible to current sorority members)were extended invitations to join the sorority. Ashley had received a "Greek Life" brochure and an invitation to participate in "rush" during a July orientation session for first-year students. The brochure listed many benefits of being in a sorority, one of which was the opportunity to make friends. Ashley thought that making friends on a large campus might be difficult, and she figured that going through rush would be an excellent way to meet people.

Two days after her arrival at Northern, Ashley began the flurry of rush activities. She was assigned to a group of 20 other women, and during the first three days of rush, she visited 15 different sorority houses and was treated to goodies and introductions at every house. Ashley began to make friends in her group of 20 and started to spend time with Melissa, who was also from a small town. Ashley and Melissa found that they had a lot in common, particularly the fact that they were excited about getting away from small town life.

Over the next two weeks, Ashley and Melissa attended sorority parties, and learned that they were invited back to the same two sororities: Sigma and Delta. Ashley was glad that the members of Sigma and Delta seemed to like her and Melissa because, during the course of rush, they decided that they would like to join the same sorority. As the last day of rush approached, Ashley and Melissa decided that they would join Sigma, as the members seemed very friendly, genuine, and fun to be around. Sigma members had taken an interest in both women, and spent a lot of time with them at parties talking, laughing, and offering advice and encouragement. In addition, Ashley and Melissa found the Sigma sorority house very elegant—much more elegant than their own homes. There was a grand piano, brand new plush carpeting, and a beautiful stained glass window with the Sigma crest hanging in the dining room (which had lace tablecloths)! Ashley and Melissa hoped that they would both be invited to join Sigma, and nervously awaited the delivery of "bids" (e.g., invitations to become a member of a particular sorority).

On the Friday that bids arrived, Ashley and Melissa decided to open their bids together so that they could celebrate or commiserate, depending upon the outcome. Each held her breath as envelopes were torn open, and then read aloud similar greetings. Much to their relief, Ashley and Melissa both received invitations to join Sigma. The invitations read, "You are cordially invited to join Sigma. We welcome you with open arms to our friendship circle! Should you decide to join us, kindly notify us of your acceptance by 3:00 P.M. on Friday. At 4:00 P.M. on Friday, we request your presence at our sorority house." They screamed and hugged. Ashley and Melissa were ecstatic, not only because they had been invited to join Sigma, but also because they would be together.

Learning and Breaking Rules

Ashley and Melissa arrived at the Sigma house just a few minutes before 4:00 on Friday, and were asked to wait outside the front door. They met 22 other women who had also been asked to join the sorority. Promptly at 4:00 a sorority member opened the front door and invited the new members inside. They were directed to sit on the floor of the living room. The woman inviting them inside introduced herself as Mallory, and noted that she was their "pledge trainer." Mallory continued by saying, "From now until the end of January, you will be known as 'pledges' of Sigma, and as members-in-training. Every Monday night after dinner here you will be instructed in the rules and regulations of Sigma and will participate in 'pledge training.' You will learn about who we are and about our purpose. You will also, over the course of the next four months, be required to spend time with each active member, one of whom will be your 'big sister.' You will also spend a great deal of time with your fellow pledges. All of this is a way to help you understand us, so that you can become members who contribute to and value what we do. I have been put in charge of helping you to become a valued member of Sigma. We are proud of this sorority and want you to be, too."

After explaining the history of Sigma to the pledges, Mallory handed out small pins in the shape of a crescent to all 24 women. "These pins are 'pledge pins.' They signify to others that you have decided to join Sigma. They should be worn while you are in public, but especially every Monday night for formal dinner, which, by the way, begins promptly at 6:00." Finally, Mallory closed the meeting by handing out the music and words to a sorority song. "I strongly advise you to learn it by Monday," she instructed with a wry smile. "I'd hate to have you regret it."

Ashley and Melissa spent much of the weekend with the other pledges learning the song. Much to their relief, they knew both the words and the tune by Monday afternoon. Ashley hummed the tune while getting ready for her first formal dinner at the Sigma house. She chose a nice pair of slacks and a top, much like what she saw Sigma members wear during rush. She ran outside to meet Melissa so that they could walk to the "house" together. Melissa was dressed in a similar manner. They sang the sorority song softly as they made their way to the house, where they arrived promptly at 5:59.

Upon their arrival, they were the only two standing outside. They cautiously opened the front door, and observed everyone inside talking and laughing . . . and wearing dresses! They were dismayed. "Damn, they're going to *hate* us!" Melissa whispered to Ashley. "We're the only ones who were late and the only ones in pants. Boy, do I feel like a jerk!" Ashley retorted, "Well, we're not psychic. How were we supposed to know that we had to arrive ten minutes early to socialize and wear a dress? Nobody *said* anything! Maybe if we sing loudly, they won't kick us out!"

Although no one looked at them in a disapproving manner, Ashley and Melissa decided to listen and observe during dinner, and tried to keep a low profile. They were intimidated by the formality of what they had observed. The dining room was set with lace tablecloths and china, and there were men dressed in white shirts, black ties, and short white jackets standing by the kitchen door ready to serve dinner. Ashley and Melissa learned that these were the "houseboys," and that they were hired to serve dinner and do the dishes on Monday nights. The housemother, introduced to the pledges as "Mrs. P," stood by the door and hushed all the women before she walked over and turned on a light behind the stain-glassed Sigma crest that Melissa and Ashley had admired during rush. She then led them into the dining room.

Ashley began to follow the housemother when she felt a gentle hand on her shoulder pulling her back. "Don't get ahead of Mrs. P or our officers," the voice commanded. The order was quickly followed by a stage whisper, "It's Amanda. We talked quite a bit during rush. I'm your big sister. It's my job to help you understand what's expected around here, despite what Mallory tells you. Sit with me during dinner and I'll help you out." Ashley breathed a sigh of relief. As she stood next to Amanda, she noticed that Mrs. P. and all the Sigma officers moved to a head table and that all the others filed in behind them, scattering to other tables of eight. As Ashley pulled out her chair to sit down, Amanda again placed her hand on Ashley's shoulder. "Not yet. First we sing grace." Ashley noticed that everyone pulled out the chair to her left prior to sitting down, rather than pulling out their own chairs. "Whew," Ashley thought to herself. "I'm glad that Melissa and I decided to observe. At least I didn't blow *that* one."

Dinner went smoothly and Ashley began to relax. Amanda kept her posted on what would be happening by saying, "Look, Ashley, I know that you weren't 'born in a barn.' But, since Monday dinners are quite formal, let me remind you of a few things. Remember to always use the utensil on the outside first and work toward your plate. Also, we pass everything to the head of the table and let that person serve herself before we take anything. And . . .," Amanda added, "serve yourself and pass everything to the left." Ashley was most grateful for the refresher course on etiquette.

By dessert Ashley was actually enjoying herself. "I'm going to get along here just fine," she thought. "Amanda sure is helpful, and I think I can ask her almost anything. I'm glad that she's my big sister. I wonder, though, why she made that comment about how she can help me out 'despite what Mallory says'?" Her thoughts were interrupted as a houseboy brought her an absolutely divine looking piece of chocolate cake covered with rich, creamy, chocolate frosting. Although she was not hungry and did not want dessert, she allowed him to put a piece of cake at her place. At that moment Ashley looked over at Melissa, who appeared dismayed. Melissa was hanging her head and her cheeks were flushed. She had been assigned Mallory (the pledge trainer) as her big sister, and Mallory appeared to be "lecturing" Melissa about something. Ashley noticed that Melissa had refused a helping of chocolate cake. "It would be tough being allergic to chocolate like Melissa," Ashley reminded herself. "Geez, I wonder why Mallory is talking so sternly to Melissa. Certainly Melissa's refusal to take cake is nothing to be lectured about."

Ashley's thoughts were interrupted as Amanda laughed and gently chided her, "If you're not going to eat your dessert, pass it down to Joan, as she would love to have seconds." Ashley complied, happy to stick to her diet.

After dinner, the housemother rang a bell for the houseboys to come and clear the dessert plates. Sigma members engaged in lively chatter until the houseboys had completed their task. As the last plate was removed, the Sigma president rose and announced, "We will now close dinner with a sorority song that the pledges were instructed to learn. After that, all pledges will meet with Mallory in the T.V. room while the rest of us attend Chapter." Amanda leaned over to Ashley and offered her some encouragement. "Now's your first chance to show that you want to belong. Go for it!" Ashley sang in as animated a fashion as she could. While she sang, she noticed that (despite her *faux pas* of arriving late and wearing pants) several sorority members were looking at her while they smiled and nodded approval.

At the pledge meeting after dinner, Mallory approached them in a very stern manner. "Despite the fact that you have been invited to join Sigma, realize that you are not yet permanent, active members. You have to prove to us that you are worthy of active membership. From what I saw tonight, not many of you want a place in our sorority. Frankly, your singing was abysmal. You'd better learn quickly how things work around here if you want to be initiated! It's my job to teach you the rules, and I don't want you to make me look bad. Here is a list of house rules of conduct. Memorize them by next Monday. By the way, Ashley and Melissa, you will be fined $5.00 for wearing pants to Chapter dinner. You can pay next week. Also, make sure that you get together with your Big Sisters at least twice this week. Meeting adjourned. I'll see you next week."

Ashley and Melissa quietly left the house, and Ashley could sense that Melissa was upset. Once they were out of earshot of the other pledges, Melissa sobbed, "I hate Sigma. I just had the most horrible dinner of my life! I can't believe that Mallory is my big sister. What a wretch! She rode my butt throughout dinner and treated me like I was stupid. All she did was criticize me in front of all the others. I've never been criticized in front of other people before. In my family if someone bugged us, we would talk it out privately with them, not in front of an audience! We also never ate formally at my house. We don't even own a lace tablecloth. We're just not like that. What difference does it make which way you pass a damn dish? Who cares which fork you use as long as you chew with your mouth closed? I can't stand this! And, to be fined five bucks for wearing pants! How the hell were we supposed to know? What stupid idiot decided that?" Ashley tried to console Melissa, but with no success. Ashley was worried that Melissa might decide to leave Sigma, so she decided to talk with Amanda the following day.

When Ashley poured out Melissa's problem to Amanda, she found her big sister supportive, yet firm. "I feel very bad for Melissa," Amanda proclaimed. "Unfortunately, she is stuck with Mallory, as we don't change big sisters after they have been assigned. I guess that we shouldn't have given Mallory the task of being both a big sister and a pledge trainer. Perhaps it's too much for her. However, in Mallory's defense, I must say that learning proper etiquette is something we take very seriously. It is very important later on in life." Amanda continued, "That aside, I am very angry that you both got fined, although it is something that I would expect Mallory to do. Over the summer,

Mallory turned into a by-the-book person. She was much more relaxed before we elected her as our pledge trainer. It almost seems like a little bit of power has gone to her head! In July she took it upon herself to rewrite the house rules of conduct, and is determined to stick by them, though we haven't closely adhered to house rules in the past. While the house rules need to be enforced, there should be some room for flexibility. It's unclear to me whether or not we should fine pledges, particularly for a first-time violation. Let me talk with the President and see what can be done. If past practice is followed, people do not pay the first time they are fined." Amanda concluded, "I understand that it's difficult to learn new ways, but that's what pledge training is all about. Some things you will be taught directly, like our house rules. Other things you just pick up by observing what is going on or by being corrected, like at dinner last night."

"Dinner last night . . .?" Ashley pondered. "Oh, you mean when you reminded me to pass the mashed potatoes to the left?"

"Well, sort of," replied Amanda. "Remember when I told you to give your chocolate cake to Joan? You may not have realized it, but taking dessert even when you don't want it is very important around here. During formal dinner, we are only allowed one helping of dessert—it's Mrs. P's hard and fast rule. Some people would like to have more than one dessert. So, even if you don't want dessert, you should take one and save it for anyone else at the table who wants seconds."

Amanda continued. "As long as we're talking about dinner last night and how to behave during formal meals, I should tell you that Joan mentioned to me that you did not talk with her at all. You simply handed your cake to her at my request. It is a pledge's responsibility during formal dinners to initiate conversation with every active member seated within comfortable talking distance. So, you should be sure to talk with any active members sitting on either side of you or directly across from you at the table. You're considered arrogant if you don't talk to everyone seated near you."

Ashley was relieved. She left the house feeling much better and was anxious to tell Melissa what she had learned. Yet she was also beginning to think that making new friends outside of Plains was not going to be as easy as she thought. "Dinner at Sigma is certainly unlike anything I've ever experienced. Geez, all the formality," she mused. "Oh, well, I guess that's why I joined. I'll get used to it, I'm sure."

Ashley talked with Melissa and explained everything that she had learned from Amanda. They acknowledged that Mallory was rigid (not to mention a bit power-hungry) but that she probably had Melissa's best interest at heart when she corrected her. However, they decided that when the time was right, Melissa would explain her feelings about the public reprimand to Mallory. "Hopefully Mallory will ease up a bit as time goes on, and I will be able to talk with her," Melissa said wishfully.

After thoroughly discussing Melissa's relationship with Mallory and what could be done to improve it, Ashley laughed out loud. "I just have to tell you this," she giggled. "You won't believe it. When I was talking to Amanda she told me that everyone always takes dessert during formal dinner whether or not they want it. They then save it for people at the table who want seconds, because Mrs. P won't allow anyone to have seconds from the kitchen! I'll make sure that I sit next to you every time we have chocolate, so you can give me your dessert. Do we have a deal?"

"No," said Melissa as she giggled. "I noticed that Mallory wolfed down not one, but two pieces of cake at dinner. I'd better make sure I offer my dessert to her!"

"Fine," Ashley said, feigning anger. "Let her eat cake!"

Endnote

[1] The author is indebted to Grace Harris and her two sorority sisters Casey and Jackie for their insight and comments about an earlier version of this case.

For Further Thought and Reflection

1. It is said that communication rules help prescribe expectations for behavior. What general communication rules do you see operating throughout this case?
2. It is said that communication rules are used to evaluate, justify, correct, predict, and/or explain behavior. How do communication rules in this case function to evaluate, justify, correct, predict and explain behaviors?
3. What implicit (unstated prescriptions for behavior) and explicit (clearly stated prescriptions for behavior) rules did you see? Which appear to have more importance?
4. When is it appropriate to break rules? How were rules broken in this case? How are people supposed to know when and if it is acceptable to break a rule?
5. What is discussed in this case are rules of organizational socialization (e.g., learning the ropes of how to behave in a new situation). How might the types socialization rules identified here apply to other situations and contexts you have experienced?
6. Sororities and other organizations often have relatively formal rules for when and how to communicate. In more casual relationships rules tend to be less formal, conscious and explicit but equally present. Can you identify rules that guide how you and others act when your family has dinner, or when you and friends go out to dinner together?

References

Allen, D. G. (2006). Do organizational socialization tactics influence newcomer embeddedness and turnover? *Journal of Management, 32*, 237–256.

Ashforth, B., Harrison, H., & Corley, K. (2008). Identification in organizations: An examination of four fundamental questions. *Journal of Management, 34*, 325–374.

Bach, B. W. (1990). Moving up on campus: A qualitative examination of organizational socialization. *Journal of the Northwest Communication Association, 18*, 53–71.

Bullis, C. A., & Bach, B. W. (1989). Socialization turning points: An examination of change in organizational identification. *Western Journal of Speech Communication, 53,* 273–293.

Gossett, L. M. (2002). Kept at arm's length: Questioning the organizational desirability of member identification. *Communication Monographs,* 69:385–404.

Shiminoff, S. B. (1980). *Communication rules: Theory and research.* Beverly Hills, CA: Sage

Becoming a "Real Family": Turning Points and Competing Discourses in Stepfamilies

10

Dawn O. Braithwaite, Leslie A. Baxter, Paul Schrodt

Key Terms

stepfamily development, turning points, relational dialectics, rituals, caught in the middle

Lonnie was lugging the last of her clothes down the stairs. The large trunk made a loud "thump!" as she dragged it down the worn steps. "Which of you kids is making all that racket?" her mother, Gail, called brightly. Lonnie smiled to herself. Even though she was 18 years old and off to college, she still loved to bug her mother. "Here, let me help you, for goodness sake!" Lonnie smiled and offered her mother one handle of the trunk. "Where are Tim and Celia? I want to get going soon so the baby will sleep while we're on the road." Lonnie pointed out to the driveway where Tim and her sister, Celia, were shooting hoops next to the van, packed with Lonnie's treasures. "Thanks, mom! Go get Emily and let's roll!"

As she stood at the bottom of the stairs, Lonnie felt strangely sad. It didn't seem that long ago that she hated this house. Now the day to leave for college had come and all Lonnie could do was think back to all her family shared in this old yellow house. In some ways, it was even hard to remember what life was like before they lived there, but as she stood waiting, she remembered other moving days.

Dad Moves Out

Lonnie had known this day was coming. It was just two weeks after her 12th birthday. Her parents, Gail and Gene, had a huge fight the night before, the worst Lonnie and her nine-year-old sister, Celia, had ever heard. Things had been bad between her parents for some time. For many years, the family had enjoyed a weekly family dinner at a local diner, Flo & Mo's. For nearly a year now that ritual had degenerated with her parents bickering all the way back from the restaurant. Lonnie and Celia would try to be extra good so as not to set their parents off.

Finally, one warm July night, Gail and Gene called Lonnie and Celia together after dinner and explained that they had tried to work things out, but that "sometimes moms and dads just can't make things work." Their father was moving out. They had decided that the girls would be better living with their mom, and they would have dinner with him on Wednesdays, and spend every other weekend and part of each summer with him. Lonnie was not unfamiliar with this arrangement, as several of her friends whose parents were divorced had similar schedules. Despite this, Lonnie and Celia were devastated by the news. Lonnie worried about how her life might change.

The Single Years

For the next two years, Lonnie and Celia lived with Gail in their house on Evergreen Street. They didn't have much money, and they missed having their mom and dad together. Once their dad got on his feet and bought a condo, Lonnie and Celia shared a huge bedroom with their own flat screen TV. In contrast, things were tight financially at home with mom. They turned their dad's old office into a bedroom for Celia and painted a second-hand bed and dresser for her. Each sister had her own room at least, and Lonnie relished her privacy.

Gail was working hard to support them, while also going to night school. Lonnie knew about their financial problems, as her parents fought about money whenever they talked. They passed messages back and forth through Lonnie. "Tell your mom your sister needs new skates" or "Bring a check from your dad for the dentist's bill. I just can't cover it." Lonnie liked to be in the know on what was happening, but talk about money made her feel uncomfortable. And she hated it when one of her parents criticized the other. All too often her parents took their anger out on her when she delivered a message.

Lonnie took on a lot of responsibility and learned to cook. She often had dinner waiting when her mom dragged herself home. The three of them enjoyed really talking when they went out for pizza on payday and then went window-shopping. While they ate and as they walked along looking in the shop windows, their mom asked them about what was going on in their lives, and they shared their concerns and questions. At times, as Celia skipped ahead of them, mom also began to share a lot of her own worries, and Lonnie began to feel as though her mom treated her more like a close friend than a daughter at times. In one sense, this made her important and closer to her mom, yet it also felt uncomfortable now and then. Sometimes her dad would text or call during these outings and, even though she felt bad doing it, Lonnie would not answer during their special times with mom. She struggled, as it was hard to please them both at the same time.

Tim Arrives on the Scene

That summer she and Celia had spent a month with their dad and his parents at the lake. It was great to be with Nana and Grandpa, but Lonnie missed her mom. When they arrived home, Gail ran out to meet them, and Lonnie noticed that her mom had a new hairstyle and was wearing new earrings. When she asked about it, Gail blushed and said, "Oh, we'll talk about it." They went out to Flo and Mo's and on the way home, mom said, "Well, girls, I hope that you don't mind, but I am going to the movies later tonight." Lonnie was surprised and asked, "Going out? With Betty?" "No, well, um . . . with Tim." Mom stammered, "Tim Bartino, a man I've been seeing." Lonnie felt sick. "You mean you've been dating someone and you didn't tell us?" "No, Lonnie, well, yes I, I met Tim at school last spring. We had coffee a few times, but the last couple of weeks we have been going out. Don't worry—it's nothing serious." Lonnie and Celia didn't say anything, because they didn't want to hurt their mom's feelings, but as the two of them talked that night they shared their anger and disappointment that their mom wasn't home on their first night back. Both of them wondered how their dad would react when he found out that their mom had met someone else.

Over the next few months, "nothing really serious" became "something serious" as Gail and Tim began spending more time together. Lonnie and Celia were wary of Tim at first—unlike their dad, he was a quiet man, a studious engineer who was working on his Masters degree. He was divorced with two children—Tony, who was a high school junior, and Tina, who out had dropped out of high school in her senior year. Tony and Tina lived with their mother, three hours away, and it was six months before Lonnie even met them.

Tim was spending much more time with them; in fact, he was staying at their house most of the time now. At first, all of Lonnie's conversations with Tim were brief, awkward, and filled with small talk. However, once they had worked through some of the initial nervousness, like seeing Tim at breakfast, things fell into a fairly normal routine. For the first time, life seemed kind of like it was before her parents' divorce. She knew something had changed in their lives the first time Lonnie found herself telling a friend that she had to be home for a "family dinner." It was nice and, well, just normal to have the four of them together, and their mom seemed so happy. At the same time, this bothered Lonnie too. Had their mom been unhappy with just the three of them? Was her dad really that replaceable? One evening when Tim asked her what time she would be coming home from a party, she blurted out, "Hey you're not my dad! I am not ready to trade dads this year!" He looked very hurt.

On Thanksgiving weekend, Tim moved in for good. Her mom called a "family meeting," and the four of them discussed the move. Tim said he had already spoken with Tina and Tony and said, "they are looking forward to spending our first Christmas together." At first Lonnie felt strange when her mom used the term "family meeting"—were they a real family? She didn't feel the same as she had with her real family, yet, as Tim moved in, it seemed like a new period had started in their lives. Family-like routines had developed, and things began to feel different. As she got to know him, Tim was a little easier to talk to. She began to open up a little more with him and to share with him what was going on with some of her friends at school. Lonnie started watching football with him on Sundays, as they both loved sports. She didn't tell her dad about getting closer to Tim because she didn't want him to feel bad.

Things changed in their household. Whereas Lonnie was used to taking care of her mom and making dinner, now Tim often made dinner, and she had to admit he was a great cook. Gail would come home and make a huge fuss, "Oh, I am the envy of all my friends!" One of the things that really irked Lonnie was that Tim now went along on their payday dinner and window-shopping nights. Celia and Lonnie missed talking with just their mom, and both felt like they had to compete with Tim for their mom's attention. When Lonnie brought it up, Gail seemed irritated, "Now, Lon, Tim is just trying to be part of the family. Give him a break!" Pretty soon they stopped having their nights out altogether.

The Wedding

Spring and the summer after her first year of high school were a busy and happy time. Gail and Tim announced their engagement in April and planned an August wedding. Lonnie was glad to see her mom so excited, and she had to admit she genuinely liked Tim and the way the family was going, especially when it was just the four of them. Tony seemed OK, but things were tense when Tina was around. Since they would not be living with them, Lonnie figured it really didn't matter.

Before he asked Gail to marry him, Tim took Celia and Lonnie out to lunch and asked how they felt: "I don't ever intend to replace your dad, but I love your mom and I know we can have a good life together." It meant a lot to Lonnie that Tim respected them enough to consult them. It also showed Lonnie that he was sensitive to the prospect of dealing with "two dads." Nonetheless, Lonnie had some mixed feelings about it all and she worried how her dad would react. She had to admit that she certainly felt much more at home with Tim and mom these days than she did with her dad. She liked Tim a lot, and it was hard to imagine their family without him now. The younger Celia didn't seem to be bothered by any of it and was excited that all four kids were to serve as attendants at the wedding.

In June, Tim and Gail began looking for a larger house. Just before the wedding they bought a big old yellow farmhouse on three acres of land. It was definitely a fixer-upper, and Gail was excited about the huge kitchen and told the girls they would finally be able to have a garden and maybe even a horse! The problem was that the house was 20 miles away from their present home. Lonnie protested, "Mom, this means I will have to leave all my friends and start a new school for my sophomore year! I don't want to attend South High!" Gail seemed too busy to even hear her concerns.

As the wedding day approached, Lonnie felt mixed emotions, "How can I feel so happy and so sad at the same time?" The night before the wedding Lonnie told Celia, "I know this sounds stupid, but I guess till today I always thought mom and dad might get back together." Celia agreed, "I know what you mean—I wish Tim and mom weren't getting married! And I am not going to call Tony and Tina my brother and sister!" Despite these mixed feelings, it was a nice wedding and, as Tim and Gail exchanged their vows, Celia and Lonnie cried—for all they had lost and for all they had gained.

On Saturday they had the wedding, on Sunday they moved to the yellow farmhouse, and on Monday, the girls started at new schools. These were among the darkest days of Lonnie's life. She missed her friends, and she absolutely hated the "stupid, drafty old house." Most importantly, she resented Tim and her mom's time alone together when she desperately needed her mom's attention and support. Tim and Gail put off their honeymoon to work on the house. During the home repair period, Lonnie and Celia had to share a room, and they fought constantly. The low point was when Tina came for the weekend and slept in their already crowded room.

The First Christmas

By the holidays, things had settled down. Lonnie had joined the choir at her new school and had a date for the Holiday formal. Christmas had always been special in their household and Gail promised, "I plan to make it very special for us all." Her family had always come together on December 24th to decorate the tree with all their family ornaments and sing Christmas carols. They went to Christmas Eve Mass and then spent a quiet Christmas Day at home—just the family—opening gifts and enjoying a huge turkey dinner.

Gail had everything ready for Tony and Tina's arrival the morning of the 24th. When they arrived—late—Tina said, "Geez, it doesn't look much like Christmas around here. Don't you people even have a Christmas tree?" They filled her in on the day's activities, but she did not seem interested. As Gail, Lonnie and Celia decorated the tree, Tim and Tony sat and watched and Tina texted her friends. Tony and Tina refused to go to church. On the bright side, Tim had gone shopping on his own (and he hated shopping) to buy a special present for each of the four kids. Tina complained that "my dad does this every year and comes home with the most goofy stuff," but Lonnie was touched by his efforts and the sweet music box he chose for her.

On Christmas day Lonnie, Celia, and their mom worked on the traditional Christmas dinner and Tim joined in. Tony and Tina were trying to get everyone to go to the movies, "C'mon you guys—let's get out and *do* something!" Lonnie tried not to show it, but she was really pissed off at those two. "Mom, why can't they just join in and give our traditions a chance?" Gail ran interference, saying to Tony and Tina, "Look why don't you two go to the movies, and we'll hold dinner so we can all eat together, OK?"

Lonnie hated to admit it, but she felt much more comfortable when Tony and Tina were gone and just the new family was there.

Settling In

Tim and Gail spent all their free time throughout the winter and spring months working on the house. Tim made a special effort to finish the interior of Lonnie's and Celia's bedrooms first so they could move into their own rooms. Tony came to visit much more than Tina, and Lonnie appreciated his effort to get to know the family. Tony and Tim had a long-standing routine of watching sports together on Sundays. Lonnie had always liked sports, and would join them. The three of them went to several baseball games together, and Tim and Tony started calling her "Fred" and "one of the guys." Although she could never bring herself to say it to their faces, Lonnie often referred to Tim and Tony as "her dad" and "her brother" to her friends.

Dad Remarries

Lonnie and Celia learned that Gene was seriously dating Victoria, a divorced woman with a four-year-old son. Gene and Victoria married in a ceremony at the courthouse in the late Spring. In fact, Lonnie and her sister didn't even find out about their marriage until afterward and, although she felt guilty admitting it to herself, Lonnie just could not get all that excited.

Dad said that they would now "be a family," but it certainly did not *feel* like a family. Not like what she felt as a child with her mom and dad, or what she felt with mom and Tim. In fact, it surprised her to see how strongly she felt about her new family with Tim. Lonnie had grown close to Tim over time and he knew way more about her than her own dad did. In fact, Lonnie thought about her mom and Tim as her main or primary family.

Lonnie could not say that she truly disliked Victoria, but she could not warm up to her. As time went on, Lonnie and Celia found reasons to miss their weekends with them or go home early. They loved their dad, and didn't want to hurt him by telling him how they felt. During the weekends at Victoria's and Gene's, they missed their mom, their house, and Tim.

Tina Moves In

As her junior year began, Lonnie was surprised at how happy she was. One good thing was that Gail and Gene were getting along better and had started meeting alone for coffee once a month to talk about the girls. What a change that was, and Lonnie was relieved not to be the messenger between her parents. Shortly after the school year began, Gail called a family meeting. At the meeting, Gail and Tim announced that Tina would be moving in with them for "a while until her money problems were under control."

Tina was very rude and demanding. She smoked constantly and got into fights with Lonnie in particular. When Lonnie complained to her mom and Tim, they took Tina's side: "Look, Lonnie, Tina is adjusting to a lot here and has her own problems to work through right now. Let's try and keep a lid on things, OK?" Finally, Tina got on her feet financially and was able to move out. Lonnie was really glad Tina was gone and the family went back to normal.

A Second Dad

Things were going pretty smoothly by Fall of her senior year. Tony had moved to the city to attend community college and lived in an apartment close by. He spent a lot of time with the family now and was a great big brother. School was going well and Lonnie was making college plans. Tim was especially helpful with her with college applications. While her dad wanted her to go to the community college, he and Gail had negotiated and each agreed to pay 40 percent of her expenses at the university if Lonnie would cover the other 20 percent with jobs and loans. Lonnie was surprised when Tim told her, "Let's keep this between the two of us and I'll cover some of your extra expenses when you need help."

The big family news was that Gail was pregnant and expecting a baby around Easter! Tim was ecstatic, and Lonnie had to admit that she was surprised at her own reaction—she was really excited! When she was a kid, she had hoped for another baby before her parents' problems escalated. Celia was less certain about the whole thing and worried that "they will only have time for the baby—what's going to happen to me?"

The weekend before the Homecoming dance, Lonnie was out shopping for shoes to match her dress, when she suddenly felt hot and queasy and had pains in her side. When stabbing pains doubled her over, she called home. Tim answered the phone and said he would be right there. It was all she could do not to pass out. Tim took one look at her and raced her to the emergency room. He held Lonnie's hand as he drove like a wild man. Gail showed up soon thereafter and called Gene. Lonnie's appendix had burst and she was rushed into emergency surgery. The surgeon said that Tim had gotten Lonnie there not a moment too soon.

Tim barely left Lonnie's side while she was in the hospital. She had always known he cared about her, but she never realized just how much. When her friends stopped by, Tim told them, "You better get going soon, my daughter needs her rest." He had never called her "daughter" before. Just as the words left Tim's mouth, her dad called to check in. Lonnie did not tell him how she got to the hospital and said that her mom had taken good care of her.

Baby Emily's crying pulled Lonnie back into the present. Tim shooed them into the van. "We've got to get to the university by noon," Tim reminded them. Lonnie shoved the last of her stuff into the van and they were off. Gail exclaimed from the front seat, "Oh geez, I was supposed to call your dad and let him know where to park for the parents' orientation. He'll be upset I forgot. Lonnie, honey, give your dad a call and tell him it's Parking Lot F4, will ya? It will be better coming from you." Lonnie sighed. Today of all days, she did not want to cause a stir. "It's never simple," she told herself and dialed the phone.

For Further Thought and Reflection

1. Compare and contrast the changes that occurred in the communication between Lonnie and her stepfather Tim and that occurred between Lonnie and her dad, Gene. In what ways did the conversational patterns of these dyads become more or less personal and intimate?
2. What are major turning points (important points of positive or negative change) in the development of Lonnie's original family, single-parent family with Gail, and two stepfamilies?
3. Relational Dialectics Theory claims that relationships are organized around competing discourses. One of these is openness and closedness. How do Lonnie and her parents deal with openness and closedness, and how does Lonnie end up "caught in the middle" between them at times? What other competing discourses can you identify in Lonnie's relationships in this case?
4. Rituals (routines and traditions) are important recurring communication practices that honor some aspect of family life. How did family rituals change as Lonnie's families changed? Why were they able to adapt some rituals and not others, as family circumstanced changed?
5. What is a real family? What are the communicative practices that make a family real, and how is that accomplished through communication?
6. What are different address terms (names) that these family members use to refer to one another, and how do these reflect changes in their relationships and who is regarded as family?

References

Baxter L.A., Braithwaite, D.O., & Nicholson, J. (1999). Turning points in the development of blended family relationships. *Journal of Social and Personal Relationships, 16,* 291–314.
Braithwaite, D.O., Baxter, L.A., & Harper, A. (1998). The role of rituals in the management of dialectical tension of "old" and "new" in blended families. *Communication Studies, 48,* 101–120.

Braithwaite, D.O., Toller, P., Daas, K., Durham, W. & Jones, A. (2008). Centered, but not caught in the middle: Stepchildren's perceptions of contradictions of communication of co-parents. *Journal of Applied Communication Research, 36,* 33–55.

Ganong, L.H., & Coleman, M. (2004). *Stepfamily relationships: Development, dynamics, and interventions.* New York: Kluwer Academic, Plenum.

Koenig Kellas, J., LeClair-Underberg, C., & Normand, E. L. (2008). Stepfamily address terms: Sometimes they mean something and sometimes they don't. *Journal of Family Communication, 8,* 238–263.

Schrodt, P., Braithwaite, D.O., Soliz, J., Tye-Williams, S., Miller, A., Normand, E.L., & Harrigan, M.M. (2007). An examination of everyday talk in stepfamily systems. *Western Journal of Communication, 71,* 216–234.

Schrodt, P., & Afifi, T.D. (2007). Communication processes that predict young adults' feelings of being caught and their associations with mental health and family satisfaction. *Communication Monographs, 74,* 200–228.

11

No Strings Attached: Friends with Benefits on a College Campus

KENDRA KNIGHT, CHRISTINA SHAW, PAUL A. MONGEAU
ARIZONA STATE UNIVERSITY

Key Terms

friends with benefits, hookups, dating, relational uncertainty, emerging adulthood

---

First Year Orientation

At eleven o'clock on a Friday night in September, a popular college bar called Josie's Grill has a line out the door and snaking down the block. Inside, men in polo shirts and women in high heels crush against the bar, vying for the bartenders' attention. Whitney, a college freshman, who got into Josie's using her older sister's ID, wraps her small hands around six shot glasses full of a pink liquid and squeezes through the mob back to her table. She sets the shots on the high-top table to cheers and feigned groans from her friends.

Her roommate, Lindsay, who also entered the bar using a fake ID, holds her shot glass up in the air and turns a clumsy pirouette, shouting "Woo-hoo!" The gang downs the drinks in unison.

Lindsay stumbles and yelps in pain as a guy at the next table steps back onto her foot. "Ow! Look out!"

The young man reaches toward Lindsay, spilling half his beer trying to catch her. "I'm so sorry!" He shouts over the roar of the crowd.

"No worries!" Lindsay shouts back over the music. "Here, let me buy you another beer!"

"Okay, thanks! What's your name?"

"Lindsay."

"Nice to meet you Liz."

"No, *Lindsay!*"

"Sorry! *LINDSAY.*" He extends his hand. "I'm Jerod."

Homecoming

Whitney opens her eyes on a Saturday morning. Because she has lived in her dorm room only a few weeks, some mornings it still takes her a little while to remember where she is. The room is completely dark except for a ribbon of light shining around the door. Her roommate, Lindsay holds the door ajar with her foot while she whispers to someone in the hallway. Lindsay is saying goodbye to Jerod, who has shared her tiny dorm room bed the last three Friday nights. Whitney clicks on her bedside lamp as Lindsay squeezes back through the door.

Lindsay says, "Oh, sorry, I hope I didn't wake you up."

Whitney replies, "No, I woke up because I'm starving. What time is it?"

"Almost ten. We've gotta hurry if we're going to make breakfast at the dining hall." They slip on sweats and flip flops and shuffle down the hallway toward the stairwell. Whitney teases, "So, this is the third weekend in a row with Jerod? Getting pretty serious, huh?"

Lindsay rolls her eyes, "Not even *close*. We're not even dating."

Whitney says, "Well, you're sleeping together, aren't you? I hope you didn't lock me out of our dorm room until 3 A.M. because you were just talking!"

Lindsay says, "No, we *are* hooking up . . . but we're not dating. We're . . . I don't know . . . friends with benefits."

"I thought you had to be *friends* before you could be friends with benefits. You just met him a month ago. Haven't you only hung out like three times?"

Lindsay laughs and says, "Good point. I think that, for some people, you have to be friends to be friends with benefits, but I just mean that we're not *in a relationship* or anything like that."

"Okay . . ."

"We actually talked about it last weekend. He said he wasn't looking for a relationship. He just got out of a long-term thing with his high school girlfriend, and he just wants to be single right now."

Whitney asks, "Is that what *you* want? You seemed pretty into him after that first night."

"Well, he's not looking for a relationship . . . and I guess I don't really want that either. It's my first year at school, and I'm trying to have fun without being tied down. Plus, there are so many new things to get used to, and I'm so busy with school. I don't really need a boyfriend stressing me out even more. This way, Jerod and I just have fun when we're together, and then we do our own thing the rest of the time. When you stop and think about it, it's really the best of *both* worlds."

Whitney says, "Well, if that's what you want, then I'm happy for you! Anyway, what are we having for breakfast? I'm starving!"

Fall Break

At 2 o'clock on a Sunday morning, the Phi Zeta Theta frat house is a wreck. Last year, as a first-year pledge, Jerod would have been up until dawn picking up beer bottles and keg cups while the upperclassmen crashed. Thankful to be a sophomore, and free from clean-up duties, he lounges in an armchair in the front room. One pledge, who escaped clean-up duty by volunteering as a designated driver, pulls his car into the circle driveway to haul a group of the guys for a late-night run to Luigi's Pizza. Jerod squeezes into the back seat next to his frat brother Matt and opens his phone to text-message Lindsay.

Matt says, "See if you can get some girls to meet us back at the house!"

Jerod says, "Yeah right, dude; you have a girlfriend."

Matt says, "Relax. I'm just talking about hanging out! Besides, you have a girl-friend too."

"Who are you talking about? Lindsay?"

"Don't play dumb. You haven't hung out with another chick this whole semester."

"Maybe, but she's not my girlfriend."

"Yeah well, does she know that?"

"Yes."

"Did you have '*the talk?*' "

"Yeah, actually I told her from the beginning that I didn't want a girlfriend."

Matt says, "The *very* beginning?"

Jerod says, "Well, almost the beginning—after we'd hooked up like twice."

"How did that go over?"

"Um, fine. I think she may have wanted to date at first, but once we talked, she knew that wasn't going to happen. She's cool with it now. We just hang out when it's convenient for both of us."

"Like right now."

"Yup." Jerod clicks a message into his phone: "going to luigis rt now then back to the house u coming over?"

* * * * *

Lindsay, Whitney, and their friends shuffle out of a bar called Moose's at last call. Their high heels click an irregular cadence on the cement sidewalk as they cling to each other for balance and warmth against the chilly autumn night. More than a little tipsy, and with their ears ringing from bar music, they trudge up the long hill back to campus. Lindsay's phone buzzes to life and a picture of Jerod appears on the screen. Actually, it's a picture of him and Matt, drunk at the Homecoming game. Whitney says, "Let me guess . . . it's Jerod."

Lindsay replies, "Good guess . . . Surprise, surprise."

Whitney asks, "Is there an after-party at Phi Zeta tonight?"

Lindsay says, "I don't know. He says they're picking up Luigi's and asked if I want to come over."

Whitney says, "Well, let's go then. Text him and tell him to get us a large supreme with extra cheese!

"Oh, pizza sounds so good right now! But . . . I don't know if I want to."

"Eat Luigi's or go to the house? Okay. Why not?"

"Well, it kind of bugs me sometimes that he doesn't call or text until two in the morning. Or, if we go to the bars or a party, we just get drunk, hook up, and then pass out.

"And that's a bad thing? I thought that's what you said you wanted." Whitney says.

"Well, it is . . . it was . . . I don't know . . . in some ways it's good—perfect really. I usually get to hang out with you guys and then see him later. But it wouldn't kill me if we hung out more often, outside of parties and stuff.

"Okay . . ."

"I guess I'm just a little confused about Jerod's and my relationship."

"But a few weeks ago, Linz, you said there wasn't any relationship," Whitney says.

"Well, there isn't. Or there isn't *supposed* to be anyway. But sometimes I feel like . . . I feel like I want something *more,* almost as if I *like* him or something."

"Yeah?"

"I don't know," Lindsay shrugs, "I guess I shouldn't make a big deal out of it. I should just enjoy it while it lasts."

"So are we going to meet the guys at Phi Zeta or not?" Whitney asks.

"Sure, why not? The night is young!"

Finals Week

Jerod kicks open the large oak front door of Phi Zeta Theta, holding two 10-pound bags of ice in each hand. He holds the door for Matt, who inches past him carrying a folded up gaming table.

Jerod says, "You're setting up beer pong on the porch tonight? It's going to get cold later."

Matt replies, "Yeah, I don't want a bunch of people spilling beer in the house—we don't have another deep clean before winter break."

Jerod sets the ice down in the foyer, claps his hands to warm them up, and follows Matt onto the porch. Matt's phone vibrates in his shirt pocket. "That's probably Kristin." Matt hands the table to Jerod and slides his thumb across his phone to read a text message.

Jerod says, "Is she coming tonight?"

"Yep. She finished her finals today so she's driving down for the weekend with one of her roommates from State."

Jerod leans the table on its side and unfolds the collapsible legs. "That's cool. I invited this girl Jenna from my Spanish class so I'm hoping it's not all guys here tonight."

"Oh *really*. What about Lindsay?"

Jerod shrugs. "Um, I don't know what she's up to tonight. Probably hanging out with her friends or something."

Jerod and Matt stand the table upright. As they walk back into the house, Matt says, "I'm surprised you didn't invite *her*."

"I don't know . . . I hadn't really thought about asking Lindsay. We don't have to hang out every weekend. Plus, I think I like this girl Jenna. I want to try to get to know her a little better, maybe ask her out."

Matt says, "Whatever happened to Mr. 'I just want to be single and not tied down?'"

Jerod replies, "First of all, it's just a date. Second . . . it depends on the person. Lindsay is cute and cool and we have fun, and I think our arrangement works fine. But with Jenna . . . I don't know, I think there's just something *more* there."

Matt says, "What if Lindsay comes over anyway? How are you going to explain all of this?"

"I don't think I have to *explain* anything. Lindsay and I don't really get into each other's business—it's not like we're in a relationship. On the other hand, though . . . well, I really don't know."

* * * * *

By 11:00 P.M., Josie's Grill is packed for the last party night before winter break. Whitney and her friends watch a basketball game on the big screen; their college team trails in a holiday tournament game. As the game's final seconds tick away, the group drowns its sorrows with a round of tequila shots. Whitney's phone buzzes on the table. She flips open her phone and reads a text from Lindsay: "omg im freaking out where are u"

Whitney clicks back: "josies what happened"

Lindsay's reply: "tell u when i get there"

Twenty minutes later, Lindsay arrives, teary, her mascara smeared beneath red eyes. Whitney nods toward the bathroom, and the women elbow their way through the mob toward the back of the bar. In the relative quiet of the bathroom, Lindsay fixes her makeup and tells her story to Whitney's reflection in the mirror.

"So, I told you before that I hadn't heard from Jerod all week, but I saw on his Facebook page that there was a party at Phi Zeta."

"Yeah."

"Well, I decided to go over there, just to check it out. I knew they'd be watching the game or whatever."

"Okay."

"So, when I showed up, he was talking to some other girl. At first I just blew it off and talked to some of his frat brothers for a little bit. Matt and his girlfriend Kristin were there, so we played beer pong on the porch for a while."

"Uh-huh."

"Then, when I went back into the living room, the other girl was sitting on Jerod's lap!"

"Oh geez. What did you do?"

"Nothing; I just left. What *could* I do?"

"Well . . ."

"It's not like I'm his *girlfriend* or anything. We're just hanging out and sleeping together. What was I going to say, 'I know we agreed two months ago that we were just friends with benefits and not in a relationship, but it hurts my feelings when another girl sits in your lap?' I don't think so. . . ."

"But if you didn't talk to Jerod about it, how do you know it was anything? It could just be flirting and nothing else."

"Maybe, but I *can't* talk to him about it. I definitely can't bring up my feelings. I shouldn't even have feelings about him because we're not dating. I don't have a *right* to be hurt. And if I bring it up, then I'm just '*that* girl.'"

Whitney says, "Yeah, I see your point. It sucks to look like the uptight one who needs to know what you guys '*are.*'"

Lindsay adds, "*OR* the crazy girl who said she was cool with just being friends with benefits but is suddenly all emotional now."

"True," Whitney says.

Lindsay sighs and thumps her head back against the bathroom wall. "Ugh. There was never supposed to be this kind of drama. That's exactly what I was trying to avoid since I started hooking up with Jerod. If I wanted to feel jealous and emotional, I would just have a *real* relationship."

Whitney leans against the wall beside her friend and says, "Maybe so, Lindz, but you're pretty deep in it now. So what are you going to do?"

For Further Thought and Reflection

1. How does communication (or lack of the same) help to create relational uncertainty or ambiguity in this case? How do the characters communicate in an effort to handle or manage that uncertainty? What opportunities and obstacles for interacting arise when uncertainty is present?
2. Another source of ambiguity is the nature of the words used to describe actions and experiences. What terms are used in ambiguous or different ways across conversations in this case?

3. What does Lindsay mean when she says "*that* girl" near the end of the last conversation? How does that term and what it represents inform our understanding of relationship talk?
4. Some people seem to find it difficult to maintain the friends with benefits "agreement." What factors might contribute to this difficulty?
5. How do the characters in this case fit or contradict your understanding of masculine and feminine gender norms?
6. Does this case match your understanding of friends with benefits? In what ways is it similar or different? What other types of relationships are referred to as friends with benefits relationships?

References

Arnett, J.J. (2000). Emerging adulthood: A theory of development from the late teens through the twenties. *American Psychologist, 55,* 469–480.

Bisson, M., & Levine, T. (2009). Negotiating a friends with benefits relationship. *Archives of Sexual Behavior, 38,* 66–73.

Epstein, M., Calzo, J.P., Smiler, A.P., & Ward, M. (2009). "Anything from making out to having sex": Men's negotiations of hooking up and friends with benefits scripts. *Journal of Sex Research, 46,* 414–424.

Hughes, M., Morrison, K., & Asada, K. J. (2005). What's love got to do with it? Exploring the impact of maintenance rules, love attitudes, and network support on friends with benefits relationships. *Western Journal of Communication, 69,* 49–66.

Mongeau, P., Shaw, C., & Knight, K. (2009). Friends with benefits. In H. Reis, H. Sprecher & S. Sprecher (Eds.), *Encyclopedia of Human Relationships* (Vol. 2, pp. 740–741). Thousand Oaks, CA: Sage.

Paul, E. L., & Hayes, K. A. (2002). The casualties of casual sex: A qualitative exploration of the phenomenology of college students' hookups. *Journal of Social and Personal Relationships, 19,* 639–661.

Part III

Communication Processes in Established Relationships

12 The Embarrassment of Disclosing Private Information in Public: Newly Married Couples

SANDRA PETRONIO

Key Terms

privacy, disclosure, embarrassment, rules, boundaries, marital adjustment

---

On the way over to Matt's parent's home, Jennifer asked, "Matt, why do we go over so often?" "Because my mom likes to see us," said Matt.

"But, she is always asking me personal questions about our marriage. Half the time I don't know what to say—I feel embarrassed. And, why does she insist that I call her Mom? It makes me feel funny," Jennifer confessed.

"You can say anything to her; she's easy to talk to," Matt said encouragingly. "I think she wants you to feel like you are a part of the family; that's why she told you to call her Mom." Matt got the feeling that Jennifer didn't appreciate his mother, and he was confused about Jennifer's complaints. After all, he felt so happy when he saw them spending time together.

As Jennifer sat talking to her mother-in-law, Kelly, she realized how uncomfortable she felt. She wasn't used to talking with Kelly about personal things. When she stopped to think about it, she really didn't know Kelly. Jennifer wanted to get close to Matt's mother, but Kelly expected her to act as if they had known each other all their lives. Jennifer was torn. She wanted Kelly to like her, yet she also felt that her privacy was always being invaded.

Figuring this out was going to be tough, and Matt was not going to be much help. Matt just didn't see the problem Jennifer was facing. The strangest part was that Matt's openness had been the thing that attracted her. He had no trouble telling her all about his feelings. Now, the difference in how they regulated privacy and disclosure was beginning to be a problem.

Matt's Point of View

Matt loved his family. He found Jennifer's reluctance to talk to his parents and brothers difficult to understand. "Jennifer, all my life I have been open with my family, especially my mom. Why can't you just let it go and tell them the things you feel?" "Because they are not my parents" Jennifer complained. "Well, they are now," Matt pointed out—like the time they moved into their new house after they were married. The bathroom had a separate shower with a clear glass door and large window looking out to the rest of the bathroom. The first time they were both in the bathroom together getting ready for work Jennifer was in the shower and Matt came in to shave. Jennifer yelled at him not to stare at her through the glass. She acted embarrassed—as if it wasn't appropriate even to glance her way. *We're married, for goodness sake,* thought Matt. From then on, Jennifer waited until Matt was through in the bathroom to take her shower. Matt found this behavior hard to understand.

Matt has two brothers, and his parents are still together after twenty-seven years. They never expected too much privacy when they were living together in their parents' home. When they were growing up, his parents always assumed the children would talk to them if they were facing problems. They also really liked "family talk time" around the dinner table. In fact, everyone was supposed to be home at dinnertime, and the television had to be turned off when they were eating dinner. Matt has fond memories of the way he talked with his family during these times. It wasn't just during dinnertime that the family confided. He remembers one incident that happened with his brother Jamie.

"Say, I really need to talk to everyone about something. Could we meet in the family room after dinner? I need your help," Jamie said one evening. The family agreed. They were all curious, wondering what Jamie had to say, but they knew that it was up to him to tell.

Although they were an open family, they had their privacy rules about not pushing someone to talk. Jamie seemed edgy, as if he had the weight of the world on his shoulders. Matt was afraid of what Jamie might say. But, he was his brother and would always be there for him, no matter what.

Jamie finally announced to the family that his girlfriend was pregnant. "My stomach dropped out," Matt told Jennifer after they were married. "I thought his life was ruined. Everyone was great, though. I was worried that Mom would go ballistic, but she was just concerned about Jamie, as well as his girlfriend." Matt's family talked it out. Jamie and his girlfriend, Alicia, wanted to keep the baby. He was just finishing college and looking forward to being on his own and starting a career. Jamie and Alicia decided to get married.

"We always knew that we could come to our family with problems, but after the stuff with Jamie, I was really struck by how open our family really is with each other. Even my Mom and Dad come to us and tell us when they are having some problems. I like the fact that they include us kids in their lives," Matt confessed to Jennifer.

"It gives me a sense of security that I know other kids don't have with their parents. My brothers are always telling me things about their lives, too. I really can depend on my family to listen when I need to talk. That's why I can't understand your reluctance to talk to them, Jennifer," Matt complained.

"Well, Matt, my family is completely different from yours," Jennifer replied.

Jennifer's Point of View

Jennifer grew up in a family that didn't believe in talking freely about problems. Her father, Lyle, always commented that discretion is a valuable lesson to learn in life. Likewise, Jennifer's mother, Kristen, believed that revealing too much to others would make a person vulnerable. She taught her kids that, even if you are talking to other family members, it is best to keep things to yourself and work them out on your own rather than bother everyone else with your troubles. Working your problems out showed strength. Jennifer, her two sisters, and her brother all recognized the merit in keeping things private, sometimes even among themselves.

Jennifer's family respected privacy. They believed that having thick privacy boundaries was the best way to keep solid relationships with others. When growing up, they did not pry into each other's business. They did not touch personal property; nobody barged into another's bedroom without knocking; nobody borrowed clothes, bikes, or anything without asking first. Typically, they did not burden each other with problems.

Jennifer remembers learning a valuable lesson about privacy when she was young. Her mother always warned about going through other people's dresser drawers or closets. But, when Jennifer was a child, she found that those warnings made her curious.

On one particular afternoon she was home from school, not feeling well. She stayed in bed, but as a restless ten-year-old, she wandered around the house ending up in her mother's room. Her mother was down in the basement doing the laundry. One particular dresser drawer captivated Jennifer. She had been told that she should never open up that drawer. She wondered what was in there to make her mother warn the children so many times never to touch it.

Noticing earlier that her mother had a lot of laundry to do, Jennifer headed for that secret drawer. She quietly opened it and moved the papers around. "Hum," she thought, "only papers." Then she picked one up that looked kind of old. As she read the words on that paper, they did not make sense to her. She saw that it said "Birth Certificate" on the top. She remembered that she had seen her own birth certificate and it had her whole name on it. It read, "Jennifer Johnson" with her mother's name, "Kristen Johnson" and her father's name, "Lyle Johnson." This paper looked like it was her brother's birth certificate. Yet, she was not sure. It said "William," which was her brother's name. But, the last name wasn't Johnson. Instead, it said "Cramer." Jennifer didn't know what to make of this discovery. She realized that she had been in the room a long time. She was afraid her mother would find her. So, she stuffed the certificate back into the drawer and left the room quickly.

Even at Jennifer's age, her privacy dilemma was clear. She could not ask her parents about the information she found, because she knew how much they valued privacy. She was also worried that she would get into trouble about snooping in the dresser. Nor did she think it was okay to ask her brother. In fact, she wondered if he even knew about this information. She kept the secret to herself. She wondered at times why her brother's certificate had a different name on it. Jennifer knew, though, that she could never find out from her family. She was reminded of this incident as she thought about Matt's family. His family would have discussed this information at some length. But, she could not understand how they felt so free to disclose to each other.

Talking to Matt about Kelly's request to call her "Mom" was hard for Jennifer. Usually she tried to work out a way to handle unpleasant situations like this one. Jennifer was trying to be more like Matt, yet it was not easy. "Matt," Jennifer commented, "I am not sure you know how hard it is for me to tell you how I feel about the fact you want me to be more open with your family. In my family, we don't complain to each other when we are facing problems. We just try to cope ourselves. So please know that this is very troubling to me."

"Jennifer," said Matt, "I really don't understand the fuss."

Incident with Matthew's Family

Jennifer wondered why she and Matt were so opposite in the way they thought about privacy. Part of her wanted to make Matt happy; part resisted.

One Sunday afternoon, Matt and Jennifer were visiting his family. As usual, when they finished with dinner, the family joined in to clean up amid chatter about nothing and everything. Matt loved this time most when he visited—all the family doing something together, joining in on different conversations that seemed to be going simultaneously. They always were kidding and joking with each other about things. Yet, Matt was worried about whether Jennifer would fit into his family. She did not seem to welcome or understand that teasing was their way of loving each other. One family motto was "Why tease someone you hate—it is a waste of energy."

Jennifer liked a good laugh as much as anyone did. But, often Matt's family joshed about people she didn't know, or made "inside jokes" that were never explained. Many times when they teased her, she felt embarrassed. She really didn't like the teasing; it made her feel like they were picking on her and she felt exposed. This afternoon was especially bad for Jennifer. Matt's whole family was at his parents' house, including, Matt's two brothers, Jamie and Ed, and Jamie's wife Alicia. After cleaning up from dinner, they all sat at the kitchen table talking.

Then Ed started to talk seriously about taking a job in another city. He wanted to change jobs so he could make more money. He also talked about a woman he was interested in, and asked for some advice from his parents. Jennifer wondered why someone would seek advice so openly in front of so many people. When the conversation died down about Ed's decisions, Kelly turned to Matt and asked how he and Jennifer were getting along. Matt quickly revealed that Jennifer was feeling uncomfortable about having to call her Mom. Kelly asked Jennifer why she felt that way. Jennifer wasn't sure how to respond. She had told Matt in confidence and thought that he would know not to tell his Mom. Jennifer thought that she and Matt had established a co-owned privacy boundary that made Matt responsible for "taking care of" private information that Jennifer told him. Jennifer assumed Matt would understand that he was to keep the information just between the two of them. Jennifer was embarrassed and hurt that Matt did not respect her need for privacy. Kelly realized that there was some tension between Matt and Jennifer, and saved Jennifer further embarrassment by telling her not to worry—she didn't have to call her Mom if she didn't want to. Nevertheless, Jennifer was concerned that Kelly was offended.

Just as she was thinking that she'd have to talk to Matt again about disclosing her private thoughts and putting her in an awkward position with his family, he surprised her by confessing that he and Jennifer had another, more serious problem. He told his family that he and Jennifer disagreed about when to have children. Jennifer wanted to pursue a career. She had studied hard and finished her BA degree. She was hoping to go to law school. Matt wanted to have children right away. Jennifer knew Matt's family was hoping they would have another grandchild soon. The intensity of her distress was greater because Matt raised this issue without even letting her know he was going to tell his family. His disclosure caught her off guard, because they never really fully explored all the options and now his parents were invited into the decision-making process.

Jennifer had already felt miserable about Matt telling his mother that she did not want to call her "Mom." Now she wanted to scream and run away, maybe even be swallowed up by a big sink hole because he told his whole family they were having this problem. Jennifer's ears began to ring; she thought that she might become sick on the spot and lose the fine dinner she just enjoyed.

How could he be so insensitive! she thought. *The nerve of him to humiliate her like that!* When Jennifer calmed down enough to hear how the family was responding, she just couldn't take any more of it. Every member of the family had an opinion about their problem. Some of his brothers were mad at her for putting a career first. Jennifer tried to explain her feelings but the family was on Matt's side. She felt so mortified that she ran from the room.

Matt and his family were not sure why Jennifer reacted this way. They were trying to help Matt and Jennifer with their problem. However, to them, Jennifer seemed so unwilling to be helped and talk like they always did about a problem. "What's up with Jennifer?" asked Ed. "What is her problem?"

"I don't know exactly. I better go and talk to her," said Matt.

Time for Understanding

"Jennifer, why did you run out of the room?" asked Matt. "My family was only trying to help us with this decision."

"You just don't get it, do you, Matt?" said Jennifer.

"No, please help me understand," Matt responded.

"When you talked about our private life with your family, I felt betrayed because it is not just yours alone to control" said Jennifer. "Our private life belongs to you and me now. It is like you drew a circle or boundary around our private information and marked it only yours. Because we are both responsible for our private lives, I should have as much a say as you do in how we reveal that information to other people. When we talk about our private lives, we are telling things about both of us, and the information belongs to us mutually. If one of us takes control over the information, it is unfair to the other. Neither one of us should make independent judgments about disclosing the information. We need to talk about it first. We need an agreement about the kinds of things we can say to others, even your parents."

"You are comfortable with your family—you have known them all your life," pointed out Jennifer. "I, on the other hand, just met them. I don't know them at all; they are strangers to me. My family has rules about not disclosing private information, even sometimes to other family members," noted Jennifer. "For me, talking about personal matters even with you is difficult. I have been working on this, but I cannot deal with telling your whole family things that should be kept private between us."

"I still don't get it and now you want me to change the way I talk to my parents," said Matt.

"I think it is up to us to decide when we have children. Your family should not be involved in the discussion. Tonight I felt embarrassed and like a villain. It was more than I could tolerate. I don't think I can look at your family, never mind have dinner with them anymore," said Jennifer.

From Jennifer's point of view, this information is something they both should manage together. Interestingly, Matt is not used to this kind of sharing. Although he is very open about his feelings, and expects Jennifer to be open as well, jointly agreeing on when to disclose and when to keep something private between the two of them is unfamiliar to him. His family privacy rule is to be open; that is the rule he has always used. Now, he is expected to consult Jennifer whenever something is about the two of them, before he tells anyone else.

Matt knows it is going to take a real effort for them to work this out in a way they both feel comfortable. He is worried about how this is going to affect his relationship with his family, and wonders how Jennifer will ever get close to them if she will not open up to them. But, from their discussion, he is beginning to see that they have very different ways of defining private information. He never thought about the possibility of families being secretive, even with each other. Having this conversation, though painful, is helpful in beginning the long process of negotiating some basic ways to mutually manage information important to both of them. Matt loves Jennifer and knows that, although this is going to be a lot of work, they both want to build a life together. Part of the building blocks is learning how to blend values and attitudes that are different. It is funny, because Matt never even thought that this kind of thing would be a problem. He is sure that Jennifer never questioned her family's way of dealing with privacy, or thought it would be a problem either.

Endnote

[1] This case represents a composite of experiences found in open-ended questions about private disclosures by newly married couples. The names and circumstance are fictional.

For Further Thought and Reflection

1. Many newly married couples do not talk about expectations or the values they have for disclosing private information. Privacy rules are often assumptions people make without confirming another's point of view. Beside the points raised in this case study, what other ways do you think Matt and Jennifer might have conflicts over privacy in the future?
2. Why is managing private information so important in a marriage? What is the difference between remaining private and lying?
3. Matt and Jennifer grew up with different privacy expectations about information. How are they different and where do they have similarities?
4. Jennifer and Matt talk about privacy rules and how are they changing for this couple?
5. Why does Jennifer feel embarrassed? Would you? Why?

References

Caughlin, J., & Petronio, S. (2004). Privacy in families. In A. Vangelisiti (Ed.), *Handbook of family communication,* (pp. 379–412). Mahwah, NJ: LEA Publishers.

Petronio, S. (2002). *Boundaries of privacy: Dialectics of disclosure.* Mahwah, NJ: LEA Publishers.

Petronio, S. Olson, C., & Dollar, N. (1989). Privacy issues in relational embarrassment: Impact on relational quality and communication satisfaction. *Communication Research Reports, 6,* 216–225.

Petronio, S., & Durham, W. (2008). Understanding and applying Communication Privacy Management theory. In L.A. Baxter & D.O. Braithwaite (Eds.), *Engaging theories in interpersonal communication* (pp. 309–322). Thousand Oaks, CA: Sage Publications.

Serewicz, M.C.M., & Canary, D.J. (2008). Assessments of disclosure from the in-laws: Links among disclosure topics, family privacy orientations, and relational quality. *Journal of Social and Personal Relationships, 25,* 333–357.

A Place for Connecting and Disclosing: Facebook and Friendships at the Dawn of College Life

Andrew M. Ledbetter, Texas Christian University
& Joseph P. Mazer, Clemson University

Key Terms

self-disclosure, social connection, warranting, Facebook

Ben barely noticed the change in weather as a soft July rainstorm fluttered against his bedroom window. On this late Friday afternoon, Ben knew that many of his high school friends would be gathering together somewhere, doing something social. He'd been to several such gatherings during the summer—this intermission, this pause between the end of high school and the new life of college. Already he had heard his cell phone ring several times, then the chime of a voice mail, then the bleep of a text message. But tonight, as he clutched his Xbox controller, Ben was content to stay home and do some of the things he loved most, perhaps reading part of a novel later tonight. *This game is so much more controllable than my world right now,* he thought.

His mom's familiar knock echoed from his bedroom door. "Come in," Ben yelled as he paused his game.

She cracked open the door. "Got the mail, and there's a letter for you from Lasher State."

"Really?" Ben said as his mom handed him the envelope. As he opened it, he sized it up—it looked official, like everything else from Lasher State, but felt thin, unlike the huge amount of promotional material they sent. During senior year. *Every. Single. Week.*

His eyes scanned the single sheet of paper inside. "What is it?" his mom asked.

"Looks like information about my roommate." Ben was surprised they'd sent the information this quickly. He had only completed the roommate preference form two weeks ago.

"Who is he?" his mom asked excitedly, stepping through the door and turning to see the paper. "David L. Bradford, from Hill City? I wonder if he knows the Woodsmiths?"

"Maybe," Ben shrugged. "Probably. There's only about 5,000 people living there."

"Well, his e-mail address and phone number are right here; maybe you should try to give him a call after dinner."

Ben felt his gut tighten. The last thing he wanted to do tonight was talk to anyone else. Much less talk about college. "We'll see; perhaps later this weekend."

"Just don't wait too long. You'll have to make some plans with him before school starts!"

"I know," Ben said, picking up his Xbox controller again as his mom left. He unpaused, fired another shot, and dodged a missile. But then he paused again, curiosity creeping into his brain. *I wonder . . . what can I find out about this David guy online? Google? Maybe even Facebook?* He moved to his computer, noticing he had new e-mails, but it took a moment for him to realize that one message was from David Bradford! But wait, it wasn't a "real" e-mail; the subject line read, "Dave Bradford added you as a friend on Facebook . . ."

The knot in Ben's stomach tightened a little bit. He had only created his Facebook account about a year ago, and mostly to keep in touch with a few close high school friends. At the time, he hadn't thought about how Facebook might help build friendships at college, but thinking about it now, it made sense that it would. He moved to click "accept," but then hesitated. This felt weird. *Honestly, it's strange to accept a request from someone I don't know . . . but I guess I will know him. But then again, what if we don't get along? Will he be upset if I don't accept the request?* For a moment, he stared at the screen, hovering in indecision. Then, with firm finality, he clicked the button. *Now, let's see what my new roommate is about.*

In Dave's profile picture, he was wearing a football uniform, hoisting a medium-sized trophy above his head, enthusiastic teammates and students cheering around him. Ben's eyes moved further down the left side of the page. *What? He has 732 friends? How did he get that many?* Last time he checked, Ben's friends barely numbered 100. *Obviously David likes football . . . U2, of course . . . in a relationship but "it's complicated?"* Ben skipped reading the list of brainless comedy movies Dave seemed to like and started reading Dave's wall. The first post was from someone named Annabelle Watkins, a gorgeous girl with what looked like some kind of alcoholic drink in her hand. "Hey man!!! Life of the party last night!! Won't be the same in h-town w/o u!!" The next post was from Jason Vernum, also wearing a football uniform: "What you doing sending me a FB message at 3 AM?? Oh wait, it's you, ha ha." Most posts were written by girls.

Ben leaned back, looked up, and blew air between his lips. In his mind, he saw his dorm room, plastered with Dave's ridiculous football posters. He saw himself trying to get some sleep while Dave partied into the late hours of the night. He saw Dave trying to hit on every girl that passed down the hallway. And he could almost smell the lingering scent of beer Dave would surely bring into their room. This had been his nightmare about college life: a roommate who would derail his vision of studying hard and being the first person in his family to earn a college degree. How had the housing office messed up so badly? He had made it so clear he wanted someone who prioritized grades. Did Ben just happen to get the last roommate available?

He navigated back to his own Facebook profile. *I list myself as single, but I think there are still a few pictures up with my girlfriend from junior year. Some of the bands under "Favorite Music" seem a bit dated . . . I still list The Crazy Monkeys? That's gotta go. And he's going to think I'm such a big nerd with "reading" as my first listed hobby. And, oh wow, the most recent post on my wall is even from grandma.* Looking up, his eyes scanned his "Religious Views" and "Political Views." *I kinda listed those reluctantly. Maybe I should take them down before the fall?*

With a level of intensity that surprised him, Ben closed the browser window and turned back to his video game. This was the last thing he wanted to think about on a summer night.

* * * * *

Ben felt a small burst of glee as he plugged his Xbox 360's video cable into Dave's flat-screen TV. *This is going to be so much better than my old TV! And so far only one ridiculous football poster. Maybe Dave won't be so bad after all.* He heard a knock behind him and turned.

"Hi. Looks like you have quite the TV there?" said a tall girl with straight blond hair.

"Yeah, it's Dave's," Ben replied, setting the cable down. He extended a hand. "I'm Ben Hamilton."

"Allison Wickman," she responded, shaking his hand. "I live across the hall and thought I'd say 'hi.' Have you met my roommate yet? Chloe Martins?"

"I think I saw her bringing some boxes up with her mom."

Allison laughed. "Yeah, wait 'til you see how many shoes she has! But I knew that; we went to high school together. How about your roommate? Don't think I've met him yet."

"Dave? He seems OK, but we don't really know each other—just talked on the phone a few times this summer. He seems pretty athletic; spends a lot of time with the football team."

Allison opened her mouth to reply as a girl with curly dark hair tumbled out of the stairwell. The bulk of her huge cardboard box dwarfed her tiny frame.

"Allison? Um, help?" she asked, bracing herself against the wall.

Ben turned with Allison to help steady the box. As Allison grunted under the weight, she said, "Ben, this is Chloe."

"Nice to meet you," Ben breathed, helping them shove the box through the door frame. It barely fit. He heard his cell phone ring in his own room. "I should probably get that; do you have it handled from here?"

"Think so," Allison said. "Catch you later . . . look you up on Facebook?"

"Sure," Ben nodded, then dashed into his room. The phone had just finished ringing; the missed call was from his mom. Ben rolled his eyes; *third time she's called me today.* As he set the phone down, his hand brushed his laptop. He had been editing his

Facebook profile before the urge struck to set up the Xbox 360, and it was still on the screen. *Whoops. I still have The Crazy Monkeys listed. Oh well, I guess Allison will just think I have weird musical tastes.*

"Hey Ben," he heard Dave say behind him.

"Back from the weight room?" Ben asked, turning from the computer.

"Yeah," Dave replied. "Hey, thanks for setting up the Xbox!"

"Oh, I'm not quite done yet. A girl from across the hall stopped by and interrupted me."

"Yeah, I think I saw them when I came in. Pretty good looking chicks!"

Ben felt himself squirm inwardly. *Not exactly how I was raised to think about girls. Time to change the subject.* "What are you doing tonight? I heard some of the other freshmen are going to a late showing of *Titan Wars*. Want to come?"

"Oh man, I've been wanting to see that movie!" Dave closed the door and opened up his closet. "But I've got to hit the sack early tonight; I know class doesn't start until Wednesday, but ROTC starts tomorrow. Gotta be up by six, so I'm going to try to be in bed no later than eleven this semester. Been meaning to talk to you about that; hope that's OK with you."

Ben's brain took a moment to catch up with the sudden change in his expectations. "Wait . . . you're in ROTC? From Facebook, it looked like you stayed up pretty late last year!"

Dave chuckled, pulling some clothes from his closet. "Yeah . . . you probably got a strange mental picture of me from Facebook, huh? Like I'm some party animal or something?"

Ben looked down. "Well, I guess . . . "

"No need to pretend; I didn't realize until I saw your profile how it might look to you. It's pretty clear you care a lot about your grades, and your family." He paused a moment, looking uncomfortable. "I don't really want to go into too much detail right now, but I made some bad choices my junior year. I almost didn't get into Lasher State. But then some tough things happened with my family and on the football team, and I changed a lot my senior year. That's why I requested someone who studies a lot and goes to bed early on that form they sent out. Some of my old friends still post stuff on my wall, trying to make it sound like I drink and party a lot, but I don't even go near alcohol anymore."

"Wow," Ben said, feeling stunned. "Yeah, that's not the impression I had of you from Facebook. But I'm probably not as nerdy as I sounded on Facebook, either."

"I don't know about that, buddy—only a nerd would list Crazy Monkeys on the profile."

"Getting deleted right now," Ben chuckled, turning to his computer. He had a new e-mail: "Allison Wickman added you as a friend on Facebook . . . "

Before he clicked "accept," he wondered: *When she reads my profile, what impression will Allison have of me?* Knowing that accepting friend requests would probably become a routine part of his new life at college, Ben clicked "accept." He began to explore Allison's Facebook profile.

In her profile picture, Allison wore a red and white high school cheerleading uniform; an older couple, perhaps her parents, stood next to her, as well as a few friends and football players. But the most prominent friend in the picture was Chloe, also in a cheerleading uniform, her arm tightly around Allison's shoulders. Except for a new haircut, Chloe looked pretty much like she did now. The picture appeared to be taken just after a team victory. The football players looked exhausted, but happy. Everyone was smiling. Ben looked to the left side of the page—*Wow! 985 friends? Are you kidding me? That's . . .* being a bit of a math and statistics geek, Ben quickly calculated in his head . . . *that's about 250 more than Dave! I don't even think I know that many people in person.* Allison's wall was littered with postings from Chloe: "Hey gurl! I had an awesome time dancing last night. Call me la8er. xoxoxo." Another read, "what party are we going to tonight? Gotta see ya before you head to Lasher!" Ben scrolled up and clicked on the "Info" tab. Under "About Me," it read: "I'm heading to Lasher State in the Fall with my girl, Chloe! Can't wait for college! We're going to be roommates! Yay!!!" *Wow. They seem pretty close. I bet it's going to be so easy for them to live together at college.*

* * * * *

Ben looked up from his midterm study sheet and glanced out the window. "Dave, it's snowing!" he exclaimed, watching thin clusters of flakes fall toward the parking lot below.

He heard Dave blow air between his lips. "Too early, man! Too early!"

Ben chuckled. "I think you're just in denial about midterms."

A small knock sounded from their open door. "Aren't we all?" asked Chloe, peeking her head around the door jamb. "Hey, you guys almost ready for dinner?"

Ben glanced at his watch; it was 5:30. "Wow, it is that time already!" Ben thought about how he expected that, many nights, he would have dinner with Dave, Chloe, and Allison. Since the beginning of the semester, they had become pretty good friends. In addition to lunch or dinner several times each week in the dining hall, they watched movies during the week and chatted often on Facebook. *Or at least, we all did until about a week ago.*

As Ben grabbed his room key, attached to his sporty Lasher State lanyard, he thought about asking the unspoken question that had hovered among the three of them this past week. He was sure Dave and Chloe didn't see him open his mouth and close it in hesitation before he finally opened it to speak. "Hey, Chloe, where's Allison?"

Chloe looked down, shaking her head. "Ya know, Ben, lately I just don't know about that girl. She's just never in the room anymore. She leaves early before I get up. She gets in late, sometimes after I'm asleep. And she never talks to me anymore. Ever. I mean, about anything more than basic stuff. I've been wondering if I pissed her off somehow, but I just don't know."

"Nah, it isn't just you," Dave chimed in, throwing his lanyard around his neck. "Allison's been ignoring me lately too. We used to always meet in the library on

Mondays after lunch to study, but she hasn't been there the last two weeks. And get this: I was down at the health center yesterday for an appointment about my knee, and I saw her coming out. I just, like, asked her where she'd been, but she seemed upset and said she was just busy. But she also was talking really fast and hardly looked me in the eyes."

Ben fingered his keys idly, thinking. "Well," Chloe said, "I'm sure it's not a big deal; I'll just try to check in with her tonight, no matter how late she comes in."

"Wait a sec," Ben said, bending back over his laptop. "Have either of you checked her Facebook page recently?"

"Hey—isn't that kind of, like, stalking our friend?" Dave protested. But Ben had already accessed her profile. Allison hadn't updated her status message in about two weeks, and hardly anyone had posted on her wall. The exception was a message posted about two minutes ago by an elderly woman named Donna: "Hi dear—Heard from your parents about what's going on—so sorry—love always." Ben read it out loud to Dave and Chloe as they huddled around him.

"Sounds kinda serious," Dave said, his usual levity gone from his voice.

Chloe shook her head. "Maybe, but I know Donna from home; she's friends with Allison's grandma. She sometimes exaggerates things. She probably just heard about how stressed Allison is about midterms. I mean, Allison and I have been best friends since fourth grade. If it were anything really serious, she'd tell me right away. Maybe before her family."

"Guys, I know this could be important, but the dining hall is going to get crowded soon, and I'm so hungry!" belted out Dave. "I hope they don't have that stinky green-ish looking meatloaf again!" Ben returned his Facebook page to the news feed and turned to head for dinner.

* * * * *

By the time they returned to their dorm floor after, fortunately, a non-meatloaf dinner, the unseasonably early snow had stopped. "Watching *The Bachelor* tonight?" Ben asked Chloe.

"Yeah. You guys doing your post-dinner Xbox ritual?"

"Of course!" Dave exclaimed. "Study for the psych test later? About an hour?"

"Sounds good," Chloe replied as she walked past her room toward the stairwell to the basement lounge. As Ben loaded the Xbox 360 game, he saw Dave log in to check Facebook. Just as the game finished loading, Ben heard Dave draw in a sharp, startled breath.

"What is it?" Ben asked.

"Um, it's Allison," Dave replied. "Dude, you've got to read this." Ben bolted from the papassan chair to his desk, shaking his mouse to awaken his computer. Allison's note was at the top of his news feed. As Ben began to read, Dave said softly: "I don't believe it. I feel so . . . " Quickly, Ben snapped back, "Shhh, quiet. I'm reading." He read the first two lines:

"I am writing to share some very sad and very personal news. I've been diagnosed with ovarian cancer. The doctors think they caught it early. So my prognosis is good."

Ben felt stunned, his stomach twisting in knots. "This must be why Allison has been so distant," he said. "Why didn't she just tell us and especially Chloe? I know it's really personal, and we haven't known her that long, but it feels like we're good friends . . . "

"Yeah, I know," Dave replied. "Maybe she didn't tell us because it's a 'girl thing?' "

"But it doesn't sound like she told Chloe, either."

With sudden quickness, Dave dashed across the hall and knocked on Chloe's door. There was no answer. He pulled out his cell phone. "What are you doing?" Ben asked.

"Text message," Dave replied. "Asking if she's seen Allison's Facebook note." When he was done, Dave silently returned to his desk chair and opened his psychology textbook.

Ben stood for a moment, staring at Dave, then back at his laptop, then to the Xbox 360, the game's militaristic theme song droning through the television speakers. *I can't believe how normal things felt earlier tonight,* he thought. Not feeling like playing a game anymore, he turned off the Xbox 360 and the television.

Dave's phone played its text message chime. "What does it say?" Ben asked. He held up the phone to Ben: *huh? No, whats wrong? In the dorm lounge; should I come up?* "Sounds like she doesn't know," Ben said, then feeling stupid for saying the obvious.

"What should we do? You know how she's going to react. Should we tell her?"

"I . . . I don't know. Maybe Allison was going to tell Chloe later tonight? Maybe we should back off and let her share her news when she's ready?"

"But she's going to see this next time she checks Facebook, which will probably be after *The Bachelor*—" Dave stopped as they heard footsteps run down the hall, and then saw Chloe swiftly open her door and enter her room. Ben looked at Dave, and then both followed behind her. She was already bending over her computer, a tear streaming down her cheek.

"S—someone downstairs checked the note on their iPhone—" she stammered as she opened the note. Ben and Dave remained awkwardly silent as she read the first few lines, her eyes filling with fresh tears. "Why—why didn't she tell me?" Chloe breathed in, her voice trembling.

"I'm so sorry," said Dave, trying to comfort her, putting his hand on her shoulder; she violently shrugged it away.

"She should have told me," Chloe spat, tears still in her eyes. "We've been friends since elementary school. We've been through everything together! Why couldn't see just tell me to my face? But no, I get to hear about it from some guy friends after she posts it on Facebook for the whole damn world to see!"

"Well, maybe she just wanted to tell everybody at once," Ben said, not sure what else to say. "I bet it would be hard for her to tell the same story over and over. She must have so much going on in her mind, and I'm sure she didn't mean to hurt you."

Chloe collapsed on her bed. "Ben, just shut up. You have NO IDEA what things we've gone through together! She was there when my parents divorced, and when grandpa passed away suddenly, and so many other times. And I told her EVERY-THING. But—" She buried her face in her pillow, sobbing. Ben and Dave's eyes met for a moment; Dave's face mirrored Ben's concern for Chloe, coupled with an utter sense of futility at understanding her feelings, much less comforting her. Without a further word, they both turned to leave.

But before they could take a step, the door swung open noiselessly. It was Allison.

For Further Thought and Reflection

1. Ben's perception of Dave from Facebook was very different than how Dave presented himself in person. When, if ever, have you experienced a mismatch between someone's online persona and how they communicate when face-to-face?
2. Some communication research on the *warranting value of information* suggests that we are more likely to believe a Facebook member's wall posts than their own statements about themselves. Why do you think Ben so easily believed wall posts on Dave's profile? When might we believe a person's statements about themselves rather than those of their Facebook friends?
3. Why do you think Allison shared her personal information with everyone on Facebook, instead of telling Chloe, her close friend, to her face? More generally, what qualities of online communication might help some people feel more comfortable self-disclosing online?
4. Do you think Chloe should ask Allison why she did not directly share her medical problem? Why or why not? What do you think might happen next in this story?

References

Donath, J. (2007). Signals in social supernets. *Journal of Computer-Mediated Communication, 13.* Available at: http://jcmc.indiana.edu/vol13/issue1/donath.html.

Ellison, N. B., Steinfield, C., & Lampe, C. (2007). The benefits of Facebook "friends:" Social capital and college students' use of online social network sites. *Journal of Computer-Mediated Communication, 12.* Available at: http://jcmc.indiana.edu/vol12/issue4/ellison.html.

Mazer, J.P., Murphy, R.E., & Simonds, C.J. (2007). I'll see you on "Facebook": The effects of computer-mediated teacher self-disclosure on student motivation, affective learning, and classroom climate. *Communication Education, 56,* 1–17.

Tong, S.T., Van Der Heide, B., Langwell, L., & Walther, J.B. (2008). Too much of a good thing? The relationship between number of friends and interpersonal impressions on Facebook. *Journal of Computer-Mediated Communication, 13,* 531–549.

Walther, J. B. (2008). Social information processing theory: Impressions and relationship development online. In L.A. Baxter & D.O. Braithwaite (Eds.), *Engaging theories in interpersonal communication* (pp. 391–404). Newbury Park, CA: Sage.

Walther, J.B., Van Der Heide, B., Kim, S., Westerman, D., & Tong, S.T. (2008). The role of friends' behavior on evaluations of individuals' Facebook profiles: Are we known by the company we keep? *Human Communication Research, 34,* 28–49.

14

Managing Work, Life, and Family: Informal Parenting Support Systems

Suzy D'Enbeau and Patrice M. Buzzanell

Key Terms

work-life balance, support, coworkers, caregiving, choice

Brad heard a beep as he was toweling his hair after exiting the shower. He picked up his wife's text, "OMG, U got to see this!", and threw on some boxers before heading downstairs. There his wife, Janie, sat in the kitchen scanning a text on her Kindle. Her cup of coffee was forgotten. She was totally engrossed in whatever she was reading.

Brad walked over to the coffee maker and poured himself a cup. He poured some milk, added sweetener to his mug, and watched her. Suddenly her eyes rose from the screen and she looked at him.

"You've got to see this," she exclaimed and passed the Kindle to him. On it was a *Wall Street Journal* article about dating.

"Foursomes in dating?! No way. Are you telling me that I'm not exciting enough?" he laughed.

"Augh," she sighed and shook her head. "Read."

And so he did.

The article was about couples trying to set up dates with other couples so that they could form friendships after relocating to new areas. Brad sipped more coffee as he continued to read.

"So?"

"Don't you get it?" Janie asked. "That's what we've been trying to do with Sara and Mike. And the problems we had setting up a get together or 'date' aren't unusual."

"Well, we did finally manage to get together with them and we all seemed to have a nice time," Brad noted. He started to put wheat bread in the toaster and gestured to Janie to find out if she wanted some, too. She nodded absently.

"We did have a nice time. But I can't believe how long it took," Janie added. "We started trying to set it up at the alum get-together in Chicago, remember?"

Indeed he did. He and Janie had never gone to any of the Purdue alumni functions in the different cities in which they lived. But this time they noticed that an event was being held during a happy hour in a downtown restaurant noted for its martinis and imported beers. They had lived in Chicago for a couple of months and missed not having friends to call up and do things with. While they were checking out the crowd to see if there was anyone to whom they'd like to introduce themselves, they saw Mike and Sara doing the same. The couples' eyes met, and they all started smiling. Mike and Sara started heading their way.

"Caught!," Mike commented as he extended a hand to Brad for a handshake.

"Yup, I'm Brad and this is my wife, Janie. We're both Purdue alums. I was in civil [engineering] and Janie spent her time in liberal arts. She finished up in psychology, then found a job as a sales rep for a global pharmaceutical company. My work inspecting bridges enables me to travel and live just about anywhere. So when she was relocated here in Chicago a couple of months ago, we both moved. How about you?"

"I started in EE but finished up in Computer Science. I didn't care for the theory but loved to write code. Sara here did her degree in Krannert [School of Management] and picked up minors in Spanish and statistics. I'm hoping that she'll support me when I decide to quit my job and start my own company," Mike smiled as he glanced over at Sara.

"Yeah, I've heard this for the last four years since we met at a Delta [fraternity] party and he tried to hook up with my roommate," Sara laughed. "We've been in Chicago for a half year and thought that the alum association might be a good place to meet people. Our work has finally slowed down a little."

"Us, too," Janie remarked. And so the conversation began. By the end of the night, the four decided to get together in a few days and set up Wednesday to try out the new Thai restaurant on 33rd Street.

But when Wednesday afternoon arrived, neither of the couples could make it. Janie was the first to email.

"Mike and Sara, I'm so sorry. There's a guy on my project team here whose kid had to get stitches and checked for a concussion when a soccer ball hit her in the head. He's taking her to the emergency room for a CAT scan and ImPACT test so I need to stick around and get our documentation finalized. It turned out we would have had to cancel anyway because one of Brad's colleagues went into labor prematurely, so he's got to pick up the slack. He's the only one in his office without kids. How about a trip to Purdue for the Notre Dame game on Saturday? We've got a group we tailgate with. We'll bring the brats and beer. Just bring yourselves."

But when Friday afternoon rolled around, it was Mike and Sara who had to cancel this time. Sara wrote on Janie's Facebook wall that she hoped Janie and Brad would have a great time at the game and that she and Mike couldn't go after all. Janie replied and promised to post photos of the party.

While Janie and Brad were at the game, Mike was at his office. Sara had let him know that she wasn't pleased that he had to work on a Saturday morning after weeks of weekend work. They both hoped that the overload was temporary. He promised to take her out to Giordano's for Chicago pizza that evening.

Then Mike settled in to review his data and write the reports that were due on Monday morning. Rebecca, his coworker, came into the office to help him. He saw her carry a black nylon bag and wondered if she planned to spend the rest of her weekend at the office. He was looking at the bag and was just about to make a comment about snacks at the office when she interrupted him.

"Don't ask," Rebecca warned.

"Why not? That bag looks as though it is insulated and could hold enough snacks for both of us. Ah, you're holding out on me, Rebecca!" Mike concluded.

"Mike, this is a breast pump and storage bag. It may look like some black designer laptop case or briefcase, but it isn't." Rebecca saw the look of disappointment and speculation that she might be lying to hoard cheese and crackers. He would have done the same. She started to unzip the bag and pull out the pump, bottles . . .

"Stop! I believe you," Mike said.

Rebecca put the equipment away and they headed to the conference room to review data and divide up report sections. Rebecca stayed in the conference room while Mike returned to his office. They worked steadily—with only one break for Rebecca to pump—until she stopped by Mike's office.

"Mike, I hate to do this to you," Rebecca began, "but I just got a text that Nicky has a fever and some little red spots. He has been crying for the last half hour and there doesn't seem to be anything that the nanny can do to get him to stop. I've got to get home and take Nicky to the urgent care clinic. I'm sorry to leave you. But I really have to go. I can log on tonight and pick up where you leave off. But it might not be for a while. I don't know how long the clinic will take. And the nanny is supposed to be off tonight."

Mike reassured her that he was fine working on the report and that he'd contact her if he needed her input. Otherwise, she should just take care of Nicky and he'd see her on Monday.

Mike continued to work and forgot about his promise to Sara. He didn't mind finishing up the report without Rebecca. She always pulled her share and helped him out in the past. However, it wasn't just her. His two other coworkers on the project also had family issues that weekend. Yolanda had a fiftieth wedding anniversary weekend celebration for her mother and father. Marcella had a first communion party with her family. He didn't understand why Marcella's event would tie up the entire weekend but she explained that, in her culture, the event was a big deal and family was coming in from all over. Marcella's son was the first grandchild among her five siblings, and her parents and their siblings wanted to preserve family traditions. So they were all descending on her church for the Mass and were bringing food and gifts. Her parents and several aunts and uncles weren't going to leave until Sunday afternoon. They hired a photographer for family photos and ordered a big white cake and had made homemade chorizo and salsa for the event. Marcella promised to save some for Mike, and his stomach growled at the thought of all that great Mexican food.

Mike's mobile rang. It was Sara.

"Are you ready? I'm starved," she commented.

He glanced at the clock and realized that it was later than he thought.

"Sure, let me save the documents. I didn't get as much done as I wanted. Rebecca had to leave 'cause Nicky got sick. I'll have to return tomorrow."

"Can't you just work from home tomorrow?" Sara asked.

"I would, but this project has proprietary technology, and I can't run data or pull documents from home. Even the intranet system has firewalls to prevent leaks. So the answer is 'no.' I'll just come back tomorrow morning and finish it up."

He and Sara had a nice dinner and texted Brad and Janie for news about the Purdue game. Notre Dame had won in the last two minutes. It was depressing. Brad texted that he and Janie were at the University Spirit Shop getting black and gold sweatshirts for nephews before heading home. The tailgate party had been a huge success.

On Sunday morning, Sara logged into Facebook and called Mike over to see the photos. She pointed out one shot where Brad was stuffing his face with a brat and trying to smile for the camera at the same time. She also saw that Brad and Janie planned another tailgating party for the Indiana game. IU and Purdue had a deep-seated rivalry. That would be THE football game to attend. Sara and Mike checked their schedules, got online to buy tickets, and accepted Brad and Janie's invitation. Then Mike went into the office while Sara did a little work from home.

On the day of the IU game, Mike checked them into the Union Hotel on campus and headed to the tailgate section. Brad and Janie greeted them with big smiles and they all grabbed a beer.

Despite it being Autumn, the weather was hot and sunny. It didn't seem like football weather but at least it wasn't rainy or cold. The air was filled with smoke from people grilling, and the two couples could hear loud laughter from the groups of people walking around the tailgate area. Some of the people stopped by and said hello to Brad and Janie. Brad always introduced them to Mike and Sara. Mike was amazed that Brad could remember everyone's name. Brad said that some of the people were regulars who had been tailgating for years. He had hoped to introduce Mike and Sara to another couple, Kevin and Kisha, who had graduated from Purdue a couple of years before him and Janie. They had met at Harry's Chocolate Shop one night during finals week in his and Janie's sophomore year, and instantly became friends.

Brad saw Kevin and waved. When Kevin got closer, Brad asked, "Where's Kisha?" and introduced Kevin to Mike and Sara.

"Kisha is not sure she is going to make it. Her grandfather had a fall and needed an operation this past week. They've moved her grandfather into a rehab facility for physical therapy, but she and her mother needed to go to Ohio to get him settled in," Kevin noted. "She sends her best and asks that we do the 'wave' for her. She regrets not being here but is really glad that she didn't have to take off work to go to Ohio."

"What's happening at work?" Janie asked as she walked over toward Kevin.

"Oh, you know that Kisha works with a lot of young social workers and teachers at Head Start," Kevin began. "Well, the flu season has begun and most of these women have young kids. They've needed to take off work, so the intake work is backed up and the office workers are supervising classrooms. The good part is that, once this round of the flu is over, then things should settle down some. The bad news is that Kisha has been working long hours for a couple of weeks to cover for her coworkers. Even her boss has had to take time off. They don't have extra funding to bring in a temp. They just double up on some tasks and spread the rest around. The intake desk is the worst because they don't have enough people who speak Spanish. We just keep hoping that things will settle down soon. She can't keep working like this forever."

Janie nodded and noted that many of their friends had reported picking up extra work because of coworkers' sick kids, maternity leaves, eldercare issues, the flu season, and a million other things. Janie said that she understood, but it gets old when she's the one—along with a single colleague—who has to fill in.

"If we ever have kids," Janie began, "I think that I'll have emergency backup systems for my backup systems. I wouldn't let anyone know that managing work and family was a problem. It's a source of pride to be able to work it all out."

Later that night when she was climbing into bed, Janie wondered, "Why should I have to hide family problems or think that I need to work this all out for myself when nobody else seems to mind making coworkers cover for them? Why should I have to put in all the extra time to cover for a coworker's job if he or she has family emergencies? Why should I have to finish up other people's work when they leave to pick up kids from childcare? More importantly, will they be there when I need to have them be my parenting support system? And why should they—or any of us—have to do that?"

Janie said good night to Brad and turned off the lights.

For Further Thought and Reflection

1. Should co-workers have to do extra work just because a coworker has childcare or other family issues?
2. Janie seems to think that she shouldn't let anyone know if she has childcare problems. Why would she think that? Is this a realistic strategy for safeguarding her job and career? What else could she do?
3. How would you analyze this case from different interpersonal and family communication theories? Would your solutions to the case differ based on the theoretical perspectives you chose? How might you use your analyses to make proposals for change for your workplace?

References

Bernstein, E. (2009, November 3). When four play the dating scene. *Wall Street Journal.* Retrieved November 28, 2009. Available at: http://online.wsj.com/article/SB10001424052748 703932904574511432686237774.html

Buzzanell, P.M., & D'Enbeau, S. (2009). Stories of caregiving: Intersections of academic research and women's everyday experiences. *Qualitative Inquiry, 15,* 1199–1224.

Buzzanell, P.M., & Dohrman, R. (2009). Bosses, coworkers, and direct reports: Everyday communicative acts and consequences. In W.F. Eadie (Ed.), *21st Century communication* (pp. 331–339). Thousand Oaks, CA: Sage.

Buzzanell, P.M., & Liu, M. (2005). Struggling with maternity leave policies and practices: A poststructuralist feminist analysis of gendered organizing. *Journal of Applied Communication Research, 33,* 1–25.

Correll, S.J., Benard, S., & Paik, I. (2007). Getting a job: Is there a motherhood penalty? *American Journal of Sociology, 112,* 1297–1338.

Turner, L.H., & West, R. (Eds.). (2006). *The family communication sourcebook.* Thousand Oaks, CA: Sage.

Wood, J.T., & Dow, B.J. (2010). The invisible politics of "choice" in the workplace: Naming the informal parenting support system. In S. Hayden & L. O'Brien Hallstein (Eds.), *Contemplating maternity in the era of choice: Explorations into discourses of reproduction* (pp. 203–225). Lanham, MD: Lexington Press.

15 Wedding Bells or Clanging Cymbals?

Clark D. Olson

Key Terms

coming out, same sex marriage, long distance relationships, heterosexual privilege, communication privacy management

Jason was visiting New York City for a long weekend with his partner of four years, Brandon. They both loved escaping to the Big Apple, usually once a year to visit museums, eat at fine restaurants and see Broadway theatre; New York was a far cry from Albuquerque where they lived in their recently renovated home. But this time seemed even more special as they were finally living together after having endured a long-distance relationship for three years. After being discharged from the military and the oppressive "don't ask, don't tell" environment, Jason felt free enough to occasionally grab Brandon's hand as they walked on the streets of New York or strolled through Central Park. How different this was from military life, Jason thought. During his seven years of active duty he had known of several gay soldiers. Even though they were as tough and as experienced as any of the other GIs, they had to keep their sexual orientation a secret. Jason remembered several who, despite their excellent records, were expelled just because they were gay. He even had to sit on an honor council once when one gay soldier was questioned—a very awkward experience. Jason vowed never to have to endure such a humiliating experience, and was delighted to have been honorably discharged just eleven months ago.

What a difference the last year had made. Off of the military base, he was finally able to be himself, something he had kept hidden for so long. Even both his parents were finally aware of his sexuality and, although they had divorced when Jason was very young, both seemed supportive, and each had met Brandon. Now Jason was finishing up graduate school at the University of New Mexico, he and Brandon had just finished a major remodeling project on their home, and life was finally good. Jason was more than ready to put the military lifestyle behind him.

On Sunday they met up with Charles and Donald, a couple of Brandon's friends from Wisconsin who were also visiting New York. Brandon and Jason had visited them several times when they travelled back to the Midwest to visit their families, and Jason thought it seemed like Charles and Donald had been together forever. Charles, an architect, had designed the home they built in suburban Milwaukee, and Donald ran his own stained glass studio, so their house was exquisitely appointed, down to the last detail in their garden. Charles and Donald took great pride in their home, entertaining friends at their large annual holiday party, and they had even hosted a national antiques convention for collectors like themselves. Jason longed for the life they seemed to have, and hoped that one day soon, he and Brandon could live such a comfortable life.

After the two couples took in a matinee together, they were having dinner when the conversation finally turned to the coincidental nature of both couples being in New York at the same time. Just a couple of weeks ago, Donald had mentioned on Facebook that he and Charles were heading to New York for a visit. Brandon got in touch with Donald, and they had planned to spend an afternoon and evening together while both couples were in the city. As dinner was ending, Charles mentioned that he and Donald were headed to Connecticut the next day. When Brandon asked what drew them to Connecticut, Charles and Donald smiled and revealed that tomorrow they were taking the train to New Haven and were planning to be legally married the following day, which was their 25th anniversary of the day they moved in together. Connecticut was one of only a handful of states that allowed gays and lesbians to marry, and so they had carefully researched the details, and were about to become legally wed. Jason noticed there was a new excitement in their voices as they talked about every detail of their plans, down to the process of designing their matching rings. And yet, they hadn't told any of their family or friends back in Wisconsin about their upcoming marriage. Charles said this was a private moment, just between the two of them, and they wanted to make sure that no one felt left out or obligated to attend. Once they returned home, they'd tell their family and friends. After all, this wasn't a traditional wedding—they didn't need any wedding presents, since they'd shared a home for twenty-five years. They didn't want anyone feeling awkward that they had missed the ceremony or weren't invited, so they packed their tuxedos and decided to seal their personal commitment to each other by getting legally married.

Jason thought all this secrecy was odd and somewhat unnecessary for a couple who'd been together as long as Charles and Donald, and Jason wondered what issues might prompt the need for such mystery back home. However, once Jason and Brandon realized that they were the first to be told, the evening became a spur-of-the-moment bachelor party for Charles and Donald. After touring Times Square for a photo op, they settled down at a quiet neighborhood bar and ordered a round of drinks to celebrate. At that point the discussion turned to the question "How do you have a bachelor party for two people who've already lived together for twenty-five years?" After joking around a bit, they were perplexed that no one seemed to have a good answer. The traditional last night fling didn't seem quite appropriate, since the two grooms were attending the impromptu party together. Certainly they were well past the age when a night of booze and cigars was enticing. In fact, Donald admitted that this was the first drink he'd ordered in over three years. Just as Charles and Donald were somewhat puzzled at how to plan their wedding, even the bachelor party seemed a half-hearted attempt to mirror a typical convention associated with heterosexual marriage. After just a single celebratory drink, Jason and Brandon repeated good wishes for the wedding and the two couples said good night. Both couples were leaving New York the next day; Jason and Brandon were heading home to Albuquerque, and Charles and Donald were leaving for Connecticut.

Once back in New Mexico, Jason began thinking about what his wedding day would be like with Brandon. Not yet thirty, he had never really thought about having to elope, though New Mexico was still years away from sanctioning gay marriage. In his mind, his wedding would include family and friends in attendance—it would be a big celebration! He remembered what it was like telling his parents he was gay; it was a conversation he had rehearsed in his head a thousand times. He agonized about exactly how to introduce Brandon to his career military father. His only words of advice for a reluctant Brandon were, "I don't know if he'll kick your butt first, or mine." Then he remembered the huge sense of relief when his dad had really welcomed Brandon into the family, even inviting him to visit him in his home, and greeting him with a hug. Certainly that couldn't have been easy for his father.

Jason wondered what it must have been like a generation ago when Charles and Donald each had to tell their parents. Society has changed so much, he thought. But then he wondered, had things really changed that much? He still couldn't legally marry Brandon in the state where they lived. Once out of the military, he had to find his own health insurance, as he couldn't be covered under Brandon's policy at work. He had even been reluctant to change his Facebook status under relationship from the ironic "swinger" to "in a relationship," since he still had so many friends in the military and did not think they would accept him if they knew about his sexuality. He didn't feel comfortable holding Brandon's hand when they were out and about in Albuquerque. Maybe things still hadn't changed that much.

Then his thoughts turned to the possibility of raising a family. The whole notion of gay adoption seemed like a logistical nightmare as he and Brandon had heard horror stories from many of their friends who faced varying laws and much discrimination in trying to adopt children. Finding a surrogate mother would be likewise difficult, and then battling prevailing attitudes in the courts could prove to be expensive and emotionally draining. Reflecting on this, he wondered whether he really wanted to raise a family. But the issue kept nagging at him. The first question Jason's mother asked Brandon when they met was "when" they planned to have children. Clearly, with Jason being her eldest child, she was looking forward to grandchildren and thought that even though her son was gay, he had an obligation to provide her with grandchildren to spoil. Did he and Brandon really need to mirror heterosexual relationships completely?

On Wednesday evening, Jason and Brandon called Charles and Donald to congratulate them on their wedding day. Charles and Donald were elated with the news of their wedding. Although they had planned just a simple civil ceremony, once they started touring New Haven, they discovered a church with a sign that included the rainbow logo and inclusive language marker. They had walked into the office and met an openly gay minister who agreed to perform their wedding in the historic church built in 1812 on the old city green. Both being fans of Federalist architecture, this was the perfect place for them to exchange their vows. This was far better than having a justice of the peace preside over their wedding in city hall. Charles and Donald seemed almost giddy talking about how special and public their wedding had been and how much they were enjoying being back in New York for an official "honeymoon" to see plays and take in the sights of the city they hadn't toured since they'd been in New York some fifteen years ago.

After the phone conversation, Jason and Brandon began talking about what their wedding would be like. Brandon was more religious than Jason and thought they should get married in his church, as clergy in his denomination had just received authority to begin presiding over same-sex marriages. Jason was more concerned with the geographic location where they'd get married, wanting it to be convenient so both their families could attend. Then they realized there wasn't a state within fifteen hundred miles of their home in New Mexico where they could legally marry, and so they thought about Canada. Even though the U.S. wouldn't recognize their marriage for tax privileges, there did seem something more permanent about marriage rather than holding just a simple "commitment ceremony" that would attempt to mirror a wedding, but hold little legal standing. While Canada remained an option, they carefully went through the pros and cons of each of the respective states that had sanctioned same-sex marriage. Each one was not only far away, but neither Jason nor Brandon had any personal connections to any of those states, and the logistics for their family and friends would prove difficult for them all to attend. Maybe they, like Charles and Donald, would have to elope to a far-away state and then return home to have some sort of reception for their friends and relatives to share in the occasion. Still, this didn't seem like a perfect solution. The more they tried to plan their wedding, the more frustrated both Jason and Brandon became at how difficult current laws made getting married. Jason almost felt as though he was back in the military, still subject to a strict set of discriminatory regulations.

After their chance meeting in New York, Jason and Brandon called Charles and Donald more regularly. Marriage seemed to have changed the "newly married" couple. They exuded a new sense of happiness since their wedding—they were even acting like newlyweds! Jason felt a little twinge of jealousy, wishing he and Brandon could share such a positive experience together. A few weeks later as the couples were exchanging pictures of their respective trips and the "bachelor party," Charles noted that nearly everyone they told back in Wisconsin was very excited and supportive of their marriage, except his parents. Charles and Donald had even made a special trip to

Charles's parents' farm in rural Wisconsin to announce their "good news." Despite the fact that his parents knew Charles and Donald lived together, had built a home together, even vacationed with Charles's parents at their condominium in Florida for several winters, the report of their wedding came as a shock. Charles wrote in his email, "I was told I am not to speak of it again."

"Whoa," thought Jason. The reaction of Charles's parents was just what he had expected from his own parents. Now more than ever before, he was really grateful that his parents had been so accepting of Brandon. Another email a few weeks later confirmed that Charles's parents weren't softening as Charles had already missed a family reunion with his sister and her family and he wrote that he would not be visiting his dad on Father's Day. Jason felt a pang of sadness that the relationship that had existed for twenty-five years was now causing such difficulty for Charles and his parents. It seemed like such a shame that Charles' and Donald's wedding should destroy their relationship with Charles' parents. They were getting quite elderly, and Charles and Donald had even talked about having to be their primary caregivers should they become too frail to care for themselves. Now what would their marriage mean for those plans? Charles certainly didn't want to be disowned by his family, and yet here he was being frozen out of their lives. Jason wondered if his seemingly supportive family could someday turn on him as well. While so much of society was becoming more accepting of gays and lesbians, there was still a fairly large segment of society that seemed resistant to change.

Jason speculated about what society would be like when he and Brandon had been together for twenty-five years. Would every state finally have legalized same-sex marriage? Could they have to wait until they'd been together twenty-five years to finally have the right to legally marry in the state where they lived, or would they someday be traveling to a distant state or foreign country just to have their love for each other officially recognized? While there were positive signs that society was changing, Jason ultimately wondered if they'd change fast enough to really impact his life.

For Further Thought and Reflection

1. What risks are involved in gays and lesbians "coming out" to friends, family and co-workers? What communication strategies might facilitate this process?
2. How do gays and lesbians attempt to mirror heterosexual traditions? How necessary are these attempts, or are there new conventions that could be adopted?
3. Which communication theories would be beneficial to help one understand how people of various sexual orientations express their relationships privately and publicly? How do you imagine social norms have changed for Charles and Donald during their relationship?
4. Given current trends, what do you believe society will be like when Jason and Brandon have been together for twenty-five years?

References

Badgett, M.V.L. (2009). *When gay people get married: What happens when societies legalize same-sex marriage.* New York: New York University Press.

Bauer, M.D. (Ed). (1995). *Am I blue?: Coming out from the silence.* New York: Harper Trophy.

Fitzpatrick, M.A., Jandt, F. Ed., Myrick, F.L., & Edgar, T. (1994) Gay and lesbian couple relationships. In R.J. Ringer (Ed.) *Queer words, queer images, communication and the construction of homosexuality* (pp. 265–277).). New York: New York University Press.

Oswald, R.F. (2000). A member of the wedding? Heterosexism and family ritual. *Journal of Social and Personal Relationships. 17,* 349–368.

Petronio, S. (2002). *Boundaries of privacy: Dialectics of disclosure.* Albany: State University of New York Press.

Polikoff, N.D. (2008). *Beyond straight and gay marriage: Valuing all families under the law.* Boston: Beacon Press.

Ringer, R.J. (Ed.) (1994), *Queer words, queer images, communication and the construction of homosexuality.* New York: New York University Press.

Wood, J.T. (1994). Gender and relationship crises: Contrasting reasons, responses and relational orientations. In R.J. Ringer (Ed.) *Queer words, queer images, communication and the construction of homosexuality* (pp. 238–64). New York: New York University Press.

16 Shallow Talk and Separate Spaces: Dealing with Relational Conflict

Sandra Metts

Key Terms

latent conflict, conflict escalation, conflict strategies, rules for managing conflict

---

Sarah was frustrated as she drove home from work. Always too much to do and never enough time. She was working way too much and she knew it. But she didn't know how to say no when asked to do more. She was still not finished with the midyear report and, to make matters worse, she was facing an exam tomorrow night in the class she was taking for her Master's degree. She was tired and hungry, and hoped that Russell had started dinner. She turned onto the driveway and pushed the automatic opener for the garage door. By the time it was halfway up, she saw that Russell's car was not there. "Well, I guess Russell won't be helping with dinner again," she muttered half out loud. "Why is everything my responsibility?"

Just as Sarah entered the kitchen, she heard the ding from her cell phone signaling a text message. She went back and dug the phone out of her purse. The message read: *backed up at work. be home by 6. luv U. R.* "Oh, thanks, R," she said to the cell phone as she put it on the counter. "You couldn't have called sooner?"

Sarah felt her mood darken even more. No need to return the message. It was already 5:30 and she didn't feel like cooking or waiting to eat. But she looked through the refrigerator until she found the makings of a salad, leftover pork chops, and some aging potatoes. She washed the breakfast dishes in the sink as she prepared dinner. *"Geez, he can't even do the dishes when he knows that I am under such pressure,"* she thought to herself. *"Tonight after dinner I am going to ask him to give me a little help around the house, at least until the end of the semester. Maybe he'd take care of dinner and dishes during the week and laundry on Saturday."*

A short time later Russell pulled into the garage. Sarah was putting dinner on the table when he came into the kitchen. He too was tired and the residue of a stressful day still lingered. "Ugh, what a day," he said. "I thought James and Mark would never get out of my office. Get this—they want me to do a survey of the entire county by the end of the month!"

"Well at least you don't have the same stupid report from last week, still hanging around your neck like an albatross, and an exam coming up that you haven't even studied for."

"Of course I don't. But then I wouldn't let anyone walk all over me like you let those folks at C & G do to you."

Sarah bristled. "I can't help it," she said.

"Well, you *can,* but you *won't,*" Russell responded. Then looking at the table he remarked, "Pork chops? We had pork chops last night. And Sunday on the grill."

Sarah tried very hard to control her anger, but her voice was sharp. "Yes, we are having pork chops. If you want something else, then you can fix it."

Russell answered without thinking, "Let's just go out for dinner."

"Go out?" Sarah snapped. "After I made dinner? Since when can we afford to throw away food? Or is it that my cooking is just too awful?"

"I never said your cooking was awful; I just don't feel like pork chops. Lighten up."

"Lighten up? Easy for you to say. You don't have to work full time, take care of the house, do all the shopping, and work on your Master's degree."

Russell felt his fatigue turning into anger. "Oh no, it's the poor-me-routine; you give and give, and I do nothing. Aren't you forgetting that I mow the lawn, pay the bills, buy the groceries, cook as often as you do, and clean the house every weekend?"

"Oh? Since when? You never do anything around the house. It's work all week and golf all weekend."

"Oh, so it's my fault that nothing gets done? Maybe I work all week because I am not allowed to make noise in this precious house. All I ever hear from you is 'Please be quiet; I'm studying. You know, my Master's degree, my Master's degree.' It's your excuse for everything. 'I don't have time to shop, my Master's degree. Can't watch TV, I have homework. Can't go out, I have an exam. Can't have sex anymore, gotta work on my Master's degree.' At least I get a little peace and companionship on the golf course."

"Oh, you're exaggerating, as usual. I do not make you be quiet, I do more than my share around here, and we . . . we have sex. You're making me out to be a monster."

"Well, frankly, Sarah, that's about it. You have the patience of a gnat, and you're just about as much fun. We have sex when the moon is full, and we never make love any more. I practically have to beg you to come to bed, and a man gets pretty tired of begging for something from his wife that other women would be glad to give."

"What's that supposed to mean? Are you looking at other women now?" Sarah felt resentful. She knew that there were problems in the bedroom and acknowledged she was partly to blame. But she resented Russell for making her feel so guilty; it was certainly not all her fault. "Why are you saying this? I can't help it if I'm tired. Maybe if I got some help around here, I'd have more energy. I'm carrying a heavy load. You knew I was going to continue my education when we got married."

"Yeah, but I didn't know that it would consume your life and our marriage. Now I have to worship at the altar of the Heavy Load. The pressures of work and, oh, the pressures of that blessed Master's degree. All bow in honor to the Heavy Load."

Sarah felt pushed into a corner. Russell was attacking the very core of who she was—a good student, a hard worker, a high achiever. His sarcasm hurt and she wanted to hurt him back.

"Well, at least I'm capable of getting a Master's degree. I don't see you in college, Mr. Einstein. In fact, you barely got out with a bachelor's degree. We had to drag you off the golf course for graduation—or did you even graduate? I can't quite remember."

Russell stood up so abruptly that Sarah was startled. "I know that you don't think I'm very smart—certainly I'll never meet your standards. I don't know why you married such a stupid guy. But I'll tell you, Sarah, I'm a good man with or without an advanced degree! I don't need a piece of paper to prove I'm worth something, but you sure do. We've been married almost two years and you're still not a wife. When are you going to grow up?"

He moved to the door before Sarah could respond. "I'm going out to eat," he said, "and enjoy my own ignorant company."

"Well, good," Sarah yelled back. "You are the only one who can!" Sarah was agitated as she picked up the dishes and tossed the uneaten food in the trash. As she cleaned the kitchen, she fought back tears. "*Why does this always happen. I promise myself I will be rational, but I get defensive and, bang, we're on the downward slope. I didn't think marriage would be like this. Why can't he be a little more supportive of what I'm going through? 'Still not a wife'? What kind of crack is that? I'm more grown up than he will ever be.*"

Later that evening Sarah was working at the computer when Russell returned. She heard him click on the television downstairs, and she thought about going down to talk to him. Instead, she decided that if he wanted to talk he could just as easily come up to see her. "*But he probably won't,*" she thought; "*he's too stubborn. Besides, he said some hurtful things, and he owed her an apology.*"

Russell stared mindlessly at the television. He knew that he and Sarah needed to talk, but he just couldn't endure another heated argument. He knew that he shouldn't have brought up the sex thing again, but she was never "in the mood" anymore. Every night was a struggle just to get her to turn off that darn computer and come to bed. She seemed to think that Master's degree was more important than he was. She was always so serious, about everything. Heaven forbid that a smile should cross her face. And then, oh that remark about his grades—maybe he wasn't the best student in the world but he had graduated and had gotten a good job. And he was doing well. Why didn't she ever acknowledge that? Better to sit here, he thought, and keep his ego intact than to try another discussion. He loved his wife, but lately all they seemed to do was argue. "*I just can't deal with this anymore,*" he decided. "*Maybe if I just don't say anything about anything for awhile, things will settle down.*"

Russell fell asleep in the recliner and woke up some time after midnight. He found Sarah already in bed asleep. As quietly as he could, he slipped under the covers. Sarah was awakened by his movements and thought about apologizing. But the last thing she needed to hear was about how selfish she was. He didn't even seem to care about her needs, only his own—sex, sex, sex. Sarah lay there in the darkness very still, pretending to be asleep. Both lay awake for some time—feeling frustrated, rejected, angry, and hurt.

So it continued for several days. Sarah got through her exam and finished her report. Russell also got caught up at work and tried to be more helpful around the house, but only when he didn't need to be in the same room as Sarah. The distance between them was chilling. Shallow talk and separate spaces. Neither one brought up any issue that might cause conflict. They showed no affection and closed each other out. Both were beginning to feel the strain in their relationship.

On Sunday afternoon Russell was golfing and Sarah was working on her studies. The telephone rang. Her older sister, Betty, was in a good mood and began chatting about her family. The kids were doing this and that; Fred was refinishing some furniture. After a few minutes she paused. "Is something wrong? You seem sort of down?"

"Yeah, I guess I am," Sarah replied. "Russell and I had another fight."

"Oh, dear. What about this time?"

"I don't know. Just the same old stuff. He won't help around the house, but when I bring it up, he gets defensive about my Master's degree and starts complaining that we never have sex anymore. How am I supposed to feel sexy when I have to do everything around here? Besides, even when I am willing to have sex, he still complains because we aren't "making love"—whatever that means. We just can't seem to discuss anything without a big fight."

"Oh, I know how that is."

"You do? But you and Fred never fight."

"Oh contraire, sister dear. Fred and I used to fight a lot, and we still have conflict, but we learned how to 'fight fair.'"

"What do you mean?"

"Well, it seemed that most of our arguments began when we were tired. I would complain about something and instead of just saying, yeah, you're right, Fred would complain about something I did. Then I would get defensive and say he was wrong. Then he would say I was too sensitive, and I would say he was selfish. I don't know why, but we just got into these dueling matches that accomplished nothing but hurt feelings. So now, we try to take turns. If I have a complaint, we deal with that complaint, and put it to rest. If Fred has a complaint at the same time, we wait and deal with it later. It's hard sometimes, but we try not to get the issues confused and we try not to hit below the belt. To call each other stupid, or inconsiderate, or lazy, or selfish solved nothing. It made us both feel hurt or angry but did nothing to help the situation."

"Yeah, that's pretty much what happens around here," Sarah said. "Maybe we need some ground rules for our conflict. Thanks for listening. Well, I need to get going. Tell the family 'hi' for me."

"Sure, will do. And good luck," said Betty as she hung up.

Later that afternoon, Russell returned home from his golf game, a bit more re- laxed than when he had left, but still dreading the cold shoulder he was expecting from Sarah. He placed his golf clubs in the closet and decided he had best find Sarah and offer to help with dinner. He expected some kind of vague or curt reply, but he wanted to get it over with. "Sarah," he called. "Are you upstairs?"

Sarah answered from the kitchen. She had already made dinner and Russell noticed that it wasn't pork chops. He wanted to say thanks for not making pork chops, but didn't dare risk it. He expected her to criticize him for playing golf instead of staying home to do the cooking. So without saying anything, he just began setting the table. During din- ner, Sarah seemed particularly nice and even asked about his golf game. "It wasn't bad," he said. "I actually think I'm getting better with my putts. I didn't squirrel to the right so much." Sarah considered for a moment how much pride Russell took in his golf game. Not really very different from the pride she took in her academic accomplishments.

After dinner, Russell began to clear the table. But Sarah stopped him and asked him to sit with her for a few minutes and talk. "I want to apologize to you for my com- ment the other night about you not being capable of getting a Master's degree. I know you could if you wanted to. I was just angry and lashed out. But I really don't under- stand why you are so resentful of my efforts to get an education."

Russell's first impulse was to list again the zillion times that her studies intruded on his plans, his needs, his pleasures, but instead, he paused, put down the plates he had picked up and sat down across from her. He realized that she was not complaining or attacking him. In fact, he could tell from the tone of her voice and the way she looked at him that Sarah's apology was sincere and she really did want to know why her study- ing bothered him so much. He wanted to show the same sincere effort to get these is- sues resolved. His first impulse, to be sarcastic, faded away and he said instead, "I guess I just feel left out sometimes. I need time with you, too. All I ever hear is you're so tired and so busy."

Sarah didn't respond immediately, but when she did, she chose her words care- fully. "You're right. I have been complaining a lot lately about my pressures at work and school. I realize that I tend to close you out when I'm busy and I'm sorry for that. But I need your support, not your resentment."

"Oh Sarah, I'm just not as good with words as you are. I don't resent you, I'm proud of you. I suppose I should tell you that more often. I guess I just want to know there is some line that you can draw for us, some period to be placed at the end of the work day when you put it all away and relax. If that's not possible to do during the week, at least on the weekend. I want to be supportive, but I feel disconnected from you sometimes, like everything else in your life is more important than I am. I have a job too and I'm do- ing pretty well at it. I would like to know you are proud of me too, that my life matters, that I mean something more to you than a roommate who helps around the house."

Sarah was struck by the sadness in Russell's voice and realized that the burden had not been hers alone. She hadn't been physically or emotionally available to him for quite awhile. Perhaps more importantly, she had stopped showing how much she respected Russell, how much she enjoyed his wit, his energy, his accomplishments, and his ability to keep work and play in proportion—all the things that had attracted her to him in the first place. She had become much more likely to find fault than to tell him how much she valued him as her friend, her companion, her lover, and her husband. Impulsively, she leaned across the table and kissed him. Then she proposed a plan. "What do you say to this? What if we agree that when we have a complaint, we try to keep it focused on behavior, not personality, and that we really try to listen and be supportive even when we are getting very angry? And let's try to stick to one person's complaint at a time. We just keep dumping our own agendas on the table without listening to the other person's concerns."

"Well, that sounds good, but it won't be easy."

"I know, but I think we have to try."

"You're right. And how about apologizing when we are wrong instead of going on the attack?"

"You got it. Now how about helping me with these dishes and then maybe we can work out something so I can have more free time for us?"

"Ugh, I guess that means making a list of household chores and dividing them up, huh?"

"Yeah, but this time, we'll have three lists: household tasks, our own tasks, and things we want to do together."

Russell would have preferred that their life be a bit more spontaneous, especially where sex was concerned, but Sarah was such a planner. Oh well, he thought, maybe that trait was a good thing right now, given the challenges of being a dual career couple. Maybe he could quit thinking so much about his own needs and show her more appreciation. He smiled, looked across the table, and said, "Okay, I guess I need a bit of organization but can golf be on my Saturday to-do list?" Sarah laughed and replied, "Absolutely, if working on the computer can be on mine. We'll just take turns paying for the pizza we have delivered for dinner."

For Further Thought and Reflection

1. John Gottman (1994) describes four communication behaviors of dysfunctional conflict that characterize unhappy couples. As you look at the list of these behaviors below, what examples for each do you find in the conflict of Sarah and Russell?

   Criticism: Attacking a partner's personality or character, rather than his or her behavior

   Contempt: Insulting and psychologically abusing a partner's sense of self

   Defensiveness: Refusal to accept responsibility for one's actions, often done by meeting partner's complaint with a counter complaint

   Stonewalling: Actions characterized by withdrawing from interaction and keeping an icy distance

2. Sarah seems to have good intentions when she first decides to ask Russell for more help around the house. However, several factors seem to derail her original intention, influence Russell's reactions, and ultimately contribute to the escalation of the conflict. What are some of those factors? Which might be attributed to the situation and which might be attributed to the interaction?

3. Sarah and Russell come up with some rules to help them manage their conflict. What are these rules? Do you think their rules are good ones? Are there other rules you think they should add to guide their conflict, either before it starts or after it is underway?

4. What do you see in the future for Sarah and Russell? That is, do you believe they have resolved all of the important issues? Do you think there is any "latent" conflict (unresolved issues) that might influence future interactions, for example, if they have children? If so, describe the issues that might linger as problems in their relationship.

5. Conflict episodes have two "texts" or levels. One text consists of the messages that are exchanged; a second text consists of the emotions that prompt particular messages or result from receiving particular messages. Explain the emotions that you see in Sarah's and Russell's conflict, and try to associate these emotions with the messages produced and received. To what extent do you think that Sarah and Russell are competent in controlling their emotions?

References

Busy, D.M., & Holman, T.B. (2009). Perceived match or mismatch on the Gottman conflict styles: Associations with relationship outcome variables. *Family Process, 48,* 531–545.

Cloven, D.H., & Roloff, M.E. (1993). The chilling effect of aggressive potential on the expression of complaints in intimate relationships. *Communication Monographs, 60,* 199–219.

Cupach, W.R., Canary, D.J., & Spitzberg, B.H. (2009). *Competence in interpersonal conflict* (2nd ed). Prospect Heights, IL: Waveland Press.

Gottman, J. (1994). *Why marriages succeed or fail.* New York: Simon and Schuster.

Metts, S., & Wood, B. (2008). Interpersonal emotional competence. In M. Motley (Ed.), *Studies in applied interpersonal communication* (pp. 267–286). Newbury Park, CA: Sage.

Neff, L A., & Frye, N. (2009). Conflict prevalence and sources. In H.T. Reis and S. Sprecher (Eds.), *Encyclopedia of human relationships* (pp. 310–313). Thousand Oaks, CA: Sage.

Sagrestano, L. M., Christensen, A., & Heavey, C.L. (1998). Social influence techniques during marital conflict. *Personal Relationships, 5,* 75–89.

Zacchilli, T.L., Hendrick, C., & Hendrick, S.S. (2009). The romantic partner conflict scale: A new scale to measure relationship conflict. *Journal of Social and Personal Relationships, 26,* 1073–1096.

17 Yard Sales and Yellow Roses: Rituals in Enduring Relationships

CAROL BRUESS

Key Terms

relational culture, rituals, intimate play, private language, secrets, dialectical tensions

---

The back-and-forth motion of the porch swing brought comfort to Martha; she was feeling a bit exhausted from hauling boxes and cleaning out closets for their annual yard sale—a joint effort by her and her partner and kids to clean, purge and simplify—and she was feeling both the stress of preparations and the relief from making good progress that day. As she and her partner Jack sat swaying on their front porch swing, she thought back to their first little house rented during graduate school.

It had been 26 years since they had married and sat on a porch swing very similar to the one now greeting visitors to their home. During their early years of marriage, they regularly sat on the swing, late in the evening, stealing a few moments of peace after chaotic and full days of studying and attending classes. Mundane talk about their days and lives, and dreams about their future saturated such moments. Now, many years later, Martha and Jack used "porch-swing time" to reflect on their past, discuss their three grown children, and imagine the next chapter in their lives.

"Porch-swing time," according to Martha and Jack, had a few not-at-all-elaborate but absolutely essential items. First: popcorn. Since their first date in college, Martha and Jack shared a love of the fluffy white kernels. At Barnhamm Theatre, where they'd sink into the red velvety seats and attempt to watch a movie—distracted by their interest in looking at one another instead of the screen—they purchased the biggest bucket of popcorn and then playfully wrestled each other for each bite. During their early years of marriage, as they prepared for their weekly (sometimes daily) gathering on the porch swing, they would pop a huge pan of their own popcorn. Jack insisted on a mountain of salt. Grabbing a bottle of red wine and mismatched wine glasses secured at others' yard sales, they'd head for the swing.

"Those were the days, weren't they?" Martha recalled fondly as they'd adjust the hand-me-down pillows flanking them on the swing. The air was warm and moist on this August evening; the streetlight cast curious shadows onto the shakes of their early 20ᵗʰ century home. They used to dream about owning the very home in which they now felt lucky to dwell. As the motion of the porch swing brought them in sync, Jack had no doubt Martha would mentally and verbally reflect on their early years of marriage and raising children; she often did so whenever one of their children had called home with some important news. Their youngest daughter Jill, now 23, was on the phone an hour earlier with an excited voice and many details about her new job, one that would take her to Japan!

Jenny, now 29, their oldest child, lived in Green Bay, Wisconsin (Go Packers!) and worked as a 4th grade physical education teacher. Their second child, Chad, 28, recently wed his high school sweetheart and moved to Ohio.

Although both Martha and Jack loved their three children dearly, they weren't shy about admitting how much they enjoyed their empty nest! Along with developing new hobbies, they have re-initiated activities and hobbies once abandoned in favor of time with their young children. Weekday mornings, for instance, there is a sense of peace that begins the day, instead of a sprint-like beginning, which sometimes created unpleasant and tense mornings. Jack described those early years as "rushed and swirling." Martha would run frantically about the house packing lunches, filling bowls with Cheerios, making beds, and urging kids to brush teeth. Jack would be busy reviewing kids' homework, getting the car ready for the morning carpool duties, taking out the recycling, and attending to the family dog with a brisk walk, without which he'd literally tear apart the house during their absence. As a couple, Jack and Martha rarely had a chance to even speak to one another on those mornings. Now, Jack started each day by rising early and making fresh ground coffee for himself and Martha. When she awoke a few hours later, they would sit in the early morning quiet and read the daily news together. After work, because they had no kids to meet at home, no basketball games to attend, and no dance recitals to observe, they would meet for happy hour at a nearby pub, go grocery shopping, or simply take a walk. Sometime around 2:00 P.M. each day one or the other would call or text the other at work just to say "hi" or determine plans for later in the day. If the two o'clock hour passed without one or the other checking in, they felt something was missing. "It's just something we do now," Martha explained.

Jack agreed, and reflected on life with three growing kids living at home. "Those *were* the days. Remember how many schedules and activities we were juggling? I kind of miss those times."

"It does seem to be true what people say: 'They'll grow up before you know it.' Where has the time gone?" Martha also misses some of the chaos, but frequently reminds Jack of how good life felt now too. Similar, but different.

As they inched their way to the bottom of the popcorn bowl, the warm summer air blanketed them and their fond memories like a warm hug. Neither needed to actually say much in these moments; each quietly enjoyed the symbolic comfort of the porch swing—back and forth, forward and back—the bowl of popcorn nestled between them, and wine glasses held loosely in hand. In these moments, they couldn't help but recall where their lives began together.

The Yard Sale

Each spring Martha began thinking about the yard sale months in advance. "Could it really take nearly six months to get ready for a tag sale?" Jack would often joke. Although some years there wasn't much to purge from their tiny rooms or recycled/hand-me-down furnishings, the spirit of the sale was clear: connect with neighbors and refocus on their family's motto: "Live Simply; Love More." Preparations for and conversations about the annual tradition typically went something like this:

"Hey Jack, I was thinking that this year we should sell the *old twin beds* down stairs at this Spring's yard sale." (Item in italics was different each year, but Martha said almost precisely these words). Jack predictably and playfully then replies with a groan: "Do we really need to have another sale this year?" Martha ignores his insincere grumbling, knowing Jack enjoyed the haggling, selling, and friendly-shout-outs about "deals happenin' here!" and "low, low prices!" to cars rolling by. As a customer strolls up, Jack is fond of humorous tactics: "Only 10 cents for this entire box! And we'll throw that tire in for free. Buy one tie and get a dog kennel for ½ price!" More than even Martha, Jack loves yard sale day. It's an event, no question, with a long, shared history in their family.

During yard sale prep days Martha would often yell down to the basement from the top of the stairs: "Hurry up Jack! What's taking you so long?" After a pause she would think to herself "Why ask?" She knew exactly what it was. He had run across an old letter, tool, or photo, and was now captivated as he surveyed it from all angles. Sure enough, Martha would round the corner of the basement storage room and find Jack sitting crossed-legged on the cement floor, surrounded by college photos and yearbooks.

One time she found him half way into reading an essay exam written for Fr. Murray's Christian Ethics class. He had gotten an "A!" "One of the few from your college days . . ." Martha chided him. "I can pull out a few of yours if you'd like, Miss Martha Betcher!" Jack often used Martha's maiden name when he kidded her about issues of her "smarts."

Martha had nicknames and special phrases she used privately for Jack too. The most common was to call him "Fuzz." Its origins lie in a private, playful game created between them early in their marriage called "belly button search." Even after 26 years of marriage, the game will emerge when one of them least expects it. Martha explains its origins: "I would check Jack's belly button for fuzz on a daily basis at bedtime. It originated when I noticed some blanket fuzz in his belly button one day and thought it was funny! We both found it fun and teased often about the fuzz. If there wasn't any fuzz for a few days, Jack would put some in his belly button for me to find." Although none of their friends or family knows of the "belly button fuzz game," the nickname "Fuzz" is used publicly while maintaining a symbolic, private meaning for them as a couple. When asked by others where the nickname came from, they both innocently shrug their shoulders and say "Hmm. Don't really know." They love having little "secrets" from the rest of the world!

"This stuff is hilarious, Martha. Check out this photo of us with the kids at the beach!" Jack pointed to the image of their three young children and his and Martha's young faces and not-at-all-hip-anymore hairdos. "Remember how we could spend nine hours on the beach and not even know we'd been gone an hour? Those were such great times. And look at this one of us on our honeymoon. Why is *this* in this box of junk?" Jack quipped.

Martha became outwardly irritated when Jack would complain about "disorganization" or the way things were "junked up." A perpetual argument in their marriage was about who was responsible for the daily tasks and managing the house-cleaning, the organizing, and the purchasing of household items. Martha would say she was overburdened in this area of their marriage, while Jack would say he "pitches in quite a bit."

For most of their marriage, except a few years when their three children were very young, both Martha and Jack worked full-time: she as a professor at the local University and he as a high school principal. Despite their busy days, Martha, like most women in dual career marriages, took on a good majority of the "house" work (laundry, cooking, dishes, organizing kids' activities, remembering to schedule dentist appointments, etc). So, when Jack asked these kinds of questions, she got irritated. "It's in that box because you probably put it there, Mr. Organization, Mr. I-never-put-anything-away-that-would-take-some-time-and-effort! . . . Mr-I-don't-know-what-it . . ." Her voice and mild irritation end when she sees Jack trying to add a bit of lightness, probably because neither of them was in a mood for the same old argument. He was having such a great time looking at the old memories in the boxes! "Was that 93 cents or 96 cents?" He asks with a grin. Martha instantly shoots him a big smile in return.

The statement "Was that 93 cents or 96 cents?" was another of their relationship secrets, a sentence that had meaning just between the two of them. Jack's parents would often correct one another and bicker over the most trivial details. One evening Jack and Martha watched them argue for hour upon hour whether something had cost 93 cents or 96 cents. They adopted the question for use in their own marriage as a way to gain perspective when tension or conflict was emerging. When uttered, they'd often laugh at themselves and divert unnecessary conflicts. It had worked again today!

Their eyes and attention swiftly moved back to the honeymoon photo Jack had unearthed. Martha: "We look so young! That was such a great time of . . . Oh!" She interrupted herself. As she dug even deeper into the box of old stuff she thought she had lost, out fell the ribbon used on her wedding bouquet. It was yellow, just like the roses it held. Martha: "Awww. Look at this!" "Ewww" was Jack's response. "That's looking kind of moldy." Martha agreed. But she couldn't toss it. And Jack knew she wouldn't. Yellow roses and yellow ribbons, like those in her wedding bouquet, had become a means for Jack to express his adoration of Martha. Each year on their anniversary (26 and counting) he sent her one yellow rose with the same hue of ribbon attached. He vividly recalls about 10 years before when he painstakingly drove to multiple flower shops—even in neighboring towns—before he was able to locate a yellow rose. But he did, successfully. Martha looked forward to the gesture but always tried to act surprised when the rose arrives. "They remind me, every time, how much we love each other. It's very sweet of him to always do that."

"Look at this photo of me and the guys at 456!" Jack found a snapshot of his roommates posing with a gaggle of pink flamingo lawn art at 456 Western Avenue, their college rental. Although most of "the guys" had dispersed about the country since graduation, one of Jack's best friends was Tim. They not only had shared a room in that overcrowded, run-down house, they also shared many of their most personal thoughts and dreams about their futures in that space. It was during one of their late night chats at 456 Western, over a pizza and a pile of unfinished homework, that Tim had told Jack that he was gay.

Until that time, Tim had told no one—not even his own family. After settling in at college Tim had decided he needed to start telling people, to let people know who he really was. Jack helped Tim through some of the toughest days of his life: when he finally told his parents and his family; when his parents wouldn't speak to him or visit for over a year during his last year of college; when Tim began to experience some of the unthinkable, hateful actions and words from students and others at the college; and when he had seriously thought about dropping out. It was that time, during their last year of college, when Jack and Tim became the closest of friends.

"By the way" Jack said, interrupting his own wandering thoughts. "Tim called the other night and wants to add a few items to the yard sale. He said they have lots of junk to get rid of after the move." Martha was always pleased to add others' stuff to their yard sale. "The more the better" was her yard-sale-philosophy. "He's going to drop it off Friday night. He said he'll have it all priced."

Since Tim moved back to town, Jack had been very happy. He and his partner Bart decided to move to the city where Martha and Jack now lived. It was just a short drive from where Jack and Tim had gone to college, so it was a natural choice. Jack and Martha couldn't have been more thrilled when Tim had called to share the news of their move!

If Jack said it once, he had said it a hundred times: "It's so great having *Rock* back in the city." Rock was Tim's nickname, given to him by Jack. He didn't use it very frequently anymore, but it still had a special place in their friendship. It represented Tim's inner strength, something Jack always admired. Tim called Jack Doughboy because of his pasty white skin and blonde hair. Yet Tim was the only one who could call Jack that without distaste. Martha saw Tim as a brother; she loved him dearly. They had all grown close over the years and had a long, shared history—something that made their friendship stronger than some of the others in their adult lives.

Living in the same town again resulted in welcome changes in how they stayed connected. When separated by thousands of miles, Jack and Tim maintained a weekly calling ritual. Throughout graduate school, even after Martha and Jack moved another 600 miles away, Jack and Tim talked routinely; usually the call took place on Sunday nights, well after the kids were all asleep. If it wasn't on Sunday night, it was Monday for sure. They now traded in their call for a monthly (sometimes weekly) dinner and drink. It most often included their partners, Martha and Bart. The four thoroughly enjoyed their evenings together; they cherished the chance to reunite, reminisce, and get to know one another's families and interests. Their favorite spot was Luci's, a cozy, authentic Italian eatery at the edge of town where they could sit and chat for hours. The conversation flowed seamlessly from serious to silly to significant. Most often, it was just good old "talk." And that's exactly what they looked forward to most.

One of the things about Tim was that he never let life get boring! Upon returning from a two-week canoe trip to the boundary waters of Northern Minnesota a few years ago, Martha and Jack were greeted by 100 pink flamingos poking around in their front lawn. When they pulled in the drive, they simultaneously shouted in laughter "Tim!" Jack yelled into the phone. "We'll get you, buddy. And paybacks are hell!"

And so it began. Every so often, when someone least expected, the plastic pink flamingos on wire spokes would make their way into either Tim or Jack's yard. Sometimes they even dangle from the roof. They looked particularly funny on Tim's snow-covered boulevard last February. And as the prank evolved, other local friends and neighbors have happily joined in, borrowing the flamingo collection for placement in others' yards or gardens. A few years back someone even expanded the collection, adding items, creating a veritable and ever-growing plastic farm (twirling plastic daisies, the rear-view of a female gardener, and bright green bugs with waving wings).

Looking back at their college photo, Jack laughed: "Pink Flamingos. Ah. The good old pink flamingos. Where it all began!" They both laughed. "Maybe we should sell them at the yard sale tomorrow?" Martha half-seriously questioned. "You're nuts! Marty! Those things will be around until I die. Or if Tim goes first, we can use them at his funeral!" A frown came from Martha; she didn't think it was funny to joke about death.

"We'd better stop this puttering and start hauling up to the garage." Martha began to move an old rusty fan and a box of her mother's old linens toward the steps. "It's already five o'clock, and we don't even have everything cleared out yet." Jack agreed, although he kind of felt glued to the floor. "I'm hungry, Marty. What do ya say we go over and grab a burger at the counter first, and then come back to finish the hauling and tagging?"

Martha couldn't resist an invitation to "the counter," the malt shop just down the street from their house. Since the kids had moved out, it had become a new dinner ritual for her and Jack. It reminded her of the Woolworth's counter she and her dad used to go to on Saturday afternoons. She and Jack also liked it because it was similar to the soda fountain they went to when they first dated ("Sodas were a quarter then!") Martha's favorite flavor was lime; Jack preferred Cherry Coke. Suppressing her urge to keep working on the yard sale now, she said "Great idea. Let's go. But let's make it quick, eh?"

Back (and Forth)

The porch swing slowly rocked her and Jack back and forth, back and forth. She loved these "porch-swing" moments more and more as the years went by, as their children grew older, and as their relationship grew stronger. It wasn't that either of them thought they hadn't had a strong relationship from the start, but each session of remembering seemed to add clarity to the way their lives together—of memories, yard sales, nicknames, shared friendships, photos, stories, secrets, burgers, and popcorn—gave them a unique and irreplaceable history.

"Ouch" snapped Jack. "Darn mosquitoes! They're out in force this summer. I'm heading in the house." "Meet you inside," Martha responded as she gathered the empty popcorn bowl, and two glasses which had tiny red rings left at the bottom where the last drips of wine had settled. She glanced back with a peaceful smile as the swing slowly came to a halt.

Endnotes

This case represents a composite of experiences from couples participating in a research study conducted by the author and her co-researcher, Dr. Judy Pearson. All names and identifying details have been changed.

For Further Thought & Reflection

1. Members of relationships create their own "relationship culture" in and through their communication. A relational culture weaves partners together not through the activities or interactions themselves, but in the meanings partners assign to these activities and interactions. How would you describe Martha and Jack's relationship culture to someone who had not read this case? How would you describe the relational culture of one of your own relationships? What kinds of interactions contribute to the relationship maintenance of the couple in the case? What kinds of interactions sustain a relationship of yours?

2. Rituals are defined as recurring interaction patterns that pay homage to something symbolically significant to relationship members. What rituals—large or small, mundane or celebratory—can you identify in this case? Make a list. After doing so, describe what Jack and Martha's relationship might be like without any of the rituals they enjoy. Referring back to question #1, how would their relational culture change if they had no rituals?

3. What do your answers to question #2 reveal about the importance of rituals in relationships? Researchers believe rituals serve a multitude of functions for relationship members. What functions did they serve for Martha and Jack? How about for Jack and Tim? How do some of the rituals in this case simultaneously serve the contradictory needs of novelty and predictability, openness and closedness, autonomy and connection?

4. Researchers report nicknames and private language serve a number of functions in our personal relationships. What examples of private language can you identify in the case? What functions do you think it serves for Martha, Jack and Tim? After considering the case, reflect on and list as many examples of nicknames or other private codes you use in your family or friendships. What functions do they serve in your relationships? Hint: think about conflict resolution, playfulness, privacy, secrecy, and/or discussing taboo or uncomfortable topics.

5. What kind of rituals do you have in your own friendships or personal relationship? How about in your family? Make a list of all the "rituals" you can think of in one of these relationships. Don't overlook the mundane ones in favor of the annual or celebratory! As you look at your list, can you identify when and how the ritual developed? Does its origin tell you anything about the shared history and culture of your relationship?

References

Baxter, L.A. & Braithwaite, D.O. (2006). Family rituals. In *The Family Communication Sourcebook* (Eds. L. Turner & R. West, pp. 259–280). Thousand Oaks, CA: Sage.

Bruess C., & Pearson, J. (1997). Interpersonal rituals in marriage and adult friendship. *Communication Monographs, 64*, 25–46.

Bruess, C., & Pearson, J.C. (2002). The function of mundane ritualizing in adult friendship and marriage. *Communication Research Reports, 19(4)*, 314–326.

Fiese, B. H. (2006). *Family Routines and Rituals*. New Haven: Yale University Press.

Fiese, B. H., Tomcho, T. Douglas, M. Josephs, K. Poltrock, S. & Baker, T. (2002). A Review of 50 Years of Research on Naturally Occurring Routines and Rituals: Cause for Celebration? *Journal of Family Psychology, 16*, 381–390.

Goffman, E. (1967). *Interaction ritual*. Garden City, NY: Anchor.

Part IV

Serious Challenges in Interpersonal Communication

18

Serious Challenges in Interpersonal Relationships: Betrayal in the Case of Chris and Sandy

Steve Duck, University of Iowa

I am grateful to Jennifer Anderson Senchea and Cara Roberts for their help and advice about this article.

Key Terms

betrayal, trust, gossip, uncertainty reduction, relationship dissolution

Sandy and Chris had been friends at Whitby High since long before I ever knew them. They were always there for each other, always supported each other, always *had* loyally supported each other since they became friends in grade school. They would do things like standing up for each other if other people were talking trash about the other one. You know how teenagers like to talk behind someone's back. But they stood above it and protected each other faithfully even when there were all those rumors about the Bellevue High football team and what had happened at the party after the game. You know the sort of thing. Some people said they had heard about it from the folks at Bellevue High, but no-one else from our school had been there at the time. And Sandy never let on.

There was plenty of gossip about the two of them as individuals too (and of course, later, about their relationship). Sandy was regularly teased for crazy hair styles and Chris was suspected of doing drugs. Actually that probably wasn't true because I never saw Chris do anything like weed or shrooms, though I personally didn't like Sandy's hair either, nor the tendency to act big in class. You know, always looking to be the one who knew it all, trying to get a rise out of the teacher by saying outrageous things and coming back with cute one-liners, but I have to admit that I had a sneaking admiration for that kind of quick-fire comeback.

Anyone could see that Sandy and Chris liked each other a lot. You know how you can always tell things not only from the words but also from the way they acted—the nonverbal communication as I have now learned to call it in my interpersonal communication classes. They used to sit by each other a lot, look into each other's eyes, and laugh together all the time. I don't think I was really conscious of all this till I took the interpersonal communication class. Well, perhaps I did notice, but I didn't give it a label. Anyway, whatever it was, you could tell just by watching them, even when you couldn't hear what they were saying. You just *knew* they really liked each other.

And they had always been very loyal friends. Sandy would often tell a story about when Chris was called to the Principal's Office and questioned for a long time about someone saying Chris had smoked weed at the football game. But Sandy voluntarily went in and claimed to have been with Chris at the game and hadn't seen anything—in fact Sandy told the Principal it was someone else—from Bellevue—who looked like Chris. Sandy had to say they'd both been drinking some beer, though, smuggled into the game in Coke cans, and so they could not have been where the other people had said they were at the time. Sandy and Chris both got into some trouble over that, of course, but not as much as if they'd been caught with weed. So Sandy basically took half the blame instead of Chris getting all of it. That was the sort of thing they did for each another. As to whether Chris really smoked at the game, I just don't know what was true. It's just what people said. Anyway, if it hadn't been for Sandy, Chris could have been in huge trouble and really owed Sandy big time.

Sandy once said Chris was a *real* help when it came to leaving Whitby to go to college. That can be kinda scary, as you know, but Chris had helped with the move physically, then was "there" psychologically, too, always thinking of reasons to drop by the dorm and check to make sure that Sandy was doing OK. If one thing was obvious about the two of them, it was the level of trust they had in each other. We all used to talk about it. Again, it wasn't as if they kept talking to everyone saying "I really trust Sandy" or whatever, but you could tell from the way they told stories about stuff they did. They could tell each other anything and they just obviously knew a lot about the other person's "history" and emotions and inner feelings. Some of us tried to copy their friendship—or at least we hoped we'd have friends like that one day. That kind of trust and loyalty are hard to find and these days when everyone is so superficial. Like, you can talk and talk, or even be Facebook friends, but you never really feel like you truly *know* the person. LOL, have I even *met* some of my Facebook "friends"??

I like both of them. Not only as individuals but also as two really decent people. Sure, they do some of the dumb things we all do, and people like to talk about those, but they were both cool and everyone respected them. I got in tight with each of them and we were all very close at one time.

I suppose that was part of the problem. It's always harder for three people to be close than for two, you know? You get "triangulated" when there's three—you know, two against one, one complains to one of the others about some gripe about the third one and wants you to referee—or preferably to be on their side, more likely! You get to hear a lot of BS, of course. Well, who *doesn't* whine once in a while when they can talk to someone they trust? Sometimes you have to act as a counselor or a go-between for people then. When you get close to someone you get to know some of their secret fears, thoughts, hopes, and opinions about other people or whatever. And when there's three of you, some of those hopes and fears are about "the other one." But Sandy and Chris were always close. I expect they talked about me, too. It's only natural. You just hope that no-one says anything too embarrassing!! No-one wants a bad reputation, whether at high school or college. I think it's worse at high school, though, and people were forever talking about who's doing who and which boys are just out to get on the most girls and which girls are "easy." Nobody really talked about Sandy and Chris that way, though.

Then Chris started talking about Sandy in ways I couldn't believe. I mean, when you know both of them and one's telling you they suspect the other is doing it with some skanky person, what can you do? [You can't really go around telling people what's said behind their back, but on the other hand if you don't—and you know that Chris is partly concerned for Sandy, partly worried that it might be true and partly hoping you'll say you have heard it's not true, so, should you tell Sandy or not?] Or more precisely, how much should you tell Sandy about the suspicions Chris is mentioning? Or Chris for that matter? How much should you tell Chris that is really true, if you happen to know? You owe something to each of them but if you keep one person's secret, you let the other person down. But if you actually reveal what you know then you're letting a different one of them down! You're caught right in the middle!

It was harder because I really knew the truth for sure. It was a real dilemma, a big one. I guess I see how important it was to a friend like Chris to be able to continue to trust Sandy completely, and given what they'd been through together, Chris had come to expect Sandy to be absolutely honest. A rock really. You just have to be able to rely on your friends, so in this situation it was probably even harder—I mean, given what I know now about their real relationship.

If Chris had suspected a random hook-up, a one-night stand when everyone was trashed or something, I think it would all have been easier to deal with, but it wasn't like that. Fact is, the new secret relationship really *mattered* to Sandy, and it looked as if it could turn into something serious. Like, Sandy had found something that could become a real "Relationship"—and that would mean seeing less of Chris. You know how *that* goes. You get involved with someone and you start to see less of your friends so you can be with the new person and stuff. Or you get used to hanging out with a friend and, like, all of a sudden they meet someone special and now they've got no time for you, because they are off mackin' on The New Love Interest. Chris obviously suspected that was going on and could have expected Sandy would talk about it, but how do you talk about suspicion without making it into a big deal and getting into a big nasty fight or—worse—you get stuck in one of those big "Our Relationship" talks that are so uncomfortable. But as I said, their relationship was obviously changing and it wasn't really the sort of thing Sandy could easily bring up, given the circumstances.

That's one of the things about a close relationship. The more you get to know someone, the more you expect to confide in them, to check out stuff, see what they think of it, find out if you are really doing the right thing, get a respected opinion from someone who knows you well. When you have been hanging out as long as Chris and Sandy and been through so much, then you get to know how someone really thinks and feels. You know what pushes their buttons, what makes them feel mad or nervous, what they hate, or how things make them feel. So they really are great as listening posts for you too because they know you so well. You trust them, they trust you.

But in a way, that very closeness makes you vulnerable. You know how they work—so you know what hurts them too. They know how you work, too, so they could tell someone else. I mean if they ever wanted to. When you're close you have a whole lot of things that you could tell other people about your close friends if you ever wanted to. But you don't do that. That's the point about a close relationship. You don't do that.

When the relationship gets into trouble, though, all those things—those secret, vulnerable, private things—are up for grabs and if the person really starts to hate you or become an enemy or get really pissed at something you did then there's a lot of secret stuff or personal stuff that becomes a kind of blackmail they can use against you, like a set of sharp weapons. You can use the information to hurt the very person you cared so much about, just by telling what was said when you were getting close to the person.

Of course, Chris was always good to me like that. Some of the things we shared were really, really deep, and I learned things about Chris that I would never share with anyone else—the truth about the party after the game, for example. But more than that, I learned some of Chris's deeper thoughts and secrets, and in particular a few things about Chris' father that I really wish I didn't know. You don't expect most fathers to do thing like that to their little kids, and it obviously left psychological scars on Chris. It also explains a few things about the way Chris would act sometimes, though! But that sort of stuff is kind of personal and obviously this was very deep and affected the way Chris saw other people and relationships—the whole Trust Thing.

Well, when Chris first got concerned about Sandy, a lot of what happened was just the typical worrying, just "inside the head stuff," mulling it all over, wondering if it could be true—looking for evidence, replaying things that Sandy had said and done—or not said and not done. Chris was obviously looking for changes or signs that could clear up the suspicions, but without having to bring it up to Sandy directly.

Chris was really just mulling it over, getting angry alone, not really talking to anyone about it very much but obviously stewing a lot; and getting really bugged by it. You could tell because Chris was normally so outgoing but during that semester Chris just seemed to close down a lot more and go quiet and sorta moody, withdrawn. I read something for one of my Psych classes about it: the guy called it the "intra-psychic phase of relationship breakdown," where people just get worried, basically, not really knowing if anything is really wrong but thinking it over, trying to get a handle on it.

I heard a bit later from one of my old friends who is still at Bellevue High on the other side of town that Chris had talked with her about it, not really wanting it to get back here to Sandy, but needing someone to bounce things off to see if the concerns were real or if it was all just imaginary. My friend didn't really have much to say except general stuff, since she didn't really know Sandy or have a network of friends that talked about Sandy or the people here at college much. At least she wasn't sure she did.

But it couldn't go on for long like that, just staying inside Chris' head. After a while Chris became, like, totally freaked out and convinced that something was really, really wrong. Apparently some loser had told Chris that Sandy had been down at the lakeside—at that familiar hook-up spot there, a really dumb place for Sandy to go when you think about it, I suppose, unless there was some sort of unconscious desire that the whole thing would come out into the open. Maybe, by that time it didn't matter. Anyway the story got back to Chris via some poor dumb innocent guy who didn't even know that Chris and Sandy were lovers. He just mentioned the lakeside sighting all very casually, like he had heard a rumor, not having a clue about what it would do to Chris. It must have totally shocked Chris to hear that. It was, like, "WTF???"

Well Chris was mad of course, and very hurt too. I was just about the only one who knew about the real relationship between Chris and Sandy and how the friendship thing had really become an act just to cover up the real relationship. So Chris was very upset when the rumor got started, and naturally wanted to find out what was behind it.

Chris really got talking to a lot of people, and started asking around and trying to reduce uncertainty about Sandy by checking out what people knew, or suspected. Finally of course, the two of them had it out right then and there with some really deep discussion about The Future and The Nature of The Relationship. It was tough for both of them and of course I got caught right in the middle. Chris still wasn't sure if it was any more than a rumor and Sandy didn't want to let on at first, obviously, didn't want to be open about it. They both told me all about the whole thing and what it was doing to them. Sandy obviously felt a lot of guilt, Chris a lot of anger and suspicion. But it really was all over between them by then and I knew it, but didn't really have the heart to tell Chris what I thought. In any case I didn't think it was my place. I thought that should come from Sandy. And of course it eventually did but not very directly. People started talking about Chris, hearing things about the party incident that could really only have come from Sandy. Or from me I suppose, but, . . . hey! Why would *I* say anything?

And the way things are, before long there was a big set of stories going around and Chris looked like a bad person. Chris did this; Sandy did that. You've seen it before, a thousand times. The different groups of friends from school started taking sides, some with Chris, some with Sandy, obviously, but not really knowing the whole truth, which I guess we never really know, human nature being what it is. But there was a lot of talk: some people finally admitted that they'd never really liked Chris, or that they'd suspected the real nature of the relationship with Sandy, or that they were glad it was all out in the open now because it made them uncomfortable to play along with the act about the relationship. And Sandy and Chris had assumed nobody knew about them! That was a bit of an eye-opener for both of them, I think, finding out that more or less everyone knew. And people can be really mean when they talk about stuff like that, even if they don't intend to hurt people's feeling.

Mostly, though, what happened after the break-up seemed to be a big PR exercise anyway. I mean, almost anything anyone does can be seen in a good or a bad way, can't it? To know all is to forgive all, as they say in France (in French obviously! LOL!!).

Those who favored Chris soon talked about Sandy as the Beast from Hell. I mean like they had never done anything remotely like that themselves. Come ON! Never two-timed or stepped out on someone and acted unfaithfully. GET OVER IT!! Where have they been living? Anyway the different people told different stories and took different sides, spreading their versions of what Sandy did or what Chris did and how it all fit into the breakup scenario. There were some quite interesting things that came out in the open that way. It was almost like a war zone sometimes with big time gossip against one or the other of them, depending on whether you were for Chris or for Sandy. It didn't do the relationships of the whole group of us much good either, with everyone taking sides or feeling awkward around either one of them. Eventually, Chris tended to lose out and become kinda pushed to the side. There were just more people taking Sandy's view of it all.

Well Chris and Sandy split up after that, not only as lovers but also as friends, and seemed to spend most of their time telling their side of the break-up to anyone who would listen. Sandy was pretty smart about it. Chris wasn't quite so smart, but anger and bitterness can do that to a person. Chris was a bit unstable if the party story was true anyway, and had all that baggage about trust issues after the way the father had acted. Sandy was clear that Chris was basically a good person, but despite the unusual nature of their relationship and the special closeness that it brought, it couldn't ever work till they really decided where their heads were. Sandy could understand Chris's feelings or motives for saying some of the things that got said, and was really pretty saintly about the whole thing. But realistically, it was the kind of ending that Sandy had always seen coming to their relationship. Anyway Sandy needed space and time to settle into the new relationship without all these other hassles.

Chris was angrier and felt very betrayed and didn't care who knew. Chris called Sandy all sorts of names, talked about back-stabbing and called Sandy a "traitor" and actually pissed off a lot of people by being so nasty about Sandy even though when you think about it there was some justification. Anyway Chris seemed determined to make sure that no-one would ever consider going out with Sandy ever again or even risk being friends and it kinda back-fired, but you can understand why someone would try to do it. To paint that kind of picture I mean. No-one would ever want to go out with or trust someone who was basically untrustworthy and might tell other people all the secrets you shared when you were close. So I guess Chris was trying out a trick that a lot of us would use if we were in that position.

Not that it really matters, though, since most people remembered how Sandy stood up for Chris over smoking weed at the game and all the stories about "disloyalty" and "betrayal" were really easy to argue against. That story about the Principal was just s-o-o-o-o-o widely known and people had obviously come to trust Sandy for themselves. And once the truth about the party incident came out anyway, it was actually Chris who looked bad. Anyway, perhaps I'm biased. I liked them both but I have to admit that Sandy is just about the best lover anyone could wish for.

References

Anderson, J.A. (1998). Gendered constructions of sexuality in adolescent girls' talk. Doctoral Dissertation, University of Iowa.

Bergmann, J.R. (1993). *Discreet indiscretions: The social organization of gossip.* New York: Aldine de Gruyter.

Duck, S.W. (2011). *Rethinking relationships: A new approach to relationship research.* Thousand Oaks, CA: Sage.

Rollie, S.S. & S.W. Duck (2006). Stage theories of marital breakdown. In J.H. Harvey & Mark Fine (Eds.), *Handbook of divorce and dissolution of romantic relationships* (pp. 176–193). Mahwah, NJ: Erlbaum.

Wood, J.T. & Duck, S.W., Eds. (2006). *Composing relationships: Communication in everyday life.* Belmont, CA, Thomson Wadsworth.

For Further Thought and Reflection

1. What are the main communication elements that lead someone to feel or convey a sense of betrayal?
2. Does a sense of betrayal come out of particular individual acts or does it depend on your whole experience with the person who, you think, betrays someone?
3. What do you think is the role of a network of other friends or family in confirming or denying, supporting or resisting a betrayal? Does the network play a role in defining whether betrayal has occurred? How does the network serve to reinforce or undermine the sense that a betrayal has occurred?
4. In this case, who betrayed whom? [Note that you should be able to find at least three answers to this question.]
5. How should individuals who are friends with couples that are breaking up interact with and support each/both of the partners? Is it possible to be loyal to each person when a couple breaks up?
6. What sex did you attribute to Sandy and to Chris? Do their sexes and sexual orientations affect your interpretation of this case? [I get more questions about this than anything else in the chapter. Why do people get so irritated when they know that I deliberately made it impossible to tell what sex(es) Chris and Sandy are? Really?]

19

We'll Never Be That Kind of Couple: The Variability of Intimate Violence

LOREEN N. OLSON AND EMILY A. RAUSCHER

Key Terms

abuse, aggression, domestic abuse, intimate terrorism, relational violence, violence

---

Emma and Jason were exhausted; they had been moving their stuff into their new apartment all day and were just getting ready to sit down for dinner. Their move to Springfield, while a lot of work, was exciting. They both had graduated college in the spring and were looking forward to starting their careers and lives together. Emma had gotten a teaching job at the local high school, and Jason was starting work as an IT systems manager at the community college in a few days. As they settled down for a gourmet dinner of microwavable macaroni and cheese (their kitchen stuff was all still in boxes, after all), they heard a bit of a commotion starting in the apartment next door.

"How could you be so stupid as to lock your keys in the car," they heard a man yell at the top of his voice. "Now we have a $75 bill from the locksmith who had to come out after hours."

A muffled female's voice seemed to say, "I didn't mean to. My arms were full of groceries."

"Well, you ignorant, careless bitch, now we have an even larger credit card bill! You really piss me off with your stupidity!"

Overhearing this fight, Emma and Jason each found it difficult to swallow the bite of mac and cheese in their mouth. Emma shivered with fear and thought to herself, "I sure feel sorry for that woman. I wonder if this is something that happens regularly. If so, I'm not sure what I'll do. Hearing that kind of interaction between a couple, however, does make me appreciate the fact that Jason and I never fight like that." Because they didn't feel it was any of their business, Emma and Jason resolved to just having to live with the fighting next door. In fact, the neighbors fought so much that Emma and Jason had labeled them the 'he neighbor' and the 'she neighbor' (because they didn't

149

know the neighbors' actual names). Coincidentally, a month later, Emma and Jason were once again enjoying some delicious microwavable macaroni (only this time the menu was due to laziness rather than the state of their kitchen) when another fight next door started.

This time it seemed that the fight was further toward the back of the apartment, so the voices were not as clear. However, Jason shuddered when he heard 'he neighbor' say to 'she neighbor,' "You stupid slut, how could you look at that guy that way?" Jason couldn't help but wonder how a guy could *talk* to a woman like that. While he hated to admit that he had thought them on occasion, he would never say the words out loud. His thoughts were interrupted, however, by a loud thump, a door slam, and silence. Tonight's fight was longer and louder than what was typical—even for these neighbors. Emma and Jason just sat at the table with mouthfuls of macaroni, shaking their heads in disbelief and wondering if they should intervene in some way. Sitting frozen, unsure what to do, Emma softly muttered, "Jason, promise me that, even though our conflicts get pretty heated sometime, we will never be that kind of couple." I promise," Jason whispered back.

Several days after hearing the neighbor's escalated fighting, Jason and Emma sat down for their usual Thursday T.V. night, which consisted of *Grey's Anatomy* at 8, and then David Letterman at 10:30. Tonight's festivities started like any other Thursday night. Jason got home from work, he and Emma whipped up dinner, and they settled in for some steamy doctor drama. Tonight, however, was slightly different in that the first round of Major League Baseball playoffs started, which meant Jason was slightly edgy about how his precious Cardinals would fare against the Los Angeles Dodgers.

About halfway through *Grey's,* Jason switched over to the ballgame during a commercial to see what was going on. It just so happened his team had the bases loaded with one out.

"Jason, you need to switch it back. Our show has to be back from commercial by now!" Emma exclaimed.

"Emma, can't you see what's going on in the game right now?! If you miss a few minutes of the show, you can watch it on the internet tomorrow; it's not a big deal," claimed Jason.

Emma did not take kindly to missing any part of *Grey's*. After all, it was her favorite television show. They continued to argue over whether to watch the rest of the baseball inning, or switch back to *Grey's*.

"Come on Jason, turn it back on now! I'm going to give you ten seconds to turn the show back on," asserted Emma.

"Or you're going to do what, Emma? Whine at me some more?" Jason asked, in a decidedly sarcastic tone.

Emma finally was frustrated past her breaking point. "Jason, we always have to watch what *you* want to watch. We're supposed to watch *Grey's* every Thursday. You could have just watched your stupid baseball game *after* the show is over! I'm going upstairs to finish watching my show," Emma yelled.

Emma did not come back downstairs the rest of the night, and Jason did not try to press his luck by going up to the bedroom. He thought it was probably better to sleep on the couch. The chilly air between Jason and Emma the following morning was certainly not due to the Fall temperature drop. No, Emma was obviously still angry. Jason and Emma didn't speak that morning and very little that evening. When Jason tried to talk to her, Emma just turned on her heel and walked away. Slowly, however, Jason and Emma got back into a routine and got over their fight. By the following Thursday, they had forgiven each other and were back to enjoying their weekly ritual of watching *Grey's*.

Fall came and went, subjecting Jason and Emma to overhearing several fights between the couple next door, but thankfully, in comparison, their conflicts never got as heated as their neighbors. Sure, they would raise their voices at each other and call each other names, but they never used any physical aggression. One night when they were getting ready for bed, Jason and Emma heard things start getting heated between the neighbors. First they heard yelling, then they heard glass shattering, then more yelling. The voices coming from next door were muffled, but Jason and Emma could still make out much of what the neighbors were yelling about. They heard 'he neighbor' yelling at 'she-neighbor' about something she had apparently said when they went out for dinner that night.

"You embarrassed me in front of my boss and his wife! If you ever do that again, I'll smack you so hard you won't be able to eat for a week!" screamed 'he neighbor'.

"Oh, like you're ever really going to get that promotion, no matter how much you try to kiss your boss's ass. He can see what a worthless, lazy, waste of oxygen you really are. He, he only invited you to dinner because I made friends with his wife," screamed the 'she neighbor'.

"How dare you? How dare you speak to me that way!" he yelled in return.

Then, Jason and Emma heard more glass shattering, a sharp crack, and a very loud scream. For a moment, Jason was worried that 'he neighbor' really had hit her so hard she wouldn't be able to eat for a week, but then he heard her speak—she was crying and her voice was very garbled, Emma turned to Jason and exclaimed, "My God, I think he punched her in the jaw; she can barely talk. Do you think maybe we should call the police or something?"

"I don't know, Emma. It's really none of our business, and it might get worse if we involve the police in it. The guy might know it was us who called and hurt us in some way. Let's just ignore it," Jason responded.

Unsure of what to do and a bit afraid, Emma resigned herself to following Jason's lead. Both of them had trouble sleeping that night. It seemed these neighbors had gone from just loud yelling, to throwing stuff, to actual physical abuse. The next morning Emma went to teach as usual, but was still quite disturbed by what they had overheard through the wall last night. She knew one of her colleagues often volunteered at a center for battered women, so she poked her head into Rachel's office after lunch.

"Hey Rachel," Emma started, "do you have a few minutes? I need to talk to you about something."

"Sure Emma, what's on your mind?" inquired Rachel.

"Well, the couple who lives next door to me seems to be fighting a lot. Jason and I hear yelling and screaming through the walls of our apartment quite frequently. Last night, in fact, it seemed like there was even some physical abuse. I just don't know what to do. They're complete strangers. I don't know if I should even get involved by calling the police or what. I'm just not sure if this would be considered domestic abuse because it's mostly just a lot of yelling, cussing, and swearing. We do hear what sounds like things being thrown occasionally and, like last night, we thought that we heard him hit her, but I don't know for sure. And I don't know if these actions constitute real violence. I don't know if we should talk to the couple, call the police, or just mind our own business."

"It sounds like you're completely justified in being concerned, Emma" Rachel responded. "One thing I've learned in my volunteering for the battered woman's shelter is that there are many types of violence. Too often people think that the only real domestic violence is when a woman frequently and severely gets beaten by her male partner. Don't get me wrong—this happens, and it's very serious when it does. In fact, many of the women who seek shelters are coming from these kinds of relationships. But, other less severe, yet also unhealthy, kinds of aggression also exist in some relationships. There is just a big variety of violent couples—even ones that include no physical violence but a lot of verbal, psychological, and emotional violence.

So, by the sounds of things, I would say this relationship would be considered a violent one. If you don't feel comfortable talking to the woman directly, perhaps it would be best to call the police the next time you hear them arguing really violently. This way you know that a professional would be looking in on things. Or, maybe if you found the woman alone some time, you could give her our card with the hotline number on it. The crisis call volunteers could help her substantially. I hope that helps a bit."

"That helps. Thanks a lot, Rachel."

Rachel responded, "Good deal. Keep me posted, okay?"

"Will do." Emma's chat with Rachel made her feel slightly better because now she had some ideas about what to do if she felt things next door were getting out of hand.

When Emma arrived home, she found Jason in the kitchen making dinner. It was his night to cook, and it smelled like he was making homemade pizza. Emma was irritated by this because Jason *always* made pizza or spaghetti on his night to cook. She felt hurt that Jason didn't seem to care about making her something special—something that took extra thought and time. Instead, Emma felt Jason was always motivated by "what can I do the fastest?" rather than, "what can I make Emma that she would really find special?" Emma steamed silently for a while until she heard Jason clear his throat and look fidgety. Irritated already by his lack of special regard for her, Emma knew these were signs that Jason wanted to talk about something that he was uncomfortable discussing.

"Out with it, Jason. I know you've got something you want to say," Emma snapped, barely keeping in her pre-existing annoyance with him.

"Geez, Emma, you don't need to be so snappy with me," Jason replied. "But, OK, fine," he continued. "I was on Facebook today and noticed that you friended your ex-boyfriend yesterday. I'm very uncomfortable with you two being friends."

"Well, get over it, Jason," snapped Emma.

"He treated you like crap, Emma, and yet you still want to be friends with that guy. You really are stupid, aren't you?" Jason exclaimed in a loud angry voice.

"Don't call me stupid, Jason; I'm smarter than you'll ever hope to be," barked Emma.

"No, Emma, you might be book smart, but you're really just a stupid, spoiled, little brat who doesn't care about anyone's feelings but your own," yelled Jason, with anger in his voice.

"I can't believe you said that to me, Jason. You're just jealous that you were poor growing up and didn't have the things I had," Emma responded in a patronizing tone. With that, Emma picked up her plate of pizza and salad along with her soda and poured it all into Jason's lap. She'd reached her limit.

Jason bellowed and slammed his fist hard on the table. He then stood up, let the pizza and salad fall onto the floor, and went upstairs to change his pants. He came back downstairs and left the apartment, slamming the door so hard on his way out that a picture fell from the wall and shattered on the floor.

Jason didn't come home that night, and Emma woke up the next morning worried about where he was and what he had done the night before. It was Saturday, so neither Emma nor Jason had to work that day. They had originally planned to go see the new Jennifer Aniston romantic comedy that was out in theaters, but Emma doubted that would happen anymore. At about 2 o'clock, Jason finally came home. After he'd been there for 15 minutes, Emma asked if she could talk to him.

He said, "Sure."

Emma cleared her throat and quickly stated, "I'm really sorry about all the things I said to you last night, Jason. I didn't mean them. I was just tired and frustrated and took everything out on you. Will you forgive me?"

"I'm sorry, too, Emma. Of course, I forgive you, and I hope you'll do the same."

"Definitely," Emma replied as the two of them leaned toward each other and embraced.

As they flipped the calendar's pages and Emma and Jason started becoming more comfortable in their new surroundings, they had started taking more time away from each other to spend with new friends. The time apart started to become a source of contention between Emma and Jason, which led to a lot more arguing and increasing displays of competition, sarcasm, and anger. In fact, all they seemed to be doing anymore was trying to one up each other using whatever tactics it took to win an argument and get in the last word. Unfortunately, yelling and calling each other derogatory names had become a normal part of their arguments. Finally, in an attempt to resolve this increasingly negative conflict, they both decided a weekly date night might be just the ticket to getting their relationship back on track.

Their first scheduled date night was this upcoming Friday. Their plan was to go out for a nice dinner and then go bowling. The Thursday night before their impending date night, one of Jason's new friends called with tickets to a football game Friday night. Without thinking of how Emma might respond to this offer, Jason asked if they could postpone date night until Saturday.

"Jason, do you not understand the point of date night? We scheduled this because we are spending too little time together. How does going to that game with your friends remedy that problem?" Emma said snidely to Jason.

"I'm ssssoooo sorry, Emma. Forgive me for wanting to go to a one-time game when I could go on date night, which we could easily do on Saturday night," Jason responded in a sarcastic tone of voice.

"You've turned into a real wise ass lately. I don't appreciate your attitude. I don't care what you do about date night. Do whatever you want, Jason," said Emma, as she walked out of the room.

Alone in the living room, Jason realized it was wrong of him to ask Emma to postpone date night. He knew they were spending too little time together, and he should start prioritizing his relationship with her. The next night on Friday, he decided to bring home a dozen pink roses for Emma in an attempt to make amends. He was also prepared to issue a renewed commitment to tonight's date night and all subsequent date nights.

When he got home, he was met with something rather unexpected. Instead of being happy to see him and ready for date night, Emma was getting ready to go out clubbing with her friends. Jason approached Emma with his flowers. "I brought these for you, Emma, I'm really sorry about last night," said Jason.

"Oh, thanks Jason, that is nice of you," said Emma, as she walked out of the bedroom and back into the bathroom to finish applying her makeup.

"I thought we were doing date night tonight," Jason said as he followed her into the bathroom.

"You decided going to that game with your friend was more important than our relationship, so I made other plans tonight," said Emma.

"I never said for sure I was going to the game. In fact, I decided I would rather spend the evening with you," said Jason, a slight edge to his voice.

"Well, Jason, I feel like you shouldn't even have had to think about that decision. I should have come first tonight. But, whatever, I'm going out with my friends tonight," Emma replied, her tone an eerie shade of indifference.

"Emma, this is crap. I didn't do anything wrong. I brought you flowers," Jason said, his volume rising.

"I don't care, Jason. You can take your flowers to the football game and give one to every one of your buddies," Emma said, matching the anger in Jason's voice.

"Damn it, Emma! You're not going out tonight. You're going to dinner with me like we planned!" demanded Jason.

"Bite me, Jason. I'll do whatever I want," Emma yelled back at him.

"That's it. Don't ever expect me to do anything nice for you ever again. Those are the last flowers I'll ever buy for you!" Jason screamed at Emma.

Emma stormed out of the bathroom back into the bedroom. "Here's what I think of your flowers, Jason," Emma screamed as she threw the vase to the floor. The vase shattered all over the floor, the flowers flew everywhere.

At that point, Emma grabbed her keys and purse and left.

Emma returned to the house later that night to find Jason sitting on the couch waiting up for her. She walked past him and went straight to bed. The next morning Emma and Jason were both genuinely shaken about their fight. When Emma stepped out of the shower and into the bedroom, Jason said, "Emma, we need to talk about what happened between us last night. I think we crossed a line."

"Yeah, Jason, I think you're right. I'm not proud of anything I did or said last night. And after reflecting more about what Rachel at work told me about different types of aggressive couples, I'm really scared of where we're headed," Emma replied. What I learned from talking with Rachel is that there are different kinds of violence. Even though we didn't throw things at each other or hit each other, what we did is still violent."

"I know, I lost my temper, Emma, and I think you did, too. We need to promise each other that when things go a little wrong, we won't resort to violence ever again," Jason said.

"I really do regret what happened. I'm very sorry. I won't ever do anything like that again. I don't ever want to be that couple next door," said Emma.

"We'll never be that kind of couple," promised Jason.

For Further Thought and Reflection

1. What forms of unhealthy communication patterns do you see Emma and Jason and the neighbors using?
2. Do you think Emma and Jason's *conflicts* are aggressive? Why or why not? Do you think they are violent? What do you think is the difference between aggressiveness and violence? How do you think their conflicts compare and contrast to the "he/she neighbors"?
3. Many times, people think that domestic violence looks like the behaviors involved with the "he/she neighbors." However, as discussed in the case study, researchers have identified a variety of violent couples. Based upon what you have learned, do you think that Emma and Jason have a violent relationship? Why or why not?
4. Can we be sure that Jason and Emma are not "this type of couple?" From what Rachel told them, how would you describe Emma and Jason's relationship?
5. Jason and Emma experienced uncertainty about how to respond to what was happening between the neighbors. It can be difficult to know what to do. If you or someone you know are involved in a violent relationship, what would you do? What advice would you seek/give? To whom would you turn for advice or help?

References

Cahn, D.D. (Ed.). (2009). *Family violence: Communication processes.* Albany, NY: SUNY Press.

Johnson, M.P. (2008). *A typology of domestic violence: Intimate terrorism, violent resistance, and situational couple violence.* Boston, MA: Northeastern University Press.

Levy, B. (Ed.). 1998. *Dating violence: Young women in danger.* Seattle, WA: Seal Press.

Olson, L.N. (2004). Relational control-motivated aggression: A theoretically-based typology of intimate violence. *Journal of Family Communication, 4,* 209–233.

Olson, L.N. (2002). Exploring "common couple violence" in heterosexual romantic relationships. *Western Journal of Communication, 66,* 104–128.

20

Unilateral Union: Obsessive Relational Intrusion and Stalking in a Romantic Context

WILLIAM R. CUPACH AND BRIAN H. SPITZBERG

Key Terms

stalking, obsessive relational intrusion, privacy invasion, unrequited love, jealousy

---

Alex and Anna, now 27 and 26 years old, respectively, worked together in the information systems division of a large insurance company. After knowing each other at a distance for about a year, they were both assigned to work on a large development project. Alex and Anna enjoyed working together, and, about six months into the development project they started dating. That was almost two years ago. Now, they don't speak to one another and each is extremely uncomfortable if they run into the other. In their own words, Alex and Anna each provide a perspective on what happened between them, and why.

Alex's Story

From a distance, I always thought that Anna was cute. She seemed bright and friendly, precisely the type of woman I would want to spend time with; in fact, the type of woman I might eventually want to marry. I wanted to try to get a date with her, but it never seemed to work out. Our encounters at work were cordial, but infrequent and brief. I was dating other women off and on, and I figured someone as attractive as Anna must have lots of boyfriends. I almost got up the nerve to ask her out when I struck up a conversation with her at a division picnic, but suddenly other people were part of the conversation and the opportunity slipped away. Then, one day I suddenly found myself assigned to work on the same project as Anna. I secretly felt really excited, figuring I would now be able to get to know her better and lay the groundwork for dating her.

As soon as we began working together, things really seemed to click between us, both professionally and personally. We made great strides on the project and our skills seemed to complement one another. We often had to work late together, but neither of us seemed to mind. In our conversations, I tried to find out as much as I could about her, though I was never satisfied that I knew enough. I asked some colleagues at work about Anna's social life, trying to figure out if she was "available" for more than just a working relationship.

Anna was very friendly toward me. She always smiled at me, listened to me intently when I talked, and offered sincere words of encouragement and support whenever I talked about personal problems. We teased and joked quite a bit, and I could tell that she really liked me. I started to feel like we were destined to be together, so I felt I had to make my move. Confident that she found me attractive (she had given me numerous compliments), I decided to ask her out on a "real" date. We started seeing each other every weekend, and, within a month, we got together a couple of times during the week as well.

For the most part, I enjoyed our times together. We laughed, talked, and enjoyed each other's company. Sex was great! When we were not together, I thought about Anna constantly. The first few months were the best of my life. But I started getting suspicious that Anna didn't feel the same way about me as I did about her. She wanted to cut back a bit, saying she needed time for other things in her life. Whatever those other things were, I couldn't understand why I couldn't be a part of them—unless of course she was seeing someone else. I did what I could to confirm my suspicions on my own, but ultimately I simply raised the issue with her. This led to our first big fight, where I accused her of dating other men and hiding the fact from me. She denied it, but her anger made me wonder why she was being so defensive if there really was nothing to hide.

Although I was upset that Anna might be seeing another guy, I wanted to smooth things over with her. I apologized to her for not trusting her (though I had lingering suspicions). If anything, I felt I had to work even harder to win her loyalty and affection. I redoubled my efforts to show her how much I cared for her. I frequently would leave messages on her desk and bought her flowers and greeting cards. I called her or texted her almost every night, but about half of the time she wasn't available or wasn't answering. When I would ask her later what she had been doing, she sometimes told me, but often seemed evasive. If I couldn't get a hold of her until late at night, she seemed annoyed that I called.

The more I pursued Anna, the more she seemed to play hard to get. This simply fueled my desire for her. I told her I loved her on several occasions, but she never said it back to me. When I asked her whether or not she loved me too, she said she wasn't sure. I was convinced that, even if she had been seeing other guys, she loved me and was simply afraid to face such a deep commitment and admit it.

Anna seemed to be less and less available by phone. The gaps in time before she responded to my text messages grew longer. She starting making excuses for not being able to go out on nights we normally would see each other. When I asked to friend her on Facebook, she said she preferred not to because she was trying to limit her time on it. I became very frustrated as we were now seeing each other maybe once every week or two outside of work. The strain in our personal relationship began to take its toll at work.

Then one Friday afternoon, without warning, Anna broke up with me. We met for a drink at one of our favorite places, and she calmly told me that she thought our relationship had "run its course." She said she thought I was a "nice" person, but that we were incompatible. She claimed we were both unhappy and that it was adversely affecting work. She said something vaguely about remaining friends.

I was devastated. I begged her for another try, but she was steadfast. I went home that night, feeling numb and humiliated. What would everyone at work think? What would my family think? What would Anna tell people behind my back? How could she do this to me! I got drunk that night and called Anna, hoping to reconcile. She was pleasant as always, and I got a glimmer of hope when she said we should at least put things on hold.

I knew Anna just needed some time. But I also knew that persistence was the key. You don't obtain valuable things in life without effort; sometimes you have to struggle and push to get what you want. If I did nothing, Anna and I would never be partners. If I pursued her vigorously, I had a good chance of winning her over. After all, Anna left the door open for a relationship between us, and I've seen persistence pay off so many times before.

All I could think about was getting back with Anna. I felt I couldn't be happy unless I restored our relationship, so I spent lots of time plotting my strategy to win her over. I sent her cards, e-mails, poems, . . . even flowers, just to let her know I was thinking about her. I continued to call and text Anna several times a week. When she didn't (or wouldn't) answer the phone, I left her voice mail messages. When she did answer, our conversation was cordial. I felt like she was trying to be "nice" to me—but nice is not what I wanted. I was happy to talk to her, but I missed the intimacy and closeness in our talk, the physical contact, and hanging out together.

Anna posted for and got a job in a different division and she seemed pleased to be transferring to a different building. I couldn't understand why she would want to change jobs when she was so good at the one she already had. Since she still wouldn't go out with me, and since we no longer saw each other at work, I devised what I considered to be safe ways to see or communicate with her. I sent her humorous e-mail messages and interoffice notes and cartoons that I thought she would enjoy. I knew some of the bars and restaurants Anna and her friends liked to visit. I would sometimes casually show up, hoping to make brief contact with her. Sometimes I went alone, sometimes with my friend, Randy. I increasingly wondered what she was doing and where she was going. Once or twice at the end of a work day, I even waited in my car and followed her when she drove away to see where she was going.

I also would occasionally drive by Anna's house—thinking I might see her coming or going. Finally, I noticed a car parked in front of her place I hadn't seen before. *My God!* She *was* seeing someone else and she hid the fact from me. When I called to confront her, she first said it was none of my business. Then she admitted she was dating someone else, and told me that I needed to get on with my life. She said not to call her anymore. I was outraged. How could she betray me like that?!? I felt angry and hurt. Apparently I wasn't good enough for her.

Anna was now screening all of her calls and ignoring my text messages, so I had to settle for leaving messages on her voice mail. Once a man answered her phone—presumably her new boyfriend—and I just hung up. I no longer wanted to get back with Anna. I wanted to get back *at* her. I wanted her to know the grief she had caused me, and I wanted to punish her for hurting me. I wanted to scare her a little, so I made some empty threats. Because she never responded to my notes I left her, one day I left a letter opener in her mailbox to let her know I wanted her to respond to my messages. The next thing I knew, the police visited me and served me with a Temporary Restraining Order. I was told that they could send me to jail if I tried to contact Anna in any way.

Now, Anna and I are bitter enemies. I feel ashamed and embarrassed for behaving foolishly, but I am still deeply resentful toward Anna because I feel she led me on, humiliated and betrayed me. I would like to see her suffer in some way for how she hurt me.

Anna's Story

Alex seemed like a good guy—until I got to know him. Although I apparently met him a few times before, I never really noticed him until we were assigned to work together on the development project. At first I found him to be charming and attractive. I could tell he was infatuated with me, and I enjoyed the attention he showered on me. Our personalities seemed to mesh and this fostered a good working relationship between us. I respected his contributions to the project, and I felt that he admired what I had to offer as well. When Alex asked me out on a date, I wasn't surprised. In fact, some of my friends told me he had been asking all kinds of questions about me for several weeks. I was concerned that dating someone at work could pose problems if it didn't work out, but I decided to take the risk.

The first few weeks were a whirlwind. We both got caught up in the excitement of a new relationship. But it didn't take long for me to realize that Alex was not the sort of guy I wanted to spend my life with. Early on, it was apparent that Alex was very controlling. He insisted on making decisions about where we went, when, and with whom. He seemed constantly to test my loyalty to him. The attention he paid to me quickly became smothering and needy. I liked Alex as a person, and I enjoyed our dates, but I didn't like the fact that he was so jealous and suspicious of my private life. I thought to myself, "my God, how can he be so possessive when we've only been dating six weeks?!" One time when I returned from the bathroom, I found him looking through my mail lying on the kitchen counter. This angered me and sent up a red flag that I would have a difficult time trusting him.

I thought of breaking it off with Alex after a few months, but I kept putting it off. I didn't want to hurt him, and I didn't want the ordeal of defending my desire to break-up. I also knew it could become complicated dealing with him at work. So I decided to simply scale back the relationship. I made excuses so that our dates were less frequent. He compensated by calling and texting me more and more frequently, despite the fact that I would see him every day at work. If I was unavailable or didn't answer the phone, he apparently kept calling until he could reach me. One night I just refused to answer the phone and it rang every fifteen minutes. I finally couldn't stand it anymore and around 1:00 in the morning I answered the phone. I asked him to please not call me so late, but he continued to do so. I finally started turning off my phone at night so I could get some sleep. Whenever I did this, it angered him and he would make sarcastic and snide remarks to me at work the next day.

Alex began to be more of a pest than a dating partner. The more I got to know him, the more apparent it became that he had a very fragile ego. I wanted out of the relationship completely, but I feared he would go into a rage, or sabotage me at work, or worse. The more I withdrew from him, the harder he pressed. It became increasingly difficult to work with him, but it was essential to the project that we collaborate. The relationship was costing me time, sleep, productivity at work, and more, and I was getting nothing but aggravation out of it.

Because I had cooled off the relationship, Alex assumed that I was dating someone else behind his back. I wasn't, and I told him so. Nevertheless, Alex undertook a campaign of spying on me to find out for himself. He would drive by my house frequently, and sometimes come to the door, especially if I had told him earlier over the phone that I was busy. He really just wanted to see if I was entertaining another man. He also annoyed my friends by asking them my whereabouts all the time. He seemed to follow me everywhere. He started showing up at social gatherings and public places he normally wouldn't have gone to, just to "run into" me. I had this creepy feeling he might be following me or waiting for me around the next corner.

I jokingly mentioned to my friend Karla that I sometimes felt as if Alex were stalking me and that I must paranoid. But Karla wasn't so sure I was paranoid. She told me about a recent article she read on the Internet about stalking and obsession with relationships. The researchers cited in the article reported that stalking is not all that uncommon, and that it can be dangerous. I was surprised to learn that nearly two million people in the U.S. are the victims of stalking each year. I always thought that stalkers were "sociopaths" harassing celebrities. But Karla told me that the most common type of stalker is a former intimate partner, and that the vast majority of victims are female. My annoyance regarding Alex was turning into serious concern.

I decided enough was enough. I tried to break it to Alex gently because I knew he would be hurt. I wished him no ill will—I just wanted my life, my privacy, and my freedom back. I told him that we could still be friends, but that I didn't want to date him anymore.

After I broke up with Alex, he seemed to push even harder than before. He called me constantly—sometimes six or eight times in an evening. I avoided him as much as I could. Work became intolerable so I explained the circumstances to my manager and asked for a transfer, which I got, even though I hated to leave the work I was doing. Moving to another building made it difficult for Alex to badger me at work—although he managed to clog my computer in-box with unwanted e-mail, and he incessantly pestered me with unwanted text messages.

One day I answered the phone when Alex called, and I firmly told him never to call me again. After that I would not answer the phone when he called or respond to his texts. He eventually figured out I was screening his calls and started calling from other locations—his friend's house, phone booths. So I just stopped answering all calls and told my friends to leave a message when they called because I was screening.

I started dating another man that I met through my cousin. About this time, Alex was driving by my house frequently and he started leaving threatening messages on my answering machine. He would call me nasty names, like "frigid bitch," and tell me that I would pay for making him miserable. He also made derogatory remarks about my new boyfriend, though Alex really knew nothing about him. One of the things that angered me the most was that Alex tried to spread rumors about me to co-workers and friends. He told people that I was a slut and that I gave him a sexually transmitted disease—an embarrassing outright lie! I couldn't believe I ever saw anything attractive about this guy. How could I have been so wrong?

One day I came home to find a dagger in my mailbox. It really scared me. Alex's messages had become increasingly threatening, and I always had the feeling I was being watched. He would show up unexpectedly almost anywhere I went—including dates with my new boyfriend. So I finally called the police. Because I kept track of Alex's recent threatening behaviors, and because I had some of his threats recorded on my cell phone, I was able to get a restraining order against him. But it didn't keep me from being afraid. I've read too many stories where a restraining order can send the restrained person "over the edge" with anger. I really feared Alex would do harm to me. I changed my phone number and my locks. I don't walk my dog alone at night anymore. I frequently change my routine so that my schedule is not predictable.

Alex said he'll "get" me. But I haven't seen him since I took out the restraining order, except once at work, where he flashed me a sick smile and glared at me. I am anxious. I am resentful. I am angry. My life has been completely disrupted. I am less trusting of people, and men in particular. I wonder why I waited as long as I did to break up with Alex. I wonder why I couldn't see sooner that he had an obsessive personality. I wonder what I could have done differently before and after the break up to prevent his anger from escalating. Now I wonder, how can I protect myself? How can I get back to leading a normal life? Will he pop up again unexpectedly and do harm to me?

For Further Thought and Reflection

1. In what ways does Alex's communication with Anna reveal that his interest in her is obsessive and his pursuits are excessive? Are there early warning signs in Alex's behavior that, in retrospect, Anna might have relied on to alter how she communicated with Alex? In what ways does Anna's communication foster Alex's persistence in pursuing a relationship with her?

2. Our culture seems to promote a script that says persistence in pursuing relationships and potential partners pays off. Where does this "script" or societal message come from? What factors perpetuate and reinforce the belief that persistence ultimately leads to success, particularly where relationships are concerned?

3. At what point does pursuit of a relationship become obsessive? How do you know when you should abandon the goal to have a relationship with someone? Where is the line that divides normal persistence in relationship pursuit versus obsessive and inappropriate pursuit?

4. Many people enjoy seeing their partner be a little jealous. When is jealousy productive and when is it unproductive in relationships? How can you manage your own jealousy so that it doesn't become destructive?

5. Anna struggled with deciding when "enough was enough," and when Alex's behavior had become excessive. At that time, she broke it off, avoided contact, and eventually called the police and took out a restraining order. What, if anything, would you have done differently in her place? Why? What advice would you have given Anna at various points of her relationship with Alex? Why is hindsight, or the view of a friend, so much clearer than when we are directly involved in the relationship?

6. How do new and evolving communication technologies increase the risk of unwanted contact? How might they improve our ability to manage or cope with unwanted contact? Is our fascination with social networking sites making unwanted relationship pursuit more or less likely to be a problem?

References

Cupach, W. R., & Spitzberg, B. H. (2004). *The dark side of relationship pursuit: From attraction to obsession and stalking.* Mahwah, NJ: Erlbaum.

Cupach, W. R., & Spitzberg, B. H. (2008). "Thanks, but no thanks": The occurrence and management of unwanted relationship pursuit. In S. Sprecher, A. Wenzel, & J. Harvey (Eds.), *Handbook of relationship initiation* (pp. 409–424). New York: Psychology Press.

Dunn, J. L. (2002). *Courting disaster: Intimate stalking, culture, and criminal justice.* New York: Aldine de Gruyter.

Logan, TK, Cole, J., Shannon, L., & Walker, R. (2006). *Partner stalking: How women respond, cope, and survive.* New York: Springer.

Sinclair, H. C., & Frieze, I. H. (2005). When courtship persistence becomes intrusive pursuit: Comparing rejecter and pursuer perspectives of unrequited love. *Sex Roles, 52,* 839–852.

Spitzberg, B. H., & Cupach, W. R. (2007). The state of the art of stalking: Taking stock of the emerging literature. *Aggression and Violent Behavior, 12,* 64–86.

Spitzberg, B. H., & Cupach, W. R. (2008). Managing unwanted pursuit. In M. T. Motley (Ed.), *Studies in applied interpersonal communication* (pp. 3–25). Thousand Oaks, CA: Sage.

21

Head Coverings, Jihad, and Fantasy Football: Moving beyond the Stereotype

TIMOTHY M. MUEHLHOFF

Key Terms

positive stereotype, language as reflection, selection, and deflection, reducing uncertainty, labels, categorization, characterization, and correction

In an introduction to interpersonal communication course at a Midwestern university students are assigned a listening project that requires them to learn about themselves and others by selecting a representative of a group whose perspective they would not ordinarily listen to. Two days after the project is assigned, the news is dominated by the shooting rampage at Fort Hood, Texas, where the shooter, a soldier of Arab descent handed out Qurans leading up to the attack and shouted "Allah Akbar,"—God is great—as he shot and killed 13 of his fellow soldiers. Deeply disturbed by this incident, Michael, a Christian student in the class, decides to visit the Muslim Student Center on campus and listen to the perspectives of Muslim students.

Walking to the Muslim Center, Michael decides spontaneously to ask students he passes what they think of when they hear the word, *Muslim*. He is shocked at the responses. Some of the words people said: *angry, war, hatred, upset, terrorists, Allah, religious, Arab, head covering, devout,* and *9/11*. While his impromptu survey is hardly scientific, it reveals that many students have negative pictures of Muslims. Michael wonders what words the guy he's going to interview would use to describe Christians?

Michael walks into the Muslim Student Center and is introduced to Amin, an American-born Arab who is a devout Muslim majoring in religious studies and psychology. They grab coffee and settle into two large leather chairs in the lounge. Amin notices Michael's Detroit Lions football cap and congratulates him on his team winning two games this season. Michael laughs and responds that after going winless the

---

[1] Thank you to my colleague Dorothy Alston Calley who regularly challenges her students to engage in such a meaningful listening assignment and shared her idea with me.

previous year two victories is a huge success! Michael asks if Amin likes football, and Amin explains that while his dad grew up playing soccer in Saudi Arabia, he's a huge American football fan and is a fantasy football junkie. Michael says he is too, and soon they are comparing how their fantasy teams and players fared the previous Sunday. After a complete rundown of stats, the interview begins with Michael pulling out a tape recorder and asking the first question.

MICHAEL: On my way over, I asked students to tell me the first word they thought of when they heard the word, *Muslim.* They used words like, *angry, war, hatred, Allah, religious, Arab, terrorist, head covering, devout,* and *9/11.* As a Muslim, how does that make you feel?

AMIN: Well, it saddens me, but I'm not surprised. They think all Arabs are Muslims, and all Muslims are angry or unstable people.

MICHAEL: (attempting to make a joke) You did get angry when I said my fantasy team would *crush* yours if we went head-to-head.

AMIN: (in a deadpan tone) Hey, don't *ever* mess with my team. My religion, yes; my fantasy team, never.

MICHAEL: Seriously, where do you think that impression of Arabs or Muslims comes from?

AMIN: It comes from a million different voices. Movies like *True Lies, Raiders of the Lost Ark, The Mummy, Patriot Games,* and TV shows like *JAG, The West Wing,* and *The Agency,* all present Arabs and Muslims in a negative light. In fact, a media scholar named Jack Shaheen—I think that's his name—documented over 900 Hollywood films that portrayed Arabs in an offensive manner. When you see a negative or menacing image of something or someone over and over, you can't help but form an impression of it and even grow fearful of it.

MICHAEL: But don't you think we watch those shows, we know they're fiction?

AMIN: I hope so. But what about kids who are perhaps less discerning? What happens when an image is placed before them at a young age? Did you ever see Disney's movie, *Aladdin?*

MICHAEL: Of course. I remember my teacher showing it in school.

AMIN: Remember the opening song? Don't worry, I won't sing it.
Oh, I come from a land
from a faraway place
where the caravan camels roam,
where they cut off your ear
if they don't like your face.
It's barbaric, but hey, it's home.

When most people hear that song, they get caught up in the catchy tune and watch Aladdin and Jasmine, two light-skinned heroes, fight off sinister Arabs. When they hear this song and watch the movie it perpetuates an offensive stereotype of Arabs being barbaric and angry. *Look at me in the wrong way and I'll cut off your ear.* So, no, it doesn't surprise me that students responded that Muslims are upset or angry. However, the other words the students used—*war, terrorists, 9/11*—really is scary and deeply discouraging. This view of Arabs as terrorists has even found its way into my favorite comedy, *The Office.*

MICHAEL: (laughing) *The Office* is a riot. I love it. Remember the episode where Dwight unexpectedly punched Michael Scott in the gut and then they fought during their lunch break at Dwight's karate school?

AMIN: (laughing with him) Yes, absolutely hilarious. Do you remember the show in which Michael as the boss decides to do diversity training? He has everybody in the office put Post-it notes on their foreheads that have different ethnicities written on them such as Black, Asian, Mexican, Jewish, and so on. They then are to treat each other according to the stereotype; Asians don't care about food and Jews only care about money. At the end of the exercise, Michael says into the camera: "Nobody was an Arab—that would be too explosive. No pun intended." It's said for laughs, but we all know what he means.

MICHAEL: Look at an Arab in the wrong way, and he'll cut off your ear.

AMIN: (pointing to himself) Or, look at *me* in the wrong way and I'll put a bomb in your office.

MICHAEL: You mentioned that having fellow students use words like, *hatred, terrorists,* and *9/11* to describe Muslims is scary. Could you elaborate?

AMIN: Sure. Every time there is an incident involving a person of Arab ethnicity the entire Arab community holds its collective breath and fears an anti-Islamic backlash. For example, I remember reading somewhere that after the Fort Hood massacre in Texas, a mosque in Dearborn, Michigan found a disturbing package left on its doorstep. It was a hardbound copy of the Quran which had been defaced with spray paint. Inside was a note that read something like "Islam is a sickness and every Muslim should be kicked out of the USA." I know that such talk is crazy and should be ignored. When events like Fort Hood or 9/11 happen my community feels a type of double shock—shock at the tragedy itself and shock at the possible retaliation against us by people who view us negatively. Knowing that people have such twisted views of us can also make listening to the news a nerve-racking experience.

MICHAEL: How, so?

AMIN: As an Arab living in the States, when you are listening to the news and hear of a shooting or bombing your first thought can be: God, don't let the shooter be a Muslim. Did you know that right after the bombing of the federal building in Oklahoma City news outlets quickly reported suspicious Middle Eastern individuals had been seen in the area before the bombing? Of course, later we learned that it was Midwestern Caucasians who were responsible.

MICHAEL: I don't mean to offend you, but can I ask you a delicate question?

AMIN: Fire away.

MICHAEL: Hasn't Islam kind of earned its reputation of being violent? Doesn't Islam in fact believe in something called a holy war?

AMIN: Yes, we do. However, let me say two things about holy war, or as we call it, Jihad. First, not all Muslim theologians agree on what the Quran—our holy book—teaches about this topic. You are a Christian. Not all Christian scholars or pastors agree on every doctrine or passage of the Bible, right?

MICHAEL: Uh, no. We have plenty of lively and heated disagreements.

AMIN: Well, we do, too. It's impossible to boil all of the richness and diversity of Muslim perspectives into one monolithic voice. When it comes to a controversial idea like holy war, you are going to get very different ideas coming from the Muslim community. Second, most Muslims I know believe that when Jihad was started by Muhammad—the leading prophet of Islam—it was done only as a form of self-defense. As I and most of my friends understand the Quran, it teaches that holy war should only be waged in defense of life and property and never to oppress or dominate another. So, six days after the terrorist attacks of 9/11 dozens of leading Islamic scholars issued a statement that said they were grief-stricken at such horrifying events and the murder of innocents could never be justified nor tolerated by true followers of Islam. However, because media have linked Jihad to Muslims, it's all many people think of when it comes to Islam.

MICHAEL: My Communication professor said that all language simultaneously *reflects, selects,* and *deflects.* If I hear what you are saying, when people talk about Muslims and Islam, all they select is the most violent view of the holy war aspect.

AMIN: That's right. In talking about Muslims, people reflect the media's representation of us as violent people and then selectively only focus on the so-called violent aspects of Islam such as Jihad.

MICHAEL: What do you think is deflected or neglected by this pervading stereotype of Muslims as being violent or terrorists?

AMIN: Wow, a lot. First, to me, Islam is a religion of peace, not war. The Quran teaches that peace is one of the names of Allah, and many Muslims end their daily worship with the simple prayer: "O God, you are Peace." Also, when Arabs or Muslims are seen through the limiting lens of oil barons or nomads herding camels, then all the great accomplishments of Arab culture are deflected and glossed over. Few people realize that geometry, algebra, and Arabic numerals are all linked to the medieval Arab world, as well as our modern understanding of astronomy. As a fellow believer in God, you may be interested to know that one of the key arguments for God's existence, the cosmological argument, was partially developed by Islamic thinkers and is often used by Christian philosophers to debate atheists. But all of this is passed over, or deflected, when individuals selectively focus on only one aspect of my community.

MICHAEL: (smiling) This is just my opinion, but if you're trying to win people over to the Muslim perspective—particularly teenagers—I wouldn't take credit for helping to create Algebra. Just a thought.

AMIN: (chuckling) I'll bring it up at our next meeting.

MICHAEL: You mentioned that when people just focus on how others dress, so much else gets glossed over. I found it interesting that some students in my informal survey, particularly female students, mentioned *head covering* in describing Muslims. Thoughts?

AMIN: They were most likely refereeing to a *hijab*—an Islamic covering—that some women choose to wear. The word *hijab* is an Arabic word that literally means *curtain* or *covering* and is not mandated by the Quran. Some women wear them as a sign of modesty and others wear them at the request of their parents. I have one friend who has over 100 of them and she started wearing them after the attacks of 9/11 as a sign of pride in her culture and religion. I know of another woman who wears miniskirts to school and a *hijab* to the mosque. I have good friend who is Arab but not particularly religious and wears one made by the fashion designer Yves St. Laurent because she thinks it looks cool.

MICHAEL: That makes me think of a stereotype I have that's becoming clear during this interview—thinking all Arabs are Muslims or are religious.

AMIN: That'd be like saying all Americans are Christians. People don't fit into one neat category.

MICHAEL: Why do you think we like to do that, fit people into predictable, neat categories?

AMIN: Good question. I think most of us—myself included—like to keep life simple, organized, and predictable. Trying to figure out the world is tough work and we are all looking for shortcuts. In my religion class, I remember my prof saying that on average one new mosque opens each week in the United States, and that Buddhism is now the fourth most practiced religion in America. Well, imagine how messy, chaotic, and exhausting it would be to take time to form an opinion of every Muslim and Buddhist individually. It's easier, and only practical, to form an opinion about the group as a whole and then apply that general judgment to all the people in the group.

MICHAEL: So, all Muslims are angry and violent individuals who will cut off your ear if they don't like your face . . .

AMIN: And all Christians are intolerant and supported the Crusades.

MICHAEL: Touché.

AMIN: Here's a question for you. If stereotypes are an attempt to bring order to a chaotic world, then are all stereotypes by definition, negative? Could you have a positive stereotype?

MICHAEL: Don't hold me to this, but I don't see why not. Most of us have a positive perception, a stereotype, of people who take a year and work for the Peace Corp. or Teach for America. I think of them of being selfless, civic-minded, and wanting to give back, even though I've never met anyone who's actually worked for those two groups.

AMIN: I think I agree. I mean, a stereotype of students belonging to the Muslim Student Center is that they are fairly serious about their religion, culture, and so forth; a positive stereotype, and for the most part, a true one.

MICHAEL: So where do stereotypes go wrong?

AMIN: When we don't allow them to change. Once we put a label on a person, we might ignore or not notice new or contradictory information that would challenge the label.

MICHAEL: That reminds me of something we studied in one of my classes. We just had a test on it last week. One expert argued that in order to break a complex world up into more manageable, predictable pieces we continually work through a three-stage process when encountering people. What was it? I know it started with three Cs. Categorization, characterization, and . . . what is the third one? . . . Nuts, what was it?

AMIN: "Nuts" doesn't start with a "C."

MICHAEL: You're not helping. *Correction.* That's it. Categorization, charac-
                 terization, and correction. When we first meet a person we im-
                 mediately place him or her into broad categories such as liberal
                 or conservative, Christian or Muslim, and so on. Once we place
                 them into a category, we assign specific characteristics to that
                 person based on the category. The correction stage, which my
                 professor said was the *most* neglected stage, only occurs if we get
                 to know individuals and address initial judgments. The problem
                 is that our categories often keep us from getting to know people
                 on an individual basis. To be honest, if it weren't for this listen-
                 ing assignment, I would never have come into this center and
                 met you.

AMIN: Don't feel bad; I can count on one hand the number of serious
                 conversations I've had with Christians outside of my religious stud-
                 ies classes.

MICHAEL: One last question—it's kinda off the wall. What do you think God
                 thinks about stereotypes?

AMIN: (laughing) What made you think of *that*?

MICHAEL: One of my favorite writers, Eugene Peterson, says that with God
                 there is no ditto among souls. What I think he means by that is
                 that each person is created uniquely by God and could not possi-
                 bly be contained by a one-size-fits-all label.

AMIN: Well said. While labels or categories can help us organize life, they
                 can also blind us to the unique qualities of individuals within a
                 particular group. With each person we should, like God, seek to
                 see the uniqueness inherent in them.

MICHAEL: Okay, that's a perfect place to end this interview. Hey, this has
                 been really helpful.

AMIN: God's peace to you and good luck next Sunday with your fantasy
                 team.

MICHAEL: Thanks, I need both.

Surprising. That's the word that comes to Michael's mind as he walks back after interviewing Amin at the Muslim Center. He's surprised that Amin likes fantasy football,
watches *The Office,* and even jokes about being able to diss his religion but not his fantasy team—he didn't see that coming. All in all, he likes him even though he doubts
they will run into each other again. If they did run into each other, he feels they could
talk openly, even about the differences between their religions. After the interview he
is troubled by the story of the defaced Quran being left on the doorstep of the Mosque
in Michigan. How would he feel if someone did that to the Bible? He wonders if

stereotypes aren't always about merely organizing a chaotic world, but sometimes about fueling hate and wanting to feel superior to others? He also wonders if meeting Amin will make a difference in how he views other Muslims on campus or if he'll just see Amin as an exception?

For Further Thought and Reflection

1. How did Amin's noticing of Michael's sport's cap and their mutual enthusiasm for fantasy football help keep the conversation from turning defensive? Based on the results of his survey, how did Michael think his conversation with Amin would go when talking about delicate issues like Arab stereotypes or Jihad?

2. If Michael were to have passed *you* on his way to the student center and asked: "What's the first word you think of when you hear, *Muslim?*" how would you have responded? Would your response have been positive or negative? Where does your idea of a Muslim come from? What role do the media play in forming it?

3. Michael brings up a three-stage process of correcting stereotypes (categorization, characterization, and correction) and mentions that *correction* is often the most neglected stage. Why do you think correcting our stereotypes of others is often neglected or difficult?

4. In his closing observations of the interview, Michael wonders if meeting Amin will make a difference in how he views other Muslims on campus or if he'll see him as an exception. What do you think? When you meet someone who breaks a stereotype you have of a group does that change how you view the group as a whole or merely that individual?

5. Are stereotypes more about helping us organize a chaotic world, being lazy in our perceptions of others, or perpetuating hate and superiority through language?

References

Burke, K. (1966). *Language as symbolic action.* Berkeley, CA: University of California Press.

Perry, B. (2001). *In the name of hate: Understanding hate crimes.* New York: Routledge.

Peterson, E. (1997). *Subversive spirituality.* Grand Rapids, MI: Eerdmans.

Quattrone, G.A. (1985). On the congruity between internal states and actions. *Psychological Bulletin, 98,* 3–40.

Schultze, Q.J. (2000). *Communicating for life: Christian stewardship in community and media.* Grand Rapids, MI: Baker Academic.

Wingfield, M., & Bushra, K (2002). Arab stereotypes and American educators. *Social Studies and the Young Learner, 7,* 7–10.

Wood, J.T. (1998). *But I thought you meant . . . misunderstandings in communication.* Mountain View, CA: Mayfield Publishing.

22

(When and How) Do I Tell?: Disclosing Social Identity in Personal Relationships

Brenda J. Allen

Key Terms

self-disclosure, relationship development, friendship, social identity

---

Jayla Brown sighed as she closed the door to her suite in the first-year students' residence hall. She was relieved that her roommate Lisa wasn't there; she could have some time to herself. Lisa was such a ball of energy that Jayla barely had time to hear herself think. But, that didn't really bother Jayla because Lisa was such a positive person and basically a sweet girl. So far, she had been a great roommate, especially compared to other roomies she'd heard about. Jayla plopped on her bed and began to reflect on her first two and a half months at Northeastern State University. She and Lisa had hit it off from the very first day they moved in. They had so much in common it was crazy. They both were middle children, and had been on the honor rolls and the cheerleading squads at their high schools. Plus, they both had a sick sense of humor, which meant that they laughed a lot, and had similar taste in movies and TV shows. They even had the same favorite color: purple, which meant that their bedding and accessories complemented each other. In fact, they both had bought the exact same lavender desk set from Target! They each had gone with one guy during their last two years of high school, and had broken up with them right before coming to college. Most important of all, they both were reluctant pre-med majors, mainly because of parental pressure. Jayla was glad to have a roommate who really understood her ambivalence about becoming a doctor. Some days she felt positive that's what she wanted to do; other days she wished she felt free to choose her career path. But her older sister Leila already had disappointed her folks by choosing to become a professor, and Jayla knew they were counting on her. The way things were going, she and Lisa might become best friends.

Sure, they also were different from one another. For one thing, Lisa was white and Jayla was black. That didn't bother Jayla. She had gone to a predominantly white private school, and some of her best friends were white. Jayla smiled at the cliché. "Really, they were," she said aloud, and laughed to herself. Lisa, on the other hand, had never been friends with anyone black, and she sometimes relied on stereotypes when she talked with Jayla. She assumed that Jayla liked hip hop, which she did, but she also liked other types of music, as the playlist on her iPod showed. During the first few days, she had tried to "talk black" to Jayla, using slang and phrases from mainstream media like "Yo! What up?" Jayla was frustrated at first, but she decided to be patient. She felt like Lisa was trying too hard to relate to her based on her race. She gently explained that all young blacks didn't use that type of language. Lisa seemed to understand, and she apologized to Jayla. To be fair, Jayla acknowledged that she also had stereotyped Lisa because she was a white girl from California. She had figured that Lisa would talk like the Valley Girls she saw on TV and in the movies, and Lisa hadn't met that stereotype. But, she sometimes teased Lisa: one time when Lisa asked her opinion about an outfit, Jayla replied in her best Paris Hilton impression: "That's hot." She and Lisa had cracked up. Every now and then, Lisa would still use slang, but Jayla knew she was just playing around.

Jayla didn't think their racial difference was a big deal in their budding friendship. They had confided in each other about topics like being homesick, and their apprehensions about their careers. However, Jayla never felt fully open with Lisa because she was holding back an important piece of information about herself that she'd told only one other person. And, she didn't know if, when, and how she would ever tell Lisa.

Jayla exhaled deeply as her thoughts turned to the main reasons she had come to NESU. In addition to having a great pre-med program, NESU touted its racially diverse student body. This appealed to Jayla because she wanted to develop more friendships with students of color. More important to Jayla, NESU was listed online as a "gay-friendly campus." Jayla had struggled for years with her sexuality, and she had only recently become comfortable with being attracted to females. No one in her family but her older sister Leila knew about that. And, she had promised not to tell Jayla's secret, even though she had encouraged Jayla to tell their parents. Jayla just wasn't sure how her parents would react, since their church had such a strong stance against homosexuality. Indeed, one reason Jayla had tried to suppress her feelings and to be "normal" was because she didn't want to be a sinner, and she didn't want to disgrace her parents. Thanks to Leila, she didn't feel like a bad person, but she still couldn't face her parents yet.

When Jayla was a junior in high school, she visited her sister Leila at her college. They were walking on campus when two girls passed them, walking hand-in-hand, and gazing at one another lovingly. "That is so cool," her sister said. "I'm glad they feel comfortable enough to show their relationship in public." Jayla seized the moment. "I hope I can show that side of myself one day, too," she murmured. Leila stopped abruptly. "What did you say?" she gasped. "You heard me," Jayla said more firmly. "I'm pretty sure that I'm gay." "Oh, Jay," Leila said softly, as she gathered her sister in her arms. "That must be so hard for you." Jayla choked back tears as she nodded slowly.

They talked all night about Jayla's feelings and fears, and her sister had totally supported her. Since that night, they had talked many times. And, Leila had given Jayla lots of resources, including books and articles about black lesbianism. Jayla especially cherished a book by Audre Lorde called *Sister Outsider* because it discussed challenges of being female, black, and lesbian. Some authors referred to a "triple consciousness" of these three oppressed identities that made it hard for black lesbians to find a community of people who would accept them fully. They also wrote about how members of these various social identity groups sometimes forced them to choose or rank these three aspects of their identity. Jayla also had found a wealth of information online, including blogs and discussion groups written by young gay people of varying races. She realized that she wasn't alone and that she wasn't some kind of freak. She hadn't found the nerve yet to form friendships or to explore intimate relationships online, but she was comforted to have those options. Thank goodness she had come out to her sister.

Jayla wished that everyone she would come out to would be so supportive and caring. But, based on what she'd read, she knew it would be hard to predict how people would react. "It's just not fair," she sighed. She knew that she would have to come out again and again and again and again, for the rest of her life. She hoped only that the process would get easier as she repeated it.

Jayla sighed loudly again. "How naïve was I?" she thought. She had fantasized about having a multiracial network of gay and straight friends at NESU with whom she could be herself. She had read that many young people came out when they went to college. And, she figured that once she established an "out" life at school, it would be easier to tell her parents about her sexuality. She was desperately tired of feeling guilty about passing as straight. Her mom asked her almost every time they talked if she had met a nice young man, and Jayla would say she was too busy studying to think about dating. Jayla knew that her parents wanted her to have a positive, loving marriage like theirs, and they were looking forward to becoming grandparents. She dreaded letting them down, and she hated feeling like she was leading them on. She was feeling more and more urgency to tell them the truth.

Her dad had really wanted her to go to his alma mater, a black university. She had decided against that, because she had read online about challenges that some black gay students experience at historically black colleges and universities (HBCUs). And, she had witnessed homophobia and heterosexism in their family's church, which was mainly black. She knew that not all black folks were against homosexuality, and she had read that some HBCUs were becoming more welcoming. However, she hadn't found anything on her dad's college's website that led her to believe that they would welcome her. In contrast, NESU's site included sexual orientation it its diversity statement, and they had a GLBTQ student service center, which her dad's school didn't. However, Jayla felt conflicted about not going to an HBCU, because she also realized that the odds of her finding a black girlfriend would probably be higher at her dad's alma mater. But, she was open to dating women outside of her race. Jayla smiled at the thought, since she hadn't dated ANY woman yet. She basically had pretended to be heterosexual throughout high school, and she'd had a boyfriend during her junior and senior years. Mark hadn't pressured her for sex because he had taken an abstinence pledge in his church. They had kissed a few times, and she had pretended to enjoy it, but she had known since at least middle school that she was attracted to females. She and Mark had agreed to remain friends after they both decided to go to colleges that were far away from each other. Mark was one of her best friends, and he was high on her "coming out" list.

However, her plan to begin a new life by being out at NESU wasn't working out at all. She hadn't anticipated the complex web of challenges that now confronted her. For one thing, she was having a hard time finding signs of that so-called gay-friendly environment at NESU. During orientation, the Director of Jayla's residence hall cautioned girls about having boys in their rooms. She seemed to be trying to be inclusive when she said, "The same rules apply for heterosexuals and homosexuals." However, she blew it by adding: "No one wants to wake up seeing two girls in bed where a man is supposed to be." In Jayla's Intro to Communication class, all of the examples of intimate relationships in the textbook referred to heterosexual couples, and whenever her professor gave examples, she used male and female names. She hoped that the communication and diversity class she was taking next semester would be more inclusive. Most discouraging of all, every time she walked by the GLBTQ center, she saw only white males. She didn't feel comfortable entering that space to talk about her sexuality. She wondered if white lesbian students felt the same way.

Then there was the race thing. Jayla had been so optimistic about meeting students of varying races, especially other black students. When she attended a Black Student Alliance meeting, a guy had smiled at her, and said, "Welcome, my sister." Jayla wondered if he would be so warm if he knew she was gay. She met another black girl named Erika who seemed nice. Erika was a sophomore, and she told Jayla that she would help her get acclimated to NESU. Jayla wanted to take her up on the offer, but she was unsure of how and if she should tell Erika about her sexuality. She noticed another girl at the meeting with a short-cropped haircut who was dressed in masculine clothes, and she wondered if she was gay. "Shut up" she told herself. "You know you shouldn't assume." After all, she certainly didn't "look gay." Her relaxed hair was shoulder length, and she wore the latest fashions. She even had been named "Best Dressed" in high school. After attending the first BSA meeting, Jayla wasn't sure if she would become an active member. Most of the students seemed to know one another very well, even though they were friendly to Jayla and the other new students who were there. However, during the meeting, someone responded to a suggestion by saying, "That's so gay," and almost everyone laughed.

Despite the high percentage of students of color on campus, Jayla often was the only black student or student of color in her classes. Some of the white students seemed awkward around her, and some of her professors seemed to single her out when race-related topics arose. She found herself feeling self-conscious about her race in ways that she'd never experienced, although some of her black friends at church had accused her of being an Oreo because she went to a private high school. They really got on her case when she first started dating Mark, who was white. Fortunately, Lisa was receptive when Jayla expressed some her frustrations about race. She seemed genuinely concerned about Jayla's feelings, which she didn't dismiss or downplay. Jayla was learning that she could depend on Lisa to try to understand her. She had reciprocated when Lisa talked about being one of only two females in a science class where the professor seemed sexist.

Jayla exhaled deeply once again as she turned her mind to her current dilemma. Should she or should she not come out to Lisa? She had been hopeful that her roommate would be open to her sexual identity. After all, Lisa had grown up near San Francisco, which Jayla had heard was one of the most gay friendly cities in the world. Following advice from one website, Jayla had tried to gauge Lisa's attitudes toward homosexuality by asking her about her interests and experiences. During one of their first conversations, she had said, "Sooo, I understand that San Francisco is a really diverse city." Lisa had replied, "Yes, it is. We have so many different cultures there, and the city is so dynamic." "What do you mean," Jayla probed. "Oh, you know," Lisa said, "a lot of different ethnic groups and all kinds of food and music." Jayla wanted to push further, but she didn't want to seem too obvious.

Jayla knew that if she was going to come out to Lisa, her timing was crucial. From what she'd read, if she waited too long, Lisa might feel hurt and betrayed that Jayla had withheld something so important from her. Lisa might not trust her as much. But, if she had told her too soon, Lisa might not have gotten to know other things about Jayla. "It's just not fair," Jayla groaned. Why did she have to worry about disclosing her sexual identity when straight people don't have to even think about it? Of course, Lisa assumed she was straight because Jayla had a boyfriend in high school. One day when they were walking across campus, Lisa had pointed out a tall black guy, and said, "Ooooh, look at him, Jayla. You should try to get with that." Jayla sucked her teeth, and replied, "Lisa, how many times do I have to ask you not to talk like that?" Lisa grinned, and said, "OK. Sorry, girl, but you know I'm right." Jayla shook her head. In a way, she was glad that she could focus on Lisa's lame attempts to talk black as a way to deflect responding to her logical assumption that she would be interested in a guy—a black guy at that. She hadn't told Lisa yet that her high school boyfriend was white. Lisa had gone out on a couple dates since they had become roommates, and she always wanted to talk about them with Jayla. Jayla had managed to avoid or minimize talking about dating, boyfriends, and sex, but she knew that she couldn't do that much longer. After all, these were "normal" topics for female friends their age.

She exhaled deeply again. So, what might happen if she told Lisa? Lisa might be so repelled that she would ask for another roommate. Or, she might shrug it off as no big deal. Or, she might act like it was no big deal, but then become chilly. Or. . . . Jayla knew that guessing was fruitless. However, she then started thinking about the consequences of NOT telling Lisa. How could they deepen their friendship and freely discuss important topics like dating and intimate relationships or other topics that Jayla would have to either avoid or flat out lie about?

Jayla pounded her fist on her pillow. She knew she shouldn't let much more time pass. She had read lots of advice about how to have a "coming out" conversation, and she had rehearsed a couple of opening lines. She even had printed out an article about living with a gay roommate to give Lisa. Lisa was going home for Fall Break, so this would be a good time to tell her and give her time to think about it away from campus. Hmmmm. Maybe she could email Lisa while she was gone, instead of talking to her face-to-face. That might be easier for both of them. "Nah," she thought. That didn't seem right. As Jayla asked herself one more time, "What should I do?" the suite door opened, and Lisa bounded in. She smiled broadly and said, "What up, Jay?"

For Further Thought and Reflection

1. What communicative challenges does Jayla face in developing new relationships at college and in maintaining relationships in her family?
2. Are there certain topics that friends should expect to discuss and confide in one another as they develop a friendship? If so, how might those topics vary according to the friends' age, race, sexuality, and other aspects of social identity? Why or why not?
3. How do you decide when is "the right time" to disclose personal, private information to a new friend?
4. Should Jayla tell Lisa about her sexuality? Why or why not? If she should, how should she tell her? Should she already have told her? Explain.
5. Should Jayla tell her parents about her sexuality? Why or why not? If so, how should she tell them? Should she already have told them? Explain.
6. Do you agree that Jayla has an especially complex challenge with forming friendships at NESU (and other contexts) because of her social identity (i.e., female, black, and lesbian)? Why or why not?

References

Bond, B., Hefner, V., & Drogos, K. (2009). Information-seeking practices during the sexual development of lesbian, gay, and bisexual individuals: The influence and effects of coming out in a mediated environment. *Sexuality & Culture, 13*(1), 32–50.

Gortmaker, V., & Brown, R. (2006). Out of the college closet: Differences in perceptions and experiences among out and closeted lesbian and gay students. *College Student Journal, 40(3),* 606–19.

Lorde, A. (1998). *Sister outsider: Essays & speeches by Audre Lorde.* Freedom, CA: The Crossing Press.

Patton, L., & Simmons, S. (2008). Exploring complexities of multiple identities of lesbians in a Black college environment. Negro Educational Review, 59*(3/4),* 197–215.

Spradlin, A. (1998). The price of passing: A lesbian perspective on authenticity in organizations. Management Communication Quarterly, 11, 598–605.

Ueno, K., Gayman, M., Wright, E., & Quantz, S. (2009). Friends' sexual orientation, relational quality, and mental health among gay, lesbian, and bisexual youth. Personal Relationships, *16(4),* 659–670.

23 Peanut Butter Sandwiches: Making Sense of Acquaintance Rape in Ongoing Relationships

Kate Lockwood Harris

Key Terms

ambiguity of language, consent, naming, rape, sexual violence

---

I love him. I do. He has this goofy, sideways grin. No matter where you are in the room, it always looks like he's smiling just at you. Whenever he makes a PB&J sandwich, he measures out three tablespoons of peanut butter—exactly—for each slice of bread. He sings the Beatles non-stop, especially "Love, Love Me Do," and the words are just a little bit different every time. He's got four skateboards, and he always leaves them in random places in his apartment. He tells the worst jokes, I swear. And he's smart like it's nobody's business. He can have a conversation with just about anyone, anywhere, and make a friend. I love him.

My friend, Maya, can't believe that I love him. Sure, she sees all those things that I see: the charming smile and the neurotic sandwich-making technique and his wit and smarts and penchant for forgetting the words to songs. But she can't believe that I love him. Not after what happened.

It was pretty bad, for sure. And it was wrong, no doubt about it. It shouldn't have happened, but it did.

I talked to one of my friends about it the next day. The first thing she said was, "Why didn't you just kick him or something?" I couldn't answer her question. I figured she thought I'd done something wrong. So I just shut up about it.

I didn't tell anybody about it for a couple of years after that, actually. I didn't know what to say or how to talk about it. I couldn't find a way to explain it. And I was afraid that everybody would blame me because I didn't do something different.

I was so messed up afterwards. Later the night it happened, I cried a lot. I was bleeding and raw. It was so confusing. I ended up drinking a lot for about a year afterwards. I mean, not just a Smirnoff on a Friday night. I had three or four drinks most

181

nights. Margaritas were my favorite, and on weekends I'd just drink until I fell asleep. I was miserable, so depressed that I couldn't get out of bed some mornings.

At the time it happened, he and I had been dating for six months. We were definitely in love, and we told each other so. The day it happened, he and I got together at about 11am. We ran some errands, saw a movie with some of our buddies, and then had lunch. I told him then, over our three-tablespoon peanut butter sandwiches, that I didn't want to have sex that night.

I was as clear as I could have been. Plain as day, really. I said, "I don't want to have sex tonight." I had some really important reasons why I didn't want to, and I told him about them. I'm pretty sure he understood them.

We went back to my place and started to make out. I didn't say no when we got in bed. I didn't say yes either. I was so turned on. Who wouldn't be? He's cute and passionate and smart and sensitive, and he knew—for sure by that point—what got me going. I wanted him, but I didn't want to have sex.

We kept making out for a while, then everything stopped feeling right. I remember clearly what happened next. I was on my back on the bed, staring. I wasn't there. Not emotionally, not mentally. It was like I was watching a movie, and I couldn't believe what was happening. I remember looking so hard at the wallpaper. There was this repeating flower pattern on it, the kind that anybody's mom would have thought was perfect for decorating, but the kind that I found slightly nauseating. It was just a little too happy.

I don't think he was there either. At least not the guy I know. I mean, he was there, but he wasn't. That's part of what's tough about it, I guess. He seemed like a machine on top of me. I usually felt connected to him, but not then. I just lay there, not moving, not saying anything. He just kept going and going and going, fast, hard. Like it was the only thing in the world to him, just like those flowers on the wallpaper were to me in that moment.

Maya says he raped me. I don't know. I mean, yeah, he had sex with me when I hadn't agreed to have sex. And that's pretty much the definition of rape, right? But it just seems more complicated than that. I mean, if I call it rape, that makes him a rapist. He's not a rapist. He's my boyfriend. Yeah, what happened sucked, and what he did was definitely wrong. But rapists belong behind bars. And there's no way I'd be friends with, much less date, a rapist.

I guess most people think if it's rape, you've got to be kicking and screaming. I wasn't doing anything. I was just so shocked that he was doing this after I'd told him I didn't want to. It was like I was totally frozen. He didn't hold me down, but I was pinned to the bed; shock at his behavior, disbelief at his disconnection, and a sense of unreality were weights on my body. Since it happened I've thought about the million things that could have been different. I could have stayed home that night. I could have screamed when I was in bed with him. I'm pretty sure he would have listened. But I thought he had listened earlier in the day when I'd said no. If I made my wishes clear earlier, did I have to restate them? Why didn't he ask if I'd changed my mind?

Maya says I'm blaming myself. I don't think it's my fault that this happened. It takes two to tango, right? So it's at least 50 percent him. I do think there are specific things I could have done differently, like saying something at the time. That's different from thinking I caused it to happen.

Maya thinks it's his fault. In some ways, I agree. He could have made sure I wanted to have sex. And he darn well should have paid attention to what I'd said earlier in the day. I can't figure out why he didn't.

But then again, we'd had sex so many times before. Really, really good sex. I mean, the kind of sex where you're grinning for three days afterwards and you're afraid your grandma is going to be able to tell you got laid because you're so in love with the whole world afterwards.

And we'd gotten into this routine where we read each other's bodies—all that nonverbal stuff. We hardly ever said anything directly about what we wanted. It was like in the movies; we looked into each other's eyes and we could read each other. The way we touched each other said a lot. So that was kind of the norm, just communicating without words.

He wasn't reading me that night, though. Yeah, I was turned on, but when he got on top of me, I totally stopped moving, and that wasn't normal. I have no idea why he didn't notice and why he didn't find out what was going on. I trusted him, you know? I expected him to be paying attention to how I was feeling, and he always had before, even if we weren't talking about it.

Maya took a course about violence in relationships, and she told me that by the time we're done with college, one out of every four women in our class will have been raped. I couldn't believe it. I mean, when I hear "rape" I think about soldiers at war raping women, really brutal stuff. That's definitely rape. Or when someone breaks into your house in the middle of the night and holds a knife or a gun to your neck. That's definitely rape. Or those awful stories you hear about when a whole group of men takes turns on a woman—gang rapes. That's awful. Or maybe even in some really abusive relationship where the guy is threatening to kill his wife, or not let her have any money, or not let her go out to visit her friends, where he's just got total mental control over her. Even that I can see being rape. That's the stuff I think of.

So when Maya says one in four of the women I go to college with will be raped, I just have a hard time believing it. Maya has asked me a lot of questions about what I think rape means. And, like I said, seems like if someone doesn't agree to get it on and then it happens anyway, that's rape.

My friend, Jan, had a similar, confusing experience. A bunch of us went to a party the first month of our first year on campus. Everybody was having fun, and we all had a few drinks. Jan started flirting with this hot guy we'd all been drooling over. He had nice muscles, his eyes always seemed to be smiling, and he had been so considerate to all of us since we met. That made him even hotter, I think. He was definitely a nice guy. Anyway, he and Jan really hit it off. Eventually the two of them disappeared, and we all thought, "Hey, great, they're going to make out for a while." I can't remember how the night ended, but a few months later I talked to Jan. She had gone upstairs with the guy to his room (the party was at his place), and they'd talked and flirted for a while longer. They started kissing and touching, and she said she was so into it. After a while the drinks really started to have a serious effect on her. She said that she started getting really tired, and eventually she passed out. She woke up naked and he was on top of her, in her. She said she was still a little drunk so she just tried to push him off. She eventually fell back asleep, and she said the details were hazy.

"Did he use protection?" I asked.

"No, I don't think so," she said. "And I think he might have given me herpes. I broke out, and I've got to go to the doctor."

"Oh my gosh, Jan. I'm sorry that happened." I asked her what she was going to do about it. "What am I going to do about what?" Jan asked.

"Well, he raped you!" I said to her.

"Well, if he raped me then that means it's all his fault and I don't think that's right," she said.

"You were passed out. How could it not be his fault?" I asked.

"I was drunk. I chose to drink."

"Yeah, but it's not *your* fault."

"No, I don't think it is," said Jan, "But I could have done things differently."

"He *should* have done things differently," I said, angry that this guy had taken advantage of my friend. "Even if you had not passed out, you still can't give consent if you're drunk."

"He was drunk too. How come I can't be responsible for consenting when I'm drunk but he can still be responsible for initiating sex when he's drunk?" she asked.

"Wow," I said, "That's a tough question, I guess." I was uncomfortable. Clearly he'd done something wrong, and it seemed like Jan didn't want to admit it, but I guess she had a point. I mean, he definitely raped her, and I thought she should press charges against him. That's what you do when you're raped, right?

That's what Maya did. One of her friends raped her about seven years ago. She reported the incident, pressed charges against the guy, and he was convicted. Maya is very straightforward when she talks about what happened: It was rape, it was a crime, she's not at fault, and he should be punished. I wish that I had her clarity. For me there seem to be so many more factors to consider.

I know how easy it is for people to blame women for this stuff. They say, "Oh, she was asking for it. She really wanted it, and she just didn't know it. I mean, all women just want a great lay." Sometimes they say things like, "Oh, she's just saying it was rape because it turned out to be bad sex," or, "She just regrets it. Whatever."

So yeah, I don't want my story to be read that way. What happened to me was wrong. And what happened to Jan and to Maya was wrong, too. I worry that if we don't call it rape, or even if we do, people won't take us seriously.

Jan and Maya and I all got together for a picnic lunch the other day. Jan brought fruit salad, Maya brought drinks, and I brought the sandwiches, of course. He made them for us, with three tablespoons of peanut butter each. The three of us talked about all of this. Maya thinks that if we call our experiences rape, people will understand that what happened was horrible and terrible. I can't imagine that I'm dating a rapist. And Jan doesn't want to put her guy behind bars. All of our perspectives make sense to me. Is what happened to Jan really the same as what happened to me? And is what happened to us the same as what happens to women who are raped during wars? Or by gangs? I'm just not sure we have enough words to describe all of this stuff.

For Further Thought and Reflection

1. How is consent communicated? How do we know if a partner consents to having sex?
2. Based on these characters' descriptions, what are the consequences of experiences of nonconsensual sex?
3. When describing experiences like the ones in this story, what does the word "rape" accomplish? In what ways is the word "rape" limited?
4. The theory known as Coordinated Management of Meaning (CMM) suggests that not all communicators make sense of interpersonal interactions in the same way. In order to coordinate the meaning of messages, communicators may consider the context in which the communication occurs as well as what the other person(s) may be trying to accomplish. Using the CMM theory, how can you explain what went wrong between the narrator and her partner?

References

Fisher, B.S., Daigle, L.E., Cullen, F.T., & Turner, M.G. (2003). Acknowledging sexual victimization as rape: Results from a national-level study. *Justice Quarterly, 20,* 535–574.

Gavey, N. (1999). "I wasn't raped but . . .": Revisiting definitional problems in sexual victimization. In S. Lamb (Ed.), *New versions of victims: Feminists struggle with the concept* (pp. 57–81). New York: New York University Press.

Gavey, N. (2005). *Just Sex?: The Cultural Scaffolding of Rape.* New York: Routledge.

Humphreys, T. (2007). Perceptions of sexual consent: The impact of relationship history and gender. *The Journal of Sex Research, 44,* 307–315.

Jervis, L. (2008). An old enemy in a new outfit: How date rape became gray rape and why it matters. In J. Friedman & J. Valenti (Eds.), *Yes means yes!: Visions of female sexual power and a world without rape* (pp. 163–170). Berkeley: Seal Press.

Koss, M.P., Figueredo, A. J., & Prince, R. J. (2002). Cognitive mediation of rape's mental, physical and social health impact: Tests of four models in cross-sectional data. *Journal of Consulting and Clinical Psychology, 70,* 926–941.

Phillips, L. M. (2000). *Flirting with danger: Young women's reflections on sexuality and domination.* New York: New York University Press.

Part V

Change and Continuity in Long-Term Relationships

24

The Queen and Her Bee: Social Aggression in Female Friendship

ERIN K. WILLER

Key Terms

social aggression, meanness, popularity, identity, inter/intragroup comparison

---

Fire in the Hive

Mia desperately smiled with her eyes at Nathaniel as he talked to her, willing his baby browns to connect with her own. *What I wouldn't give to—*

Nathaniel's incessant chatter interrupted her daydreaming, "Just look at her. Not only is she gorgeous, but every girl in the bar wants to *be* her and every guy wants to be *with* her." They both looked across the bar at Layla, who was surrounded by a group of their guy and girl friends who were focused intently on her. "Do you think she likes me?" he asked.

Mia rolled her eyes, "Oh please, what's the huge fascination with Layla?"

Nathaniel looked surprised, "Come on, you know Layla better than anyone. You are best friends. How can you even ask me that question?"

Mia thought, *I'm going to throw up if I have to spend another minute of my life talking about Layla. In sixth grade it was, "Do you think Layla is going to invite me to her birthday party?" Sophomore year it was, "What's Layla wearing to homecoming?" Last week it was Dr. Rifken talking about how Layla is the perfect team leader for her Sudan awareness fundraiser, and now I have to listen to the hottest guy on campus plan their future together. People only like her because they don't know how two-faced she is.* "Whatever, Nathaniel, just make sure you wear a condom." *Whoops, I probably shouldn't have said that.*

Nathaniel looked back at Mia confused, "But I thought Layla had only been with one—"

At that moment Layla caught Mia's eye from across the dance floor and motioned with her head toward the ladies' room. Saved from having to respond to Nathaniel, Mia jumped up to meet Layla in the restroom.

When Mia walked in, Layla was talking to Olivia, a member of Alpha Rho, their rival sorority. *Why is Layla talking to that phony? Look at her with her fake tan and her fake personality.*

"Hey, Mia! I was just talking to Olivia about the fundraiser next weekend," Layla said. Mia rolled her eyes and responded in a tone that clearly communicated her lack of interest as she headed into the bathroom stall, "Greaaat."

When she came out, Olivia had left and Layla was pulling her hair into a ponytail. "What the hell is your problem?" she snapped.

"What do you mean?" Mia asked innocently.

"Why were you so rude to Olivia?"

"I just can't stand her or any of the Alpha Rhos. They're *so* nice; it's disgusting. Nobody's *that* nice. They're not like us Omegas—we might be mean but at least we are real."

"You are really ugly when you act like that," Layla quipped.

How can she say that? She's the one who is the queen of cruelty, Mia thought.

Smiling now, Layla's tone was more understanding, "I hear you, though. Those girls *are* fake. And did you get a look at Olivia's shoes? Hideous!"

They both laughed and Mia watched Layla as she applied a thin layer of gloss to her lips. *How can I love her and hate her so much?*

"So I saw you out there talking to Nathaniel. It looked like you were about to plant one on him the way you were staring at him. What's up with that?"

Should I tell her I'm in love with him? No, she'll steal him away like she does with every guy I like.

Before Mia could answer, Layla said, "He is so hot. Too bad he's from Rockport Valley. My dad would kill me if I went out with someone who's from that part of town! What were the two of you talking about?"

"Nothing much. He said you looked fat though, so I had to set him straight." *Just a little lie will keep her away from him.*

"What?! He must have had too many cocktails. He usually is telling me how hot I am."

The two checked themselves in the full-length mirror one more time. Mia looked at Layla's reflection and then back at her own. *I am hideous.*

"So is my gorgeous best friend accompanying me to after hours?" Layla asked.

Maybe I'll have a chance with Nathaniel if she's not here. "Na, I think I'm going to stay here a little longer."

"Please? I don't want to go without my BFF."

"No, I'm just not feeling it tonight."

"Ug, you are so lame," Layla scoffed as they headed out of the bathroom and back into the bar.

A group was halfway out the door when their roommate Avery yelled, "Hey, you two coming?"

Layla hollered over the music, "I am, but this loser is staying here."

On her way out the door she yelled at Mia, "See you at home! That is if you can avoid the walk of shame for once!"

Mia nervously laughed as everyone in the bar turned to look her way, snickering as they whispered to one another. She watched out the window as her friends piled into cabs while Layla ran around to the drivers giving them directions to the party. *Why does she have to say stuff like that?! It makes me look like such a skank. Why am I even friends with her?* Mia looked around the bar to see if she could find Nathaniel. Maybe talking to him would get her mind off of Layla and her comments. After doing a lap around the dance floor and still not finding him, she bellied up to the bar and ordered a microbrew.

A couple of hours and a few pale ales later, Mia tried to concentrate on walking in a straight line down the sidewalk that led to her house. She still was frustrated with Layla but thought that maybe she was being too sensitive. *Layla has been my best friend since we were little kids. Sure she can be mean, but she was there for me when I was so depressed I couldn't even get out of bed two years ago.* Mia stumbled a little, which interrupted her thought. She realized that she was about to pass Nathanial's apartment. Although her conscience told her she should head straight home to bed, she still was disappointed that she did not have a chance to talk with him because he apparently had left the bar to go to an after-hours party. *Maybe I'll just see what he's up to. There's no harm in that.* She knocked on the door and Nathanial's roommate answered the door. "Hey, Griffen, is Nathaniel home?"

Surprised to see her, Griffen responded, "Hi Mia. I'm not sure. I just got home. You can go check his room if you want."

Oh my goodness, his bedroom! "Ok, thanks!" Mia headed down the hallway, running her fingers through her hair and popping a mint into her mouth. She lightly knocked on the door. No one answered but she heard the T.V. murmuring inside. "Hey Nath you in here?" she said while turning the doorknob. As soon as she did, she wished she didn't. The room was a flurry as the sheets torpedoed up to cover the bodies on the bed. "Oh my goodness, sorry!" Mia screeched. *He has a girl in here. Run!*

Although she wanted to slam the door, she stood frozen after catching a glimpse of a tattooed Omega that matched the one on her own midriff. Mia's mind drifted back to freshman year when her pledge class headed to Tenacious Ink to have their letters branded on their bodies after receiving bids from Epsilon Omega. The other girls got their tattoos on their ankles, but she and her best friend thought it would be classier to have the letters on their stomachs where they could cover them.

"Mia, GET OUT OF HERE!" Her fond trip down memory lane was interrupted, snapping her back to reality. She looked up and the tattoo now was covered but Layla's face was not.

Sweetening the Sting

Layla slinked out the front door of Nathaniel's apartment, hoping no one would hear her leave. As soon as the door clicked shut behind her, she madly texted Mia, "OMG, that was so awkward! So sorry you had to see that!" *Please God let Mia see the humor in the situation. She's been so stressed out lately with school. Please don't let her have one of her usual freak-outs,* Layla thought. She stared at her phone but got no response. *I hope this means she is sleeping and not sitting up waiting to lecture me about my inappropriate behavior.* As she turned the key to the front door of her house, Layla could see a silhouette lying on the couch inside watching T.V. When she walked in, she was relieved to find that it was Avery and not Mia.

"Look who it is coming home at 4 A.M.!" Avery teased.

"Yeah, yeah. I was at—" Layla began.

"Oh I KNOW where you were. Mia came stomping in about an hour and a half ago. She filled me in on your little 'run in,'" Avery said while making air quotes with her fingers.

"She wasn't mad, was she? Wait, where is she? In her room sleeping?" Layla whispered.

"Oh no, she came in fuming about how you always steal every guy she likes away from her."

"Wait, she really likes Nathaniel? Not that she really has a chance with him, but she can *have* him. He's fun, but not exactly my type."

"Well, apparently she is in love with him."

"Oh great," Layla said rolling her eyes. "Where did she go? I have to talk to her and try to smooth things over before she refuses to talk to me."

"Why do you even care? Nobody likes her, because she is just plain nasty. She said she had to get out of here because she wasn't sure what she would do, and I quote, 'if I have to see that whore.'"

Whore? She better not have told Avery about Jamie and Dillon. "What else did she say?"

Tentatively, Avery said, "Ah, nothing much."

Sensing Avery was lying, Layla thought, *I knew Mia couldn't keep a secret about what happened with the guys.*

"She just got her backpack and left."

Exhausted, Layla said, "I'm going to bed. I am not going to try to track her down at this time of the morning." On her way to her room she noticed something was missing from the wall in the hallway. *She took down the picture of us in Cancun? Oh boy, this is not going to be pretty.*

Lying in bed thinking about what she was going to say to Mia, Layla decided to text her one more time. "I'm really sorry about Nathaniel. I had no idea how you felt about him." She paused before pushing send. "Let's talk tomorrow. Love you."

Layla woke up and checked her phone immediately. Still no response or call from Mia. *I need a latte before I can deal with her.* She walked around the corner to the Coffehouse.

As soon as she walked in, Carson, Layla and Mia's chemistry lab partner from two semesters ago, shouted "Hey LAY-la, late night last night?!"

Shocked, she turned looking at him confused. *What the. . . .* Without answering she made a beeline toward the barista's counter to avoid his question. *He's just being an idiot right? He couldn't possibly know about what happened last night.*

Not wanting to have to see him on her way out the door, Layla decided to drink her coffee there and waste some time on the Internet. After perusing the university's news website and checking the latest totals for the Sudan awareness fundraiser, she glanced over to see if Carson had left yet. *Darn, why won't that moron leave?* Needing to waste some more time, she logged onto her Facebook account. As she scrolled down her homepage, she saw the typical status updates—political rants that made her blood boil, complaints about the score of last night's football game, ridiculous posts about mundane activities. *Who cares? Why do people write—*

Her complaining was interrupted by a status update that slapped her in the face: "Mia Wallace is disgusted by what she has just seen." Carson had commented in response to Mia's post, asking what had disgusted her. Mia's response read, "My slut of a best friend."

Layla's mouth hung open and her eyes began to well. *She didn't! Oh my goodness, how many people have seen this?* She clicked on Mia's profile so that she could look at the list of Mia's Facebook friends. *Oh no, not Jose, my secret crush! And Dr. Rifken!* Layla also noticed that Mia's profile picture was no longer a shot of the two of them at last week's tailgate, but a photo Mia had taken of herself looking sullen. After clicking around on Mia's profile some more, Layla found that Mia had untagged her in all of her pictures and that all of the ones of the two of them had been deleted completely. *I am going to make her pay. Doesn't she know she has messed with the wrong person?* Layla stood up with purpose and headed toward the door.

"Leaving so soon LAY—," Conner began.

Before he could finish Layla pointed her finger at him and said, "Shut. Up."

Cowering, Conner replied with his voice cracking a bit, "I'm s-s-sorry Layla."

As soon as she was out the door, she thought, *Poor Conner. He is just an innocent bystander.* She turned around and went back inside where Conner still had a shocked look on his face. "Look Conner, I'm sorry I snapped at you. I'm just really angry right now."

"I'm sorry for giving you a hard time Layla," he said remorsefully. "And I'm sorry about Mia's status update. I figured she was joking, since the two of you are so close."

"Thanks, Conner. I have to go see if I can fix this mess."

On her way home Layla's phone incessantly chattered with text message alerts. One from her friend Jasmine read, "Girl, sounds like you had fun last night!!!"

Oh great, the gossip queen knows?!

Another one from her sorority president said, "You need to get Mia to remove her Facebook post ASAP."

Oh my gosh, the reputation of the sorority! I've worked so hard for people to see us the smart girls who are committed to community service, not the ones who are always drunk and sleeping around! I have to make this right!

Layla was on the phone. As the she listened she thought to herself, *Be assertive, but don't flip out; be understanding, but don't act like a pushover.* Just as she suspected, Mia's phone went to voicemail. Layla cleared her throat and left a message: "Mia it's me. I wanted to tell you one more time that I am very sorry about Nathaniel. I also wanted you to know that even though I understand that you are hurting, it was totally uncool for you to post what you wrote about me on Facebook. You need to remove what you wrote immediately. I know I can forgive you for what you have done, and I hope you can forgive me. This is the last message I am going to leave. I hope you don't make a stupid decision and end our friendship over this. Goodbye." *Whoops, I was doing so well until that last part. Oh well, at least she knows I am serious.*

Bumbled Bee

Three weeks after Layla had left the message, Mia lie in the dark room of her dad's house where she had been staying, and listened to what Layla had to say one last time before pushing delete. *Who does she think she is? She hopes I "don't make a stupid decision." Man, she is SO stuck up. Whatev. I can't stand her or any of those Omegas anymore.* All of them had taken Layla's side and refused to speak to Mia. She had not been to an Epsilon Omega function since the night of their falling out. Although she had been spending a lot of time in bed sleeping, when she did go out she hung around with a new group of friends who, despite their reputation for skipping class and their propensity for using designer drugs, accepted her for who she was. As she lay alone in the dark, she replayed everything that happened, not only on that night, but also over the course of their friendship. *The time when we were 12 and she teased me about my bubble butt in front of everyone. . . . In high school when she told Jackson Jones about my crush on Beyonce. . . . Last winter when she invited Avery to her parent's condo in the mountains but not me.* The more she thought, the angrier she got. She picked up her phone thinking, *It's time for me to teach that little backstabber a lesson.*

Bee Keeping?

Layla was sitting at the kitchen table when her mom walked in from the garage, "Oh, hi sweetheart. I didn't know you were coming home today."

"I just needed to get away for the day." Before her mom could ask her what she needed to get away from, Layla's story of what had been going on with Mia flooded out of her mouth. She of course edited this version, saying that Mia had burst in while she was watching T.V. with Nathaniel rather than having sex with him.

When Layla stopped to catch her breath, her mom shook her head and said, "Why are girls so mean? Just yesterday two of those Rockport Valley women drove by in a big old fancy Land Rover. I swear they were laughing and pointing at my Nissan parked in the driveway. And then at work, Justine told my boss I took an extra half an hour lunch break. What can I say? Girls will be girls."

"Mom. This is about me," Layla snapped.

"Sorry dear. What are you going to do?"

"I don't know. At first I just wanted to get back at Mia for what she wrote on Facebook about me. But now I am starting to feel sorry for her. I know she has had to go through a lot in her life. Plus, she's got really low self-esteem. She's ruined so many friendships over the years. I never thought ours would be one of them. For now, I just think it's best if I stay away from her."

"I would just hate for your relationship with Mia to be ruined over this, Layla. You've been friends your whole life. Why don't you just try calling her one more time," her mom said picking up Layla's phone that was lying on the table. Mia stared at the phone for a few seconds, and then to her surprise, it rang. Her mom looked at the caller I.D. and then said, "Speak of the devil."

For Further Thought and Reflection

1. Socially aggressive communication includes those messages that are damaging to a person's sense of self and/or her relationships with others. Mia and Layla both communicate in ways that are socially aggressive. How is their social aggressiveness both similar and different? Why do you think each of them communicates in the mean ways that she does?

2. Mia and Layla are not the same in regard to their degree of popularity within their social network. What characteristics do you think contribute to their social status? How do you think their social aggressiveness potentially factors into their popularity?

3. Mia compares herself to others inside and outside of her social network. How do these comparisons relate to her social aggressiveness?

4. Mia and Layla respond differently to one another's social aggression both mentally and communicatively. What factors do you think contribute to these different emotional and behavioral responses?

5. Layla's mom suggests that "girls will be girls," a common answer to the question "Why are girls so mean?" Researchers suggest that there are not significant differences between males and females when it comes to perpetrating indirect forms of aggression. Why do you think people perceive females as more socially aggressive than males?

References

Crick, N.R., & Grotpeter, J.K. (1995). Relational aggression, gender, and social-psychological adjustment. *Child Development, 66,* 710–722.

Hawley, P.H. (2007). Social dominance in childhood and adolescence: Why social competence and aggression may go hand in hand. In P.H. Hawley, T.D. Little, & P.C. Rodkin (Eds.), *Aggression and adaptation: The bright side to bad behavior* (pp. 1–29). Mahwah, NJ: Lawrence Erlbaum Associates.

Underwood, M.K. (2003). *Social aggression among girls.* New York: Guilford.

Werner, N.E., & Crick, N.R. (1999). Relational aggression and social-psychological adjustment in a college sample. *Journal of Abnormal Psychology, 108,* 615–623.

Willer, E.K., & Cupach, W.R. (2008). When "sugar and spice" turn to "fire and ice": Factors affecting the adverse consequences of relational aggression among adolescent girls. *Communication Studies, 59,* 415–429.

Willer, E.K., & Cupach, W.R. (in press). The *meaning* of girls' social aggression: Nasty or mastery? In W.R. Cupach & B.H. Spitzberg (Eds.), *The dark side of close relationships—II.* New York: Routledge.

Willer, E.K., & Soliz, J. (in press). Face needs, intragroup status, and women's reactions to socially aggressive face threats. *Personal Relationships.*

25

Who's the Parent Now? When Adult Children Become Caregivers for Parents

Julia T. Wood

Key Terms

parent-child relationships, gender roles, emotional conflicts, venting, honesty, sandwich generation

---

When I was nine years old, I was very sick with mumps. I was miserable—achy, uncomfortable, and feverish. I couldn't speak without strain and even swallowing was painful. I remember my mother sitting with me for hours on end. She rubbed my forehead with a cool washcloth to ease the fever and she stroked my swollen neck gently. Although I didn't realize it then, mother was neglecting other things she'd planned to do, in order to care for me. Perhaps she resented me (or my illness) for intruding on her plans; perhaps she felt frustrated at having to nurse me; perhaps she was worried about what she wasn't getting done while she sat by my bedside. If so, she didn't show those feelings. I never sensed any resentment as she sat patiently with me.

The scene I've just described was replayed 32 years later, only the second time I was the one sitting by my mother's bedside, trying to ease her pain from a terminal disease that would too soon take her from me. As I cared for her, I felt sadness and deep love for this woman who had given birth to me and nurtured me all of my life. Yet, I also felt resentment, frustration, and anger. I resented her needs because they interfered with my family plans and my professional responsibilities. I was frustrated by the unpredictability that her illness injected into my world. And I was angry at her for not acting like my mother—not taking care of me, putting her needs aside for mine—and for reversing our roles so that I was now acting like a mother to her and she was acting like a needy child.

Most of all, I felt guilty—horribly, wrenchingly guilty for feeling resentment, frustration, and anger toward my mother. I despised myself for not lovingly giving her unbounded time and comfort. Why couldn't I be as selfless for her as she had been for me?

During the process of taking my mother through her final passage and recovering from her death, I learned many things about what was happening in me and between us. I learned that the mixture of feelings I had—love, sadness, resentment, frustration, anger, guilt—were typical of many children who become caregivers for sick or dying parents. I learned that what I felt didn't make me a horrible person, and that my feelings were normal. The case that follows illuminates what I discovered about relationships in which children assume the role of parents with their own parents. The case, however, is about far more than my personal experience. It reflects insights from counselors and research on general patterns in relationships in which adult children care for parents.

* * * * *

"It's not that I don't want to take care of her; it's that I don't have the time," Kate says in an effort to explain to her therapist what she is feeling about her mother who moved into her home two months ago. "I mean, I still have my job and my marriage to Mark and our two children—those responsibilities haven't gone away just because mother is living with us and needs constant care."

"Are you saying that if you had more time, you'd be happy to take care of your mother?" Sylvia asks.

Kate nods. "Yes, of course. I'm not a selfish person."

"Is that what it feels like to you—that it would be selfish not to want to care for your mother?" Sylvia asks. Sylvia anticipates that Kate will equate not wanting to do everything for her mother with being selfish. The role of women in Western culture is so firmly tied to caring for others that it's hard for any woman not to feel she's selfish if she doesn't want to do that.

"Of course. I'd want to do it if I had the time." Kate feels compelled to answer this way, but part of her is relieved that her job and family limit how much she can do for her mother. She doesn't mind fixing meals and doing laundry or talking with her mother. Other parts of care giving, however, do bother her. She dreads helping her mother in the bathroom and despises cleaning up when her mother loses control in her bed. That disgusts her, but she berates herself for these feelings. They seem so heartless.

"Do you think your mother never resented taking care of you?"

"Of course not. She was always there for me."

"So maybe she did what you needed even if she resented it," Sylvia suggests. "Does that mean she was somehow less caring or less loving?"

Kate ponders the question. She's a mother now, too, and there are times when she is frustrated by her children's needs, or resents their demands on her time and energy. She tries to hide those feelings, but sometimes she does resent her children, just as she sometimes resents her mother.

"If love is doing only what we want to do, it's not very admirable," Sylvia says. "Perhaps a more mature, authentic kind of love is doing what others need even when we don't enjoy it."

"Maybe," Kate allows. "But it seems dishonest to act like you don't mind doing something when really you do."

"Okay, let's play that out. What would be the point of telling your mother you don't like doing some things—like changing her bed when she's dirtied it? Would that do you any good? Would it do her any good?"

"No," Kate admits. "But sometimes I just feel the need to express my anger or frustration about all of her needs and how they fall on me."

"Nothing wrong with that," Sylvia replies. "And this is a safe place for it. You need somewhere where you can vent your anger and frustration without hurting your mother and without feeling guilty yourself. You can do that with me; you can do it with your friends; you can do it with Mark. And you should."

"It just seems so selfish to feel anything but a desire to help her," Kate says. "I feel like a terrible person if I get angry when I have to rearrange my schedule for her or when I get disgusted about cleaning up after her. Those aren't nice feelings."

"So who says all of our feelings are nice?" Sylvia asks. "Does it mean you don't do what she needs? Of course not. You do it, in spite of anger or disgust. That's real love, not the storybook kind. Give yourself permission to have those feelings and express them in safe places where they won't hurt your mother."

"What I'd really like to do is express that anger to Sandy," Kate mutters. Her brother, Sandy, lives in the same town, but he never invited their mom move in with him. Actually, it would have been easier for him because his and Alice's children are older—both in high school—and their home is larger. But when she and Sandy talked about the fact that their mom couldn't take care of herself anymore, both of them had just assumed Kate and Mark would make room in their home. When Kate had suggested tentatively that maybe their mom could live 6 months of the year with each of them, Sandy had dismissed the suggestion, saying it was better for their mom to live in one place.

Since their mom moved in with Kate's family, Sandy has stopped by once a week for a short visit, and he sometimes calls between visits. What infuriates Kate most is how much her mother appreciates the little that Sandy does for her. Just last week he stopped by for only 30 minutes. After he left, Kate remembers her mother said, "It's so good of Sandy to make time out to visit me. I know how busy he is." Kate had thought "He gets praised for giving her thirty lousy minutes, and I spend hours every day taking care of her!"

Sylvia nods. Kate's situation is like that of many adult women who are caring for parents. Often there are brothers, but most don't volunteer to take over any of the care giving. Sometimes they help with expenses, but they seldom take much responsibility for the day-to-day nursing and personal care. Almost always, that responsibility falls on daughters or daughters-in-law whose husbands don't provide hands-on care for their own parents.

Sylvia reflects on the lack of change in gender roles regarding caring for others. Although the feminist movement enlarged women's political, economic, and professional opportunities, it hasn't transformed the traditional expectation that women are the primary caregivers of young children and anyone else who needs care. Both women and men continue to expect that women will do it. This sometimes creates extraordinary pressures on women in what's been dubbed the "sandwich generation"—those people who are caring for children at the same time they are caring for parents and parents-in-law. When those people are also engaged in full-time work outside of the home, the strains can be overwhelming. When more women were full-time homemakers and mothers, it was less of a strain for them to take care of relatives. Then too, Sylvia realizes, life-spans have expanded significantly, so more people are living to ages when they require assistance.

The problem is not just men who don't assume equal responsibility for caring for parents and in-laws. It's equally women who expect so much of themselves. Kate is like many of her clients, who are stretched to the breaking point to meet their responsibilities to jobs, children, husbands, and elderly parents. And still they often feel guilty for feeling strained, angry, or resentful. Sylvia wishes she could do more to help her women clients challenge the internalized feelings that they not only should care for others, but should always feel happy to do so.

"We can't control what Sandy does—or doesn't do, so let's focus on what we can control," Sylvia redirects the conversation. "Tell me more about what your resentment and frustration and anger are like?"

"Well, I just feel like I can't do it all and like I shouldn't have to," Kate begins. "It's like I have to fix all of her special meals and keep track of her medications and make sure she gets to her doctors' appointments, and everything, and nobody is taking care of me."

That's what Sylvia had been waiting to hear. Sylvia imagined Kate probably felt some sense of betrayal that her mother is no longer mothering her.

"So, not only do you have the responsibility of taking care of someone who is needy, but that person is the very one who is supposed to take care of you," Sylvia says.

"I miss my mother so much. She always took care of me, even after I was grown up and married. She was the one who would always support me and make time for me and help me."

"And now she can't do that for you and you have to do it for her? Is that what it feels like?"

Kate nods, dabbing her eyes with a tissue. "I feel like I don't have a mother anymore. It's like she's another of my children, and that feels so strange."

Sylvia nods. One of the most difficult issues when children become caregivers for parents is role reversal. Suddenly, the have to watch and protect the parents and oversee daily schedules in the home.

"Sometimes I feel like I've *become* my mother," Kate continues. "I take her dinner to her room and start talking to her, but it's her voice—not mine—that comes out. I sound like she did when she was mothering me—her words, her tones, even her gestures and facial expressions."

"That makes sense. She's your primary role model for caring. When you step into that role, it's natural for you to act like she did," Sylvia says. "Do you also hear your mother in yourself when you're mothering your children?"

"Yes, but they are children and I am *their* mother. I'm not my mother's mother; I just act like it, and she acts like my child." Kate thinks about what happened this morning before she left for her session with Sylvia. After helping her mother bathe, Kate explained that she would be gone until about 5 or 6 PM that evening. Her mother had asked if she could have tomato soup and a grilled cheese sandwich for lunch. Kate cringed, thinking about that interaction. Why would a 72 year-old-woman have to ask permission to have what she wants for lunch? Yet, the incident wasn't unusual. Her mother often asked permission for the most ordinary things as if Kate were the parent who controlled her activities.

"That's the hard part. Being with her but not having her be the person she's always been for you," Sylvia empathizes. She knows that Kate is experiencing both the loss of her mother as a mother and of her own role as her mother's child. It's a double whammy. "And it's really hard to become that person for her, to be her mother when you so much still want her to be yours."

"It really is," Kate agrees. "After more than 40 years with our roles one way, it's so hard to deal with turning them upside down. I don't want to lose our mother-daughter relationship just because she needs a lot of help now."

"Okay, that's a good thought. Let's build on it by talking about ways you might let go of the mothering role with her," Sylvia says. "Can you define the parts of your relationship with your mother in which you feel most pushed into the mother role?"

Working together over the next two sessions, Kate and Sylvia figured out that helping her mother with personal care (baths, shampoos, changing clothes) made Kate feel like her mother's mother. Fixing meals didn't make her uncomfortable because Kate or Mark fixed meals for the family anyhow. In conversation with Sylvia, Kate also realized there were benefits to having her mother live with them. She liked talking with her mom about daily life, and enjoyed seeing her mother interact with the children.

Following her discussions with Sylvia, Kate talked to Mark and then the two of them talked with her mom and Sandy and Alice. Together, they decided that they could afford to hire a nurse's aide who would come to the house for three hours each day to provide personal assistance to her mother. This relieved Kate of some of the responsibilities she disliked and allowed her to spend more time with her mother in ways that both of them enjoyed.

There are still days when Kate feels some resentment or anger. Sometimes the aide has to cancel and Kate is back to juggling her schedule and providing personal care to her mother. Sometimes she still resents Sandy. And there are moments when she deeply misses having a mother who puts aside everything for her. Even so, letting go of the bulk of mothering tasks has reduced the strain on Kate and revived parts of their mother-daughter relationship.

Discussion Questions

1. This case raises questions about whether honesty is always advisable when communicating in personal relationships. Do you think Kate should tell her mother she sometimes feels resentful, frustrated or angry? Does not telling her mother about these feelings foster a dishonest relationship?
2. This case points out that women continue to assume primary responsibility for care giving. What aspects of socialization and education might be used to foster more balance in care giving in our society?
3. In Kate's situation, it was possible to hire professional help to reduce the burdens on Kate and to diminish Kate's need to be a mother to her mother. How might Kate have coped if hiring help had not been feasible?
4. Sylvia suggests that an admirable, mature love is based on more than doing what one feels like for another person. To what extent do you think "real" love includes meeting obligations and acting beyond personal desires?

Selected References

Aronson, J. (1992). Women's sense of responsibility for the care of old people: "But who else is going to do it?" *Gender and Society, 6,* 8–29.

Gleckman, A. (2009). *Caring for our parents.* New York: St. Martin's Press.

Wood, J.T. (1994). *Who cares?: Women, care and culture.* Carbondale, IL: Southern Illinois University Press.

26   "I'm Sorry for Your Loss": Communicating with Those Who Are Bereaved

PAIGE W. TOLLER

Key Terms

self-disclosure, grief, social support, dialectical tensions

It was a beautiful spring day in May. The tulips and daffodils were blooming in brilliant shades of yellow, pink, and red. The sky was robin's egg blue and full of fluffy, white clouds. For 20-year-old Libby Johnston, it may as well have been a cold December day. Libby was standing in Oak Park Cemetery, trying to pay attention to their pastor's reading of the 23rd Psalm. Her mother's casket was only a few feet away, draped in dozens of red roses, her mom's favorite flower. Libby's dad stood next to her, tightly gripping her hand in his. To Libby, her father's face looked as numb and cold as she felt on the inside. The pastor finished reading and friends and family lined up to offer their condolences to Libby and her father. People began shaking her hand or hugging her, whispering phrases such as "at least she's not in pain anymore" or "I'm so sorry for your loss." Libby tried to say "thank you" but her throat was dry and her lips seemed to be glued shut. She just silently nodded her head as if to agree with what people were saying. Next to her, she noticed that her dad struggled to talk and was nodding his head as well.

Toward the end of the line, Susan Lawrence stood and waited to hug Libby, her best friend for more than 15 years. Susan and Libby had known each other since they were in the same kindergarten classroom. Through games of hop-scotch, braces, first crushes, homecoming dances, and the college application process, Susan and Libby had been inseparable friends. Over the years Susan had grown close to Libby's parents as well. Libby's mom, Marianne, had spent many afternoons baking cookies and giggling with the two girls about the cute neighbor boy down the street. Marianne had always been there to cheer them on during their volleyball games or yell right along with them at varsity football games. Six months ago, while on break from college, Susan had been at the Johnston's home, helping Libby and her mom bake Christmas cookies, when the doctor called and told Marianne she had late stage ovarian cancer. For the rest of that afternoon, Susan, Libby, and Marianne sat in the living room, holding each other and crying. From that day until the end of winter break, when Susan was not with her own family, she was at the Johnston's.

Although Marianne's type of cancer was aggressive, she told Libby and Susan that she was going to "beat this thing" and for nearly six months, she courageously went through chemo and radiation. Her shiny black hair fell out in large clumps and her bright, green eyes began to sink back into her face. Her petite frame became even smaller as she shrunk down to barely 95 pounds. To Susan, Marianne's bubbly personality seemed to wither as well. Susan also watched her friend Libby change. Normally adventurous and outgoing, Libby became quiet most of the time. Instead of going back to the university for the spring semester, Libby moved back home and spent every minute by her mother's side. Susan visited the Johnston's house as much as she could, but she was also a college student and her school was nearly two hours away. At least every other day Susan sent a text to Libby asking her how things were going. Sometimes Libby responded within a few minutes; other times Susan's text messages went unanswered.

The line of people had shrunk and Susan finally reached Libby. Susan was trying to think of something to say to Libby, but nothing came to mind. Susan swallowed the huge lump in her throat and managed to croak out "Hey, Libbers." Libby's eyes began to spill over, "Hey Susie-Q. I'm glad you're here." They both stood there for a few seconds before Susan opened her arms and reached out to Libby. Grabbing on to each other, they held one another and cried for what seemed like a very long time. Noticing that there were others waiting to speak to Libby, Susan mouthed "call me" and began to walk away. Libby nodded and began shaking the next person's hand.

Two months had passed and summer was in full swing. Except for a few emails, Susan and Libby had not been in contact since the funeral. The Fourth of July was in two days and Susan was looking forward to a weekend of cooking out and boating. She had recently reconnected with Jeff, a former high school sweetheart, and was excited that he was coming to town to spend the weekend with her and her family. Jeff and Susan had dated for two years in high school before breaking up at the end of their senior year. Although Susan had dated other guys while in college, none of them seemed to measure up to Jeff. Apparently Jeff felt the same way about her and had contacted her via Facebook a few months ago. Things were going well between them.

As excited as she was about the upcoming weekend, Susan was concerned about Libby. She had stopped over at the Johnston's a few days ago to see if Libby wanted to go boating with them during the holiday weekend. She thought maybe it would do Libby some good to get out of the house and hang out with people her own age. It seemed that Libby and her dad were attached at the hip these days. Libby rarely went anywhere and, if she did, her dad was usually with her. Jeff was bringing Mark, his college roommate, home with him for the weekend, and Susan thought Mark and Libby might hit it off. As she walked up the sidewalk, Susan noticed Mr. Johnston mowing the yard. Always thin, he had lost even more weight. Susan wasn't sure, but she thought his hair even looked a little grayer. Susan waved to him and he stared at her for a few seconds before finally waving back. "That's odd. Doesn't he recognize me?" thought Susan, as she rang the doorbell.

Libby opened the door to Susan's smiling face. "Hey Libbers, what's up?" Susan cheerfully chirped. "Not much. Come on in. I'm just doing some laundry." "Lib, I can't believe you have any laundry to do. Every time I see you you're in the same pair of pajama pants!" Susan joked. Libby smiled weakly as Susan continued talking, "Anyway, girlfriend, you'd better make sure your cutest tank top and shorts are clean, because I know someone who's dying to meet you. His name is Mark Walters and he is super cute. He's a communication studies major at Eastern Tech and is on the rugby team. Oh, did I mention that he's Jeff's roommate and that he's super cute? Lib, are you listening? Hey Lib, I'm talking to you!" Libby was staring off into space; something Susan had noticed her doing a lot the last two months.

"Huh? What? Oh yeah, Suz, um, I don't know if I'll be able to go with you or not. I'm not sure what Dad's got going on this weekend." Trying to hide her disappointment, Susan said softly, "Well, why don't you come out with us for a little while." "Okay, Suz. Well, I think I need to go put stuff in the dryer. Guess I'll see ya around." "Uh, yeah, sure Lib. See you around. I'll let myself out." As Libby went into the laundry room, Susan walked toward the front door. What was up with Libby? Sure, Susan realized that her mom had just died and both Libby and her dad were really missing Marianne, but it wasn't like Libby to not be excited about going boating. Libby was a fantastic water skier and usually was out on the water as much as possible in the summer. Libby just wasn't the same person anymore, and Susan wished she knew how to get her old friend back.

Tossing clothes into the dryer, Libby Johnston was angry. Her best friend Susan had just left after bugging her to go on a boating date with some new guy this coming weekend. Dating! As if Libby cared about dating these days! Frankly, Libby didn't care much about anything except spending time with her dad and taking care of him. "I can't believe Susan thought I'd want to go boating. Gosh, my mom's only been gone two months and she acts all upset because I don't want to drop everything and go hang out with her and some guy I don't even know. Boy, she's got a lot of nerve!"

Libby continued to angrily hang clothes in her parents' closet until she ran across one of her mom's old bathrobes hanging toward the back. As her eyes began to swell with tears, Libby lifted the robe to her nose, hoping that it might still smell of her mom's favorite lotion. She breathed in deeply, and rubbed the soft cotton against her cheek. Tears began to spill onto the robe and that all too familiar ache began to spread through Libby's chest. God, if she could only hug her mom one more time. If she could only sit and talk with her mom just once more. She would give anything just to have one more minute with her mom; one more second even.

In some ways, her mom was still with her, as Libby felt her presence everywhere. Everything at home somehow reminded Libby of her mom. Her mom's garden in the backyard was blooming with the perennials her mom planted years ago. Every time she cleaned up the kitchen, Libby thought of the many hours she and her mom spent cooking and laughing. Even going through the Starbucks drive-thru made Libby think of her mom and how much her mom loved coffee. Although Libby was glad she could still feel her mom's presence, sometimes it made that ache inside hurt even more.

Many times Libby would talk to her mom throughout the day. As she cleaned the bathrooms or cooked dinner, Libby would often say out loud, "Well Mom, looks like the china cabinet needs a good dusting" or "What do you think Dad wants for dinner tonight?" While her dad was at work, she would sometimes go into their bedroom and sit in her mom's favorite rocking chair. She would grab one of her mom's favorite sweaters, hold it close, and sob and sob until she had no tears left. Even though she and her father had cleaned out her mother's closet and taken things to Goodwill, there were a few items that were just too hard for her or her dad to donate. Libby was so glad she had kept one of her mom's old sweaters. It was almost like her mom was still there. Almost . . . but not quite.

Libby wished she could talk to Susan about her mom and some of the things she was feeling, but she didn't think Susan would understand. Susan would probably think something was wrong with Libby if she knew that Libby talked out loud to her dead mother. Heck, sometimes Libby thought it *was* crazy to talk to her mom. Sane people didn't talk to dead people, or hold their old sweaters, right? All Libby knew was that it made her feel better to talk to her mom throughout the day and hug her things, and right now she was willing to do anything to make the pain a little less.

Susan had a great time boating with Mark and Jeff, although it wasn't the same without Libby there. In the weeks that followed, Susan texted Libby every now and then or left her voicemails, but she didn't really know what to talk to Libby about. About a month after they went boating, Susan ran into Libby at the grocery store. As they greeted each other Susan couldn't help but notice how awkward it was between them. "Hey Lib, how's it going? What are you up to these days?"

"Oh hey Suz, not much. How are things going with you?"

"Oh, pretty good I guess. I've been working at the Gap this summer. Great employee discount you know."

"Oh yeah, I bet so. Are you still dating, uh, um, gosh, sorry. I forgot his name."

"Jeff. Yeah, we're still together. He's a really great guy."

"I bet so. Well, it was good to see you."

"Yeah, Lib, it was good to see you, too. Well, gotta run. See ya around."

As she walked toward the checkout, Susan couldn't believe that she'd just had a conversation with her best friend. It was like talking to a stranger. Libby used to be so bubbly and talkative, but now was so quiet and withdrawn that it made Susan uncomfortable to be around her. Susan just didn't know what to say to her. What do you say to someone who seems completely lost and heartbroken? How do you talk to someone that you don't even know anymore? Would it be okay to bring up Libby's mom in front of her? Susan really missed Libby and wanted to spend time with her again, but she didn't know how to connect with Libby anymore.

At the other end of the store, Libby was also upset about their conversation, but she was glad that Susan had at least spoken to her. In the last few weeks, Libby noticed that people she knew were avoiding her. Just last Friday one of her high school classmates had seen her at the mall and acted as if she didn't know her. At least Libby thought that's what happened. Maybe the girl really hadn't recognized her, although they had been on the cheerleading squad together for two years. Good grief, what was wrong with her? Was she becoming paranoid?

Anyway, what was the deal with Susan? Before her mom had died Susan was incredibly supportive and was around a lot. Now that her mom was gone, it seemed that Susan rarely stopped over and was always nervous around her. Of all of the people that she thought would have been there for her, Susan was at top of her list. Now it seemed like Susan didn't even know her anymore. Great, not only had she lost her mom, but now she'd lost her best friend too. Libby wished she could talk to Susan about their relationship, but frankly, she didn't have the energy to do so. Most of the time, it was major effort to even get out of bed and get dressed. It had only been four months since her mom died, but it felt like an eternity. Libby wished someone would talk with her about her mom, or at least mention her name. Libby felt like people expected her to just forget about her mom. Just because a loved one dies, that doesn't mean you have to forget they existed, right? Or maybe you were supposed to forget them? Libby just didn't know.

The rest of the summer went quickly and it was time to start the fall semester. Susan had already returned to her college two hours away, while Libby had started classes again at the local junior college while continuing to live at home. As Susan was finalizing her schedule for the fall semester she noticed a death and dying class still had a few seats. On a whim, Susan enrolled in the course. She wasn't sure why she was taking this course, but she thought maybe it might help her understand Libby better. She hadn't seen Libby since that day in the grocery store over a month ago. She really missed hanging out with Libby and wanted to find some way to reconnect with her, if that was possible.

The first two weeks of class went smoothly and so far Susan really liked her death and dying class. The course was being taught by Dr. Harrison, a clinical psychologist with a background in grief counseling. A warm, soft-spoken woman in her early 40s, Dr. Harrison struck Susan as compassionate and knowledgeable. After class on Thursday Susan approached Dr. Harrison to see if she could talk with her about Libby. Susan figured if anyone could understand what was going on with her best friend, it would be Dr. Harrison. "Dr. Harrison, I was wondering if you had a few minutes to talk with me?" "Oh yes. Susan, right? I would be happy to talk. What's on your mind?"

Susan spent the next hour in Dr. Harrison's office, talking about Libby's mom and how Libby was acting since her mother's death. She told Dr. Harrison how much she missed the "old Libby" and how awkward she felt around her. Dr. Harrison was very understanding and helped Susan better understand what the grieving process is like. Apparently, losing someone you are very close to, like a parent, really impacts who you are as a person. According to Dr. Harrison, most people who go through a huge loss become different people, and part of grieving for them is to create a "new normal." That didn't mean that Libby would never be a fun person again; it just meant that for some time she would sad and withdrawn.

Dr. Harrison suggested that one way Susan could support Libby would be to accept the fact that Libby was not going to be herself for awhile. Another way Susan could support Libby would be to listen to Libby talk about her mom and her feelings, if that was something that Libby wanted to do. Most of all, Susan could really help Libby by just letting her be wherever she was in her grief. As Dr. Harrison said, grief is not a step-by-step process where someone "gets over it" in just a few months. Instead, grief was something that ebbed and flowed. Sometimes a grieving person would feel better for awhile and then out of the blue they would feel intense sadness again. Susan was really glad she had talked with Dr. Harrison. She realized that it was normal that Libby wanted to spend a lot of time at home with her dad. Rather than encouraging her to go out and have fun, Susan could spend time with Libby and her dad. In time, Libby might feel like going out again.

A few more weeks passed and soon it was the first Saturday in October. Susan had driven home for the weekend and was headed to Oak Park Cemetery. Today would have been Libby's mom's birthday, and Susan was pretty sure Libby would be at the cemetery. As she walked toward Marianne's grave, she saw Libby putting red roses by her headstone. Libby looked up and seemed surprised to see Susan. "Suz, what are you doing here?"

"Hey Lib, I thought you would be here. Today is your mom's birthday isn't it? I bet you really miss her." Libby began to cry and Susan wrapped her arms around Libby's small shoulders. "Oh Suz, I miss her so much." "I can't imagine Lib. I really can't. Lib, I'm really sorry I haven't been there for you. Can we talk?"

For Further Thought and Reflection

1. What are some of the reasons that Susan is having difficulty communicating with Libby following her mom's death? What are some of the reasons that Libby is having trouble communicating with Susan as well?
2. If you were in the same situation as Susan, how easy or difficult would it be for you to talk with Libby? As Libby's friend, how would you try to communicate caring and support?
3. What, if anything, could Libby do to help Susan better communicate with her?
4. Some communication scholars have found that grieving individuals often experience the relational dialectics of openness-closedness and presence-absence. Relational dialectics is a theoretical framework that says that people in relationships

often experience competing needs or goals simultaneously. For instance, the dialectic of openness-closedness is characterized by wanting to disclose information and not wanting to disclose information at the same time. Likewise, the tension of presence-absences occurs when people continue to feel the emotional presence of someone, even though the person is physically absent. What instances of openness-closedness and/or presence-absence did you see in this case study?

References

Baxter, L.A., Braithwaite, D.O., Golish, T.D., & Olson, L.N. (2002). Contradictions of interactions for wives of elderly husbands with adult dementia. *Journal of Applied Communication Research, 30,* 1–26.

Goldsmith, D. (2004). *Communicating social support.* Cambridge, UK: Cambridge University Press.

Lehman, D. R., Ellard, J. H., & Wortman, C. B. (1986). Social support for the bereaved: Recipients' and providers' perspectives on what is helpful. *Journal of Counseling and Clinical Psychology, 54,* 438–446.

Rando, T.A. (1988). *Grieving: How to go on living when someone you love dies.* San Francisco: Jossey-Bass Inc.

Servaty-Seib, H.L. & Burleson, B.R. (2007). Bereaved adolescents' evaluations of the helpfulness of support-intended statements: Associations with person-centeredness and demographic, personality, and contextual factors. *Journal of Social and Personal Relationships, 24,* 207–223.

Toller, P.W. (2005). Negotiation of dialectical contradictions by parents who have experienced the death of a child. *Journal of Applied Communication Research, 33,* 44–66.

27 Friends of the Heart: Communication between Long-Term Friends

MARY E. ROHLFING

Key Terms

friendship, familial bonds, sex differences in friendship, cross-sex friendship

---

Sophie had stood alone in her father's now empty house for close to fifteen minutes. Knowing she'd never return to this place again, she wanted to allow herself time to experience the feelings of relief and sadness pulsing through her heart and gut. She visualized her father as she had often seen him during her annual visits "back home," seated at the kitchen table, bathed in low a light, smoking cigarette after cigarette. She remembered the ever-present stacks of now discarded magazines and newspaper clippings he piled neatly on the floor near his feet. As she blinked back the tears filling her eyes, she turned one last time to look out the window overlooking the creek and meadow where just this morning she had seen three deer grazing in the knee-high grass. She tried futilely to remember the names her father had given each one, remembering how nearly every time he had called her, he'd talk endlessly about them, and how she almost invariably would tune him out. Now, she wished she'd paid closer attention and knew which was which. Realizing that this thought, too, was hopeless, she dropped her face into her hands and sobbed.

Nothing would ever be as it had been, and she simultaneously ached to bring her father back and struggled to let him go. Dabbing at the tears that had begun to flow less freely, Sophie knew there was nothing now to do but go on. She sighed and said aloud, "That's it." Quickly and definitively she strode to the back door, opening it and shutting it tightly behind her.

Stepping outside, Sophie squinted and blinked as her moist eyes adjusted to the bright sun. She saw Jay leaning comfortably against the driver's door of the rented moving truck parked in the driveway, noticing that at his feet were three stubbed cigarette butts. "Now's a good time to quit that nasty habit," she called out as cheerfully as

211

she could. "We have 2,000 miles of highway ahead of us, and you are NOT going to smoke in that truck!"

"Please," Jay muttered sarcastically. "Is there anything more annoying than a holier-than-thou ex-smoker? I don't think so. After all I'm doing for you, you won't let me smoke in the truck? Really? It's going to take us three weeks to get to Oregon, because we're going to have to stop every fifty miles so I can have a fix." Sophie laughed, and as she did, made a noise like a horse. Realizing what she'd done, she laughed harder. "There you go, snorting already." Jay shook his head in mock disgust. He reached toward her to take her suitcase. "You think I'm kidding? This provokes a lot of anxiety for me, Sophie. Driving and smoking go together like Jay-Z and Alicia Keys. Each is good alone, but together? Perfection."

Sophie had walked around to the passenger door of the truck and Jay noticed that she was tugging at the locked handle to let herself in. He pulled the keys from his pocket and tossed them in a high arc over the cab of the truck to her. Sophie snatched the keys from the air, unlocked the door and got in. As they settled into their seats and Sophie handed him the keys, she said, "That song is tired and old, Jay, just like you and smoking. It's time for you to quit."

Ignoring her, Jay said, "Let's go, Thelma. Time to get this show on the road, hit the bars, blow up an oil truck, and drive off the cliff." Sophie smiled as she thought of her partner Melissa's parting comments as she dropped them off at the airport four days before. Hugging Sophie, Melissa looked over her shoulder and spoke to Jay, "Now don't go pulling any Thelma and Louise crap out there. Don't stop at bars, don't blow up any oil trucks, and for God's sake, don't go near any cliffs." The comment had humored them for the last three days. As they cleaned out Sophie's father's house, they had frequently referred to one another as Thelma and Louise.

As Jay adjusted the mirrors, Sophie poured herself a cup of coffee from the thermos and reached for the iPod on the seat between them. Before she'd turned it on, Jay muttered, "If I hear a single Lady GaGa song, I will leap from this truck. I haven't had enough coffee for that yet."

"What makes you think I would have Lady GaGa downloaded? she asked incredulously. As the engine began to purr, the first strains of a Lady GaGa song cranked loudly through the speakers. Sophie stared at Jay, waiting for him to answer.

Jay caught her gaze then looked out over the meadow, "Well, let's see. Maybe because I've known you for, what? Thirteen long, painful years? Maybe because your girlfriend warned me that you have some weird ritual that requires you start road trips by playing Lady GaGa to 'bless the trip.' Maybe your musical taste is more predictable than a 'Friday The 13th' movie? Gee, Sophie, I don't know, how could I have known?" They smiled and he barked, "Now pour me a cup of coffee, woman, and let's blow this popsicle stand." Sophie snorted again as she poured, then pretended to nearly spill the cup in his lap as she handed him the steaming mug. "So help me, I'll kill you," Jay sneered as he took the cup from her.

Jay placed the cup on the dashboard then leaned forward to lower the volume on Lady GaGa. Gently placing his hand on her knee, he looked at Sophie and asked, "Are you ready?" Sophie smiled weakly and nodded her head. "You sure?" She looked away, knowing if she kept his gaze a moment more she would burst into tears. "OK," Jay said, realizing it was time. "Thelma" he yelled, as he turned up the stereo to a near deafening-volume, "let's drive off this cliff!"

As he maneuvered the long, over-loaded truck out of the driveway and onto the street, Jay began to sing along, and Sophie couldn't suppress a smile. Minutes before she had been ready to break down, but now she was light-hearted and excited. Aside from Melissa, who couldn't come along since she was just two weeks into the new school year in a new position, Sophie could imagine no one she'd rather be with. "Hey, wait a minute," she said watching her father's house disappear in the side mirror behind them. "Did you call me 'Thelma,' Thelma?" Jay nodded affirmatively. "I thought I was Louise and you were Thelma. We need to get this straight."

Jay beamed. "To tell you the truth, Louise, I don't know which one's which. You be whoever you need to be. You be Angelina, I'll be Brad. Hell, you be Brad, I'll be Angelina."

Sophie thought of how they often delighted themselves arguing over pop culture trivia, and the great lengths to which each would go to prove the other wrong. They had dubbed these disagreements, the "culture vulture" wars. She recalled how they had gotten into arguments at parties over who had written this song or who had directed that movie. Invariably, they would notice that they had cleared the room and were left alone. "Well," Jay would say at such moments, "we've once again run off the competition with our superior knowledge of all things popular and all things cultural."

For the first few hours of the trip, they barely spoke, but Jay could tell that Sophie was restless. He noticed her open the glove box to retrieve the insurance and rental agreement, which she dropped to the floor. Cursing, she scooped it up and fished a rubber band from her pocket to bind the papers together before putting them back. Next, she thumbed through her phone, talking to herself as she deleted old messages and contacts. Finished with that task, she reached under the seat to fetch the road atlas, setting it neatly on the seat between them. Seeming to have run out of chores, she momentarily leaned back in her seat, then quickly jerked forward to adjust the balance of the speakers. With the sound just right, she settled in again, but not for long. Once more she opened the glove box, this time removing a crisp, new pocket notebook and pen. Shifting in the seat to face Jay, she asked, "How many miles have we gone?"

He shrugged his shoulders and coughed. "Eighty miles? One hundred? I don't know."

Sophie admonished him. "Jay, look at the odometer. What's it say?"

Jay looked crossly at her. "It reads," he said elongating the word to indicate that she had misspoken, "1,982 and six tenths of a mile." Sophie sighed and rolled her eyes.

"Didn't you zero out the odometer at the beginning of the trip?" Jay shrugged again. Perturbed, Sophie whined, "Jay, I need to keep track of this shit."

"What?" he asked. "What are you keeping track of?"

Sophie made no attempt to hide her irritation. "The miles, the gas, the hotel bills, how much we spend on food. That's what!"

Exasperated, Jay asked, "Why? Who cares how many miles we go, how much gas we use, or what the rooms cost? Don't go anal on me." He looked away from Sophie to avoid her glare.

Sophie responded, "I'm not anal. I have to keep track to be reimbursed. You know how my brothers are." Jay was unconvinced. The two times he'd met Ron, he seemed like an easy going guy, albeit tough to get to know. Her older brother, Mike, lived in California and had never ventured to Oregon to see his sister, nor had she ever gone to see him. He didn't think Mike or Ron would be counting pennies under the circumstances. After all, she had saved them both a lot of grief by taking on the task of dealing with their father's house and belongings.

Sophie yanked open the glove box and tossed the notebook inside. She remained silent as they drove west on the Pennsylvania Turnpike passing one farm after another. Jay considered apologizing, but he wasn't sure why. He knew Sophie was trying to maintain her generally jovial demeanor, but the events of the last three weeks were beginning to wear on her. Although she'd sworn she could handle the aftermath of her father's death alone, and claimed that she would relish "driving solo" in the rental truck across country, Jay had insisted on coming along. No way would he or Melissa let Sophie face all the emotional and physical work that had to be done by herself. Since he was between jobs, he was the best choice to accompany her. Jay knew, though, that Sophie was too proud to admit she needed him, so instead, when they talked about the trip, he would say the main reason he was coming along was to visit the east coast with someone who had grown up there.

In their 13 years of friendship, Sophie and Jay had been through a great deal. They first met when Jay was 26, and Sophie was 25 years old. When Sophie missed a college class both were enrolled in, Jay offered Sophie his notes. He invited her to his house to get them, and they instantly became friends. Sophie liked to say that had they been heterosexual, theirs would have been a classic case of love at first sight.

As Jay got to know Sophie better, he revealed that his lover, Zach, had recently died of AIDS. Ever since his death, Jay had remained single and celibate, telling anyone who asked that Zach had been his "one and only," and that he couldn't be "replaced." As the years passed, Sophie came to believe Jay's reluctance to become involved romantically with anyone new was just a means of protecting himself from ever being hurt so deeply again. A few years back, she had begun to encourage him to date, working up the courage, finally, to tell him what she thought was at the root of his long spell of solitude. Doing so had been a mistake. Jay stormed out of Sophie and Melissa's house half-way through the birthday dinner they had prepared in his honor. He accused them of meddling in his life and told them both to "fuck off!" For three weeks, he refused to return their calls, and once, when Sophie stopped by his house to try to talk things out, he yelled at her through the closed door that he wanted to be left alone. She stood outside his door, telling him how much he meant to her and how deeply she missed his friendship. Realizing he was not going to let her in, she finally walked away, unsure that she'd ever see him again. Then, a week later, he stopped by her office and asked her to lunch. As she tried again to apologize, he cut her short. "You did that already. Don't belabor the point." After that, Sophie never raised the issue with Jay again.

As he drove, Jay remembered how five years into their friendship, Sophie had faced her first real heartbreak when her lover left her for another woman. When she told Jay that what she missed most was having someone to say goodnight to, he called every night for the next six months to "tuck" her in. He happily stopped doing so, when, one night, Melissa answered the phone. He had known Mel for years and had long thought that she and Sophie would make a great couple. Now that the two of them had been going strong for seven years, he knew he'd been right.

Jay looked over at his friend. He noticed how tired Sophie looked, and asked if she wanted to move the atlas and lie down on the seat to sleep. She shook her head and continued staring out the window.

Sophie had known for years that her father's health was fragile. Still, she was shocked when he died. Three days before his death, she had phoned to tell him that she and Melissa were off for a week-long hike in the wilderness. When she asked how he was, he said he was "a little under the weather," but it was "no big deal." As they bid each other goodbye, he told her to have a great time and to send his "love to Mel." While Sophie and Melissa were hiking in the Cascade Mountains, Sophie's father had "slipped away" due to a massive infection in his lungs.

Sophie's big brother, Mike, was the first to hear of their father's death, and after two days of failing to reach his sister, Ron advised Mike to call Jay to find out where they were. Jay told Mike that Sophie and Melissa weren't due home for four days and that they were 30 miles from where a phone might work. He volunteered to hike in where he thought they would be to tell Sophie what had happened, but Mike refused Jay's offer, thinking it best that they enjoy their trip. Their father had been cremated and there would be no funeral. Mike was assured that their father's attorney could handle the other details. Since none of the children wished to return to Pennsylvania and live in the home their father had bought after their parents' divorce, all that remained to be done was for the house to be cleaned out and put up for sale.

Talking with Mike, Jay understood why Sophie found him so difficult to connect with. While Mike was friendly, he was terse and officious, offering no hint that he felt much sadness about his father's death. Mike, Sophie said, thought their father had "lacked ambition" and was to blame for their parents' divorce. In his eyes, their father was not a "real" man. Despite knowing all of this, Jay thought it odd that Mike could be so cool. Before the conversation with Mike, he'd always thought Sophie was too hard on her brother. After talking with Mike, he understood why she was.

Sophie loved her brothers, but was not as close to either of them as she was to most of her good friends. Mike's values, she felt, were exactly opposite of her own. He was a staunch and vocal conservative whose conversations were frequently laced with sexist and racist remarks. He'd been married three times, and each wife was younger than the last. On those rare occasions when they spoke, Mike answered her questions about how he was in financial terms. Sophie, on the other hand, didn't much care about money. She didn't make much at the homeless shelter, but Melissa had a well-paying job as a school administrator. They had plenty. Still, Sophie thought Mike believed she was less than successful in life. That she was a lesbian didn't sit well with him, and it hurt that he never asked her about Melissa. Jay knew Sophie thought Mike was a bigot and tried to dismiss him, but also that she was hurt by Mike's disapproval of her.

Ron, Sophie's younger brother was nearly ten years her junior. He admired Sophie, but since he and his girlfriend lived three hours away from Sophie, only once or twice a year did they get together to visit. Sophie felt closer to Ron, but he had been only eight years old when she left home for good. In her mind, it was as though they had grown up in two different families.

Hoping to break the silence that had engulfed them, Jay turned on the radio. He noticed that Sophie was tapping her foot to the beat of the song. Although he'd known her for over a decade, and felt more comfortable with her than anyone else, he realized that it wasn't until he made this trip back to where she had been born and raised that he felt he had real insight into her life. He asked Sophie about her favorite places, what she had done as a teenager, and what it was like, at eighteen years of age, to drive cross-country alone to go to college in Oregon. Sophie warmed to the questions, providing details she had never before shared with Jay. She was animated as they made their first stop for food and gas, and told him a funny story about traveling with her family when she was ten, and how at this very Howard Johnson's, her mother had absent-mindedly driven off without Mike before he returned from the men's room. It wasn't until they were three miles down the road that Sophie realized Mike wasn't in the car and screamed loudly for her parents to go back to get him.

After they ate and filled the truck with gas, Sophie took over driving as Jay curled into a fetal position, using his wadded up sweatshirt as a makeshift pillow. Sophie drove for close to four hours when she realized that she was too sleepy to go any further. She pulled off the highway and stopped at the nearest hotel. As she parked, Jay awoke and asked what was going on. She told him it was time to stop for the day. Jay rubbed his eyes and looked at the hotel sign. "Let me wake up, and I'll go in and register with you," he said quietly as he tried with little success to flatten his mussed hair. Stretching his mouth so as to regain feeling in his face, he asked what time it was. Sophie told him and he asked, "Have I really been asleep that long?"

"Yes. Thelma," Sophie answered. "And by the way, you're fabulous company on a road trip. Your insightful remarks, pointed questions and generally interesting patter are really making the miles fly by, pal."

Jay blinked his eyes and rubbed them, "I'm sorry. I should have stayed awake to talk to you." He yawned and stretched his arms. "I just couldn't. These last few days have been rough on this old queen. Packing this truck and carrying all that heavy furniture is more labor than I'm used to. You would have done better bringing some big, butch dyke, my darling." Sophie laughed as he continued, "Now, when we get to Oregon and start trying to figure out how to mix your dad's furniture with that funky, Bohemian college student decor of yours and Mel's, I'll be a real Martha Stewart. At the moment, though, I'm just a warm body."

Sophie stroked his hair helping to smooth down a stray strand or two he'd missed. She then reached up to the dashboard and grabbed Jay's cigarettes. She shook one loose from the pack and put it between her lips. "Got a light?' " she asked. Saying nothing, he reached into his pocket and pulled out his lighter. Sophie took it from him and lit the cigarette. He noticed that although she had quit two years ago, she didn't cough as she inhaled. Before handing it to him, she took another drag. Exhaling, she said, "This will help you wake up."

Jay was genuinely confused and quickly turned to roll down the window so the smoke could escape. "I thought this was a non-smoking truck."

"It was. I can't ask you to go all day without smoking. You stay here and enjoy it." Before he could thank her, she had opened the door and jumped out.

After showering, writing postcards, and clicking through the channels on the television, Jay popped up from his bed and announced, "I'm going to get a six pack and some burgers. Please take advantage of my absence to call your sweetie and do that kissy-face thing. I don't want to be subjected to that crap."

Sophie smiled and waved as he walked to the door. "Wait," she said. "I have to tell you something." Jay turned back to look at her. She continued, "I've been a jerk today. I just, I just, oh, Jay, how can I repay you? You're so good to me. You've been such a huge help these last few days. I could never have gotten all that done without you."

When it appeared that she might tear up, Jay cut her off. "Sophie, you know I despise this kind of verbalized sentimentality. Stop before I vomit."

"No," she said seriously. "Most of time I honor your inability to link words to feelings. Just shut up and hear me out." Jay rolled his eyes and sat down. As he did, she said simply, "I love you, friend."

Jay sat looking at her, expecting Sophie to continue. Realizing that she was through talking, he exclaimed, "That's it? That's all you have to say to me?" They began to chuckle. "You are so incompetent as a woman sometimes, Sophie." Standing to leave, he said, "So, that was the big heart to heart? You're pathetic."

As he opened the door, he turned back. "Tell me again, which am I? Thelma or Louise?" She shrugged, unable to recall. "OK, well, whichever one slept with Brad Pitt is the one I'm going to be, got it?" As he walked out the door, he called over his shoulder, "I love you, too, Sophie. And when you call Melissa, tell her I only thought about killing you twice today."

She knew he wouldn't hear her but called after him anyway. "You have to love me, I'm your best friend, Thelma!"

For Further Reflection and Discussion

1. Some researchers have claimed that men and women enact friendship in different ways. Can you see differences in how Sophie and Jay communicate their feelings of friendship and love for each other?
2. Many people believe that men and women cannot have successful friendships. What has been your experience with cross-sex friendships? How do those friendships differ from ones you have with same-sex friends?
3. Identify aspects of Sophie and Jay's communication that reflect the history of their friendship? How might their communication be different if they had been friends only a short time?

References

Metts, S. (2006). Hanging out and doing lunch: Enacting friendship closeness. In J. T. Wood & S. W. Duck (Eds.), *Composing relationships: Communication in everyday life* (pp.76–85). Belmont: Wadsworth/Cengage.

Rohlfing, M.E. (1995). "Doesn't anybody stay in one place anymore?" An exploration of the under-studied phenomenon of long-distance relationships. In J.T. Wood, & S. Duck (Eds.) Under-studied relationships: Off the Beaten Track (pp. 173–196). Thousand Oaks, CA: Sage.

Wood, J.T., & Inman, C.C. (1993). In a different mode: Masculine styles of communicating closeness. Journal of Applied Communication Research, 21, 279–295.

28

Distance Makes the Heart Grow Anxious: Managing Long-Distance and Commuter Relationships

Marcia D. Dixson

Key Terms

communication technology, long-distance relationships, self-disclosure, social support

---

Lindsay has just finished unpacking the last of her DVDs when she hears four taps followed by two quick taps on her dorm door. She smiles knowing the "tapper" to be her brother Lance, a junior at the same college where she would begin taking classes tomorrow. She opens the door and is amazed to be still struck at how "cool" she thinks her older brother is. Of course, he enhances this effect by standing languidly in the hall, leaning against her doorframe with one of his best "you'd be lucky to know me" poses. The pose gives way to a big smile and very uncool hug for his little sister as soon as the door opens.

"So, Sissy, how do you like life at U of I so far?" Lance asks, sprawling across her bed.

"Fine, but you know I hate being called Sissy! I have since I was twelve. Don't you think that now I'm in college you could quit?"

"Sure, Sissy!" he responds with a grin. "Seriously, is there anything you need? Want to know where the best bars are? Need to know where to get cash after midnight? I might even be able to hunt up the library if you're interested."

"No, thanks. I went on the first-year students tour. I can probably show you where the library is, as well as the writing center, the speaking lab, the foreign language lab! Geez, I hope I don't end up needing all the special help they have here!"

"So, what about that guy you've been seeing, Tom, John, Lon?"

Lindsay responds by sitting in her oversized chair and looking glum but determined, "It's Ron, oh feeble minded one. We've decided to stay together even though we're at colleges 450 miles apart. We'll call, email and text, and we've both got Skype now; it'll be fine. Besides he's the greatest guy I've ever dated. He's kind, smart, thoughtful, gorgeous, funny, and a gentleman. Hey, come to think of it, he's

219

everything you're not! Maybe that's Freudian or something, looking for the perfect man who's everything your brother isn't?"

"Very funny! And this from a woman with a vast repertoire of, what, two other dating experiences?" her brother responded sarcastically but then continues in a more serious tone, "Are you sure this is what you want to do? How can you have a relationship when you don't see each other? Besides you'll miss out on half the fun of college if you can't go out and enjoy yourself."

"Why wouldn't I be able to go out and have fun? I may not be dating other guys but I don't have to sit home and vegetate! Yes, I'm sure. Ron is really special and he's too important to me to blow off just because of an inconvenience like a few hundred miles. Besides, haven't you heard? Love conquers all. Speaking of which, what about that girl Terrie, Carrie, or Mary you were dating last spring?"

"Oh, Jerrie, she went back home for the summer. I don't know if she came back to school or not. Maybe I'll run into her at our frat party next weekend. That'd be ok. She's kind of cute and fun. You coming to the Phi Kappa party? I don't want you going to other parties; I won't be there to protect you, ya know."

"Right, big brother. I think my black belt in TaeKwanDo will protect me just fine. I'll be there. See ya then."

Two weeks later at the party, Lindsay finally spots her brother across the room.

"LANCE!" Lindsay tries to get her brother's attention over the music and voices.

"Hey, you made it! You remember Jerrie?"

"Hi, Lindsay, it's nice to see you again. Do you have a date or would you like for Lance and me to introduce you around?" Jerrie inquires as they move to a quieter corner.

"No thanks, Jerrie. I'm seeing someone," Lindsay responds.

"Oh, where is he? I'd like to meet him."

"He's not here. He's in Indiana—he goes to Purdue."

"Yuck, that's not much fun!" says Jerrie.

"Oh, it's not so bad."

"Don't you miss him? Don't you wish he were here?"

"Yeah, I do miss him. But what's odd is that while I miss going to parties like this and movies and stuff, I miss just being with him even more. You know, like on Sunday afternoons he'd watch football and I'd listen to music. Just having him around is what I miss the most."

"Really? I'd think you'd want someone here for the really important stuff. You know, to take you to frat parties or sneak into your dorm room, huh, Lance?" Jerrie looks at Lance suggestively.

As usual, Lance is paying little attention, "What? Oh yeah, sure, I told her this long distance thing wouldn't work but she's like our old dog, loyal to the end . . . unhh."

A quick elbow jab finishes Lance's sentence for him.

"My roommate and I came together, do you see her?" Lindsay asks to change the topic. "Oh, there she is, leaving with some guy!"

"Uh, I know that guy, I wouldn't expect her back soon," Jerrie whispers conspiratorially.

"Come on, let's see if Lance misses me while we go get something to drink."

The next day, over pizza, Lindsay notices Lance's nauseated expression and says, "Judging by how you look, the party went pretty late last night."

"Yeah, I was there 'til three. Did you have a good time? You looked kind of like a lost puppy."

"You can stop with the dog descriptions any time. The party was fine. I just felt a little out of place. I have the same problem with my friends and roommate. I don't want to go guy hunting with the single girls, but I can't double date with the girls who have boyfriends. I don't fit. My roommate keeps telling me to lighten up 'cause it's not like I'm in a REAL relationship! I wish people would see that it's a real relationship, even if he isn't here."

"Well," Lance interjects while his sister takes a breath, "you could date just for fun you know. That might get people to leave you alone."

"I don't think I should have to go to those lengths just to be left alone!" Lindsay objects. "And by the way, the Phi Kappas have the same problem. They kept hitting on me, saying that Ron was probably out partying with other girls anyway. Do I have to carry proof of relationship involvement or something to be taken seriously?"

"I told you this long distance thing wasn't going to work out. Why don't you give it up before you've wasted the entire rush season?" Lance reminds her.

"Because Ron happens to be more important to me than the entire rush season, thank you very much. I just wish we could see each other more often. But, we've worked out a plan. We make sure we are in on Friday afternoons for our Skype date. We text every day and email several times a week. But we don't expect each other not to have friends and go out. We've both agreed that while being apart is a pain, it does lessen the distractions from accomplishing what we're here to do, which is get an education so we can both get good jobs, get married, you know."

"Yeah, but isn't the distance a real problem?" Lance asks.

"Well it's changed our relationship in some ways I didn't expect. Not all bad, we don't argue about stupid stuff anymore because the time on Skype is too important to waste that way. If there is something really important that might cause a conflict, it has to wait until we see each other in person. We both know that we need open, honest communication. That means telling each other about how hard it is to have a long distance relationship. But, we won't give up! Hopefully, I can visit him soon. Speaking of giving up, how is Jerrie?" Lindsay ends, determined to change the subject and be optimistic.

"Don't ask. I have no idea what her problem is. We have only been seeing each other again for two weeks and you would think she owns me! She got all ticked off last night for no reason that I could figure out. Something about me missing or not missing something. I have no clue. She was great when we first started seeing each other, interested in lots of the things I am. Now she always wants me to take her to stupid sorority events and if I don't call her everyday she pouts. She has to share every detail of her life with me or she's not happy. Frankly, her life isn't that interesting! She's way too much trouble."

"Wow, short relationship! I'm glad Ron isn't like you. He still listens to me when we get the chance to talk. Maybe good relationships are good whether or not they are long distance."

Lance responds with his best looking-out-for-little-sister tone, "So, you're really happy? Even though you rarely see Ron?"

Lindsay seems pensive as she considers her answer, "It's hard. Last night seemed weird because everyone was pairing off. I wondered how Ron would act at a party. I missed him so much I called him, even though it wasn't our night to talk. Big surprise, he didn't answer. He was probably out with his roommates or something and couldn't hear his cell, right?"

"Are you trying to convince me or you?"

"Both, I guess. I have no reason to think that Ron would ever cheat on me. He talks about this girl, Pat, who is just a friend. They have a lot of classes together since they're both Engineering majors. I don't know or particularly care about the structure of bridges and skyscrapers, but Ron gets all excited talking about what he is learning. I guess I'm a little worried. I feel like I'm missing out on so much. When we were together I knew what was happening with him everyday. I don't really have any reason to worry. I have male friends here. That doesn't mean I'm looking or anything. I'll get better once I get used to this, won't I? Do you know I actually checked Facebook to see if he had updated his status? I saw a picture of Pat. She's pretty. That didn't help. And she had written on his Wall 'Great bridge builder—weak drinker.' What does that mean? Were they partying together?"

"OK, Facebook is not a good way to keep a relationship on track. You know people have no control over what other idiots write on their wall. Look at the stuff some girls have written on my wall! And, no, don't say it, it's not all true!! If you aren't careful, you'll be one of those people wasting time everyday lurking on Facebook just to check out Ron's wall and updates. I'm worried about you, if the relationship is going to cause you this much stress, is it really worth it?"

Lindsay considers for a moment before answering, "Yeah, it is worth it. We just have to figure out how to do the long distance thing."

"Is there anything I can do to help?"

"No, but thanks for listening to me whine."

"Aw, what are big brothers for? Hey, how about seeing a movie this afternoon?"

"What, with you and Jerrie so I can feel like a third wheel again?" Lindsay answers dubiously.

"Naw, just you and me, a family thing."

Three weeks pass before Lance and Lindsay see each other again. When they do, it's a Monday morning and Lance spots his sister on the way to class. "Lindsay, hey wait up!" he calls to her.

"Hey, Lance, how was your weekend?"

"Fine, I think I'm in love!"

"With Jerrie?" Lindsay asks surprised.

"Nah, she's history. I had a date with Jessica, one of the volleyball players. She's hot, I mean attractive. Oh, she's also smart and nice, so you and Mom would approve. How'd your weekend go? Wasn't this the BIG VISIT?"

"Yeah, I went to see Ron at Purdue. Of course, now I miss him more than ever but I think that will be better in a few days when I get used to him not being around again. It was great but it was also weird. I had dreams of how romantic it would be after being apart for so long and how he would meet me with flowers and a dinner reservation at a nice restaurant. Guess my expectations were a bit too high. Instead, when he first picked me up at the bus station, it was like we barely knew each other. I mean it's only been a couple of months so we haven't changed that much, but it was still strange. It took us a while to get comfortable again. We talked about the pressure we felt, you know, to have a perfect time together, to not waste a minute since we don't have that much time. Then it was better. We decided to spend most of our time by ourselves, but I still wanted to see the campus and meet some of his friends.

"I met his roommates, so now I have faces to go with the names when he talks about them. I also saw the campus and the town. It makes it easier to picture him when I have a setting to put him in. We had a great time. It was romantic and new and wonderful. He really missed me!"

"Was there any doubt? Who wouldn't miss my little sister! He's lucky to have you."

"Yeah, well it was nice to hear it from him and be able to hold his hand when he said it. Talking on Skype or over the phone is great, but it still not the same as face to face. And we talked a lot! I had so many questions."

"You didn't make the poor guy talk about the relationship, did you? Guys hate that."

"Well, guys may hate it but when you are apart as much as we are, I need to talk about the relationship."

"What's there to talk about? Are you still worried about that girl Pat?"

"No, I'm not worried about 'that girl' Pat. I met her this weekend. Ron thought I'd feel better if I knew her. He was right. She's pretty and very nice. I liked her."

"If she's all that then why do you feel better about it?"

"Well, I trust Ron and I trust her, and I also met her girlfriend."

"You mean she's a lesbian?" inquires Lance.

"Yep. I don't know why I always assume that everyone is heterosexual. I mean, I'm not stupid; I know better. But I have to admit I do feel better knowing that Ron really isn't her type. I don't know why I would worry. Ron would never do anything like that—he is totally trustworthy and honest and wonderful!"

"That's dumb, Sissy. No one is TOTALLY trustworthy and honest and wonderful."

"Calling me 'Sissy' is dumb!" Lindsay punctuates this with a smile and a jab to his right arm. Lance notices that his sister seems less nervous and happier than she has since she started the semester, but he has the nagging feeling that she still doesn't seem entirely secure in this relationship. He only hopes she doesn't let this long-distance relationship get her down.

A week passes before Lindsay and Lance reconnect and then it is by phone.

"Hello," Lindsay says.

"Hey, Sissy!"

"Would you please stop that, Lance! How are you? How's the latest love of your life?"

"I'm great, Jessica's great, life is great. How about you and Ron?"

"We're marvelous. We talk and text everyday and email several times a week. I feel like we get to keep up now, ya know. Plus, we started playing the new Call of Duty game online on Wednesday evening, so we are actually playing the game together. And, we decided to both start watching this new crime drama so we can text about it. It feels great to be sharing some things even though we are far apart. I complain about my loads of homework or my roommate by email or text so I don't feel like I'm wasting our Skype time each week. We still Skype on Friday afternoons, but now I can ask about the little things going on in his life, because I know what they are! I feel much more connected. And guess what?"

"What?" Lance answers.

I met a girl in my communication class, Cassie, who is also in a long-distance relationship. She and I hit it off right away and she knows a couple of other people who are in LDRs."

"LDRs?"

"Yeah, it's short for Long Distance Relationship. There is a ton of advice on the web about how to make an LDR successful. Did you know communication and psychology researchers have actually done quite a bit of work in the area? Just Google it! One of the ideas is to find other people who are in LDRs. That way you have someone to talk to and hang out with even if you don't have a 'date.' "

"You mean a support group or something?" Lance inquires incredulously.

"Kind of, but more a group of friends going through the same thing. Someone I can go to your frat parties with and not feel like they are going to dump me to take off with some guy."

"Isn't it weird, being around all those lonely lover types?"

"Not really. And, by the way, I learned in my communication class that missing someone is not the same as being lonely!"

"Is it really a good relationship if you have to work so hard?" Lance queries.

"It is not a lot of work. The websites say it's mostly little things like buying a card or sending Ron a video of me, or just texting him about little stuff (which I already do). Another of the coping strategies is not to talk about the relationship too much when we do see each other but to just try to enjoy the time together."

"Well, I told you that!"

"And, yes, it is a good relationship even if we have to work at it. As a matter of fact, there are some advantages to LDRs. We don't argue about little things because our time together is too important, we don't take each other for granted, and we have better communication even though we don't have as much. Maybe more importantly right now, I have more time to spend on all of my homework. When I'm not around Ron, I can make school my priority."

Lance shakes his head. "Still sounds like an awful lot of work to me."

"All good relationships involve some work. You know, Lance, that may explain your relational score card. Maybe you should use some of these ideas to try to make ONE relationship in your life last longer than a month."

"Ha!" Lance replies, undefeated. "Not if I have to go to that much work! Hey, that reminds me, do you want to meet Jessica? We are having another party at the house this weekend and I thought you might want to come, that is if Ron doesn't mind."

"Ron won't mind. He knows he has no competition. I'm looking forward to meeting this latest goddess."

"Great, see you at the house Saturday night. Bye, Sissy!"

"La .a.a.ance!"

For Further Thought & Reflection

1. Technology has changed the way we communicate in long-distance relationships. What technologies do Lindsay and Ron take advantage of to stay in touch? How does their use of text seem to differ from Skype or cell phone calls? What technologies do you use to communicate with friends and family who are not geographically close? Are there any technologies you could use more effectively?
2. What seem to be some of the advantages and disadvantages of being in a long-distance relationship? How can you minimize the disadvantages?
3. Lindsay experiences at least two forms of social support that help her cope with being in a long-distance relationship. For each form of support you identify, discuss the differences each makes to Lindsay.
4. Is there any self-disclosure in the relationship between Ron and Lindsay? If so, what kind seems to have occurred? How does it affect their coping with being in a long-distance relationship?
5. Research on LDRs consistently finds that couples in LDRs are more likely to idealize their partner and their relationships than couples in geographically close relationships; is this happening with Lindsay and Ron? Is it a good or a bad thing?

References

Christofedes, E., Muise, A., & Desmarais, S. (2009). Information disclosures and control on Facebook: Are they two sides of the same coin or two different processes? *CyberPsychology & Behavior 12*(3), 341–345. doi: 10.1089/cpb.2008.0226

Pempek, T.A., Yermolayeva, Y.A., & Calvert, S.L. (2009). College students' social networking experiences on Facebook. *Journal of Applied Developmental Psychology, 30,* 227–238.

Sahlstein, E.M. (2004). Relating at a distance: Negotiating being together and being apart in long-distance relationships. *Journal of Social and Personal Relationships, 21*(5), 689–710.

Sahlstein, E.M. (2006). Making plans: Praxis strategies for negotiating uncertainty-certainty in long-distance relationships. *Western Journal of Communication, 70* (2), 147–165. doi: 10.1080/10570310600710042

Stafford, L. & Reske, J.R. (1990). Idealization and communication in long-distance premarital relationships. *Family Relations, 39* (3), 274–280.

Utz, S. (2007). Media use in long-distance friendships. *Information, Communication & Society, 10* (5), 694–713. doi: 10.1080/13691180701658046

Walther, J.B., VanDerHeide, B., Kim, S., Westerman, D., & Tong, S.T. (2008). The role of friends' appearance and behavior on evaluations of individuals on Facebook: Are we known by the company we keep? *Human Communication Research, 34,* 28–49.

CPSIA information can be obtained
at www.ICGtesting.com
Printed in the USA
LVHW112034161121
703533LV00004B/11